'Elegantly written . . . His subject is of engrossing interest as a crucial episode in the development of our state, but even more so as a route into the minds of those who were party to it . . . Clever and illuminating' *The Times*

'Outstanding: a thrilling tale of retribution and bloody sacrifice, unflinching idealism and craven miscreancy . . . Like all the best history books, it succeeds not only in telling a remarkable story, but also in illuminating the entire age' Jessie Childs

'It is a credit to Spencer's skill that he both creates a vivid and enlightening picture of the age – a fevered time of denunciation and reprisal – and draws out the touching moment of human drama and sentiment from the stories of imprisonment and execution' *Independent*

'The virtues of a thriller and of scholarship are potently combined' Tom Holland

'Spencer's attention to the gruesome sights and smells of hanging, drawing and quartering is cinematic: throughout, he shows an eye for the details, gory or intimate . . . Spencer has a gift for set-pieces' *Guardian*

'Perfectly balanced . . . One of the best books on the 17th century I have read since CV Wedgwood's book, *The Trial of Charles I*' AN Wilson, *Evening Standard* Books of the Year

'It is gripping material and Spencer more than does it justice . . . Although he is, of course, uncle to the future king, Charles Spencer's admiration for [the] pious, brave and principled regicides shines through the book' *Literary Review*

A NOTE ON THE AUTHOR

CHARLES SPENCER was educated at Eton College and obtained his degree in Modern History at Magdalen College, Oxford. He was a reporter on NBC's *Today* show from 1986 until 1995, and is the author of four books, including the *Sunday Times* bestseller *Blenheim: Battle for Europe* (shortlisted for History Book of the Year, National Book Awards) and *Prince Rupert: The Last Cavalier*.

Althorp: The Story of an English House
The Spencer Family
Blenheim: Battle for Europe
Prince Rupert: The Last Cavalier

KILLERS OF THE KING

The Men Who Dared to Execute Charles I

Charles Spencer

BLOOMSBURY

LONDON · NEW DELHI · NEW YORK · SYDNEY

For Charlotte

Bloomsbury Paperbacks
An imprint of Bloomsbury Publishing Plc

50 Bedford Square
London
WC1B 3DP
UK

1385 Broadway
New York
NY 10018
USA

www.bloomsbury.com

BLOOMSBURY and the Diana logo are trademarks of Bloomsbury Publishing Plc

First published in Great Britain 2014
This paperback edition first published in 2015

British Library Cataloguing-in-Publication Data
A catalogue record for this book is available from the British Library.

ISBN: HB: 978-1-4088-5170-8
        TPB: 978-1-4088-6285-8
        PB: 978-1-4088-5177-7
        ePub: 978-1-4088-5171-5

4 6 8 10 9 7 5 3

Typeset by Hewer Text UK Ltd, Edinburgh
Printed and bound in Great Britain by CPI Group (UK) Ltd, Croydon CR0 4YY

MIX
Paper from
responsible sources
FSC® C020471

To find out more about our authors and books visit www.bloomsbury.com. Here you will find extracts,
author interviews, details of forthcoming events and the option to sign up for our newsletters.

'The fury of civil wars, when the battle has ceased, is almost invariably reserved for the scaffold.'

Malcolm Laing, historian of Scotland, 1802

Contents

Author's Note

Spellings: For ease of reading most of the letters and other documents here transcribed are given with the spelling corrected to correspond with modern usage. Many of the main characters' names were spelled in a number of ways ('Ludlowe', 'Cooke', etc.) in the seventeenth century, but I have plumped for their modern version.

Sources: The original writings of Edmund Ludlow have been edited by many writers for their political ends, with his Puritanism often downplayed and those views that chimed with radical Whig philosophy frequently amplified. However, as A. B. Worden, the pre-eminent historical expert on Ludlow, affirms, 'The work, which supplies vivid accounts of Ludlow's military and political career, can still be profitably consulted.'

Prologue

The English Civil War began in 1642, the result of escalating political, social and religious tensions between Charles I and Parliament. The English Crown had received insufficient revenue for decades, and was, periodically and reluctantly, forced to seek Parliament's aid in granting it financial assistance. However, in return, Parliament increasingly expected to be heard by the King, on grievances relating to three of the key aspects of seventeenth-century life: rights, money, and God.

From 1629 to 1640, Charles elected to reign without Parliament in order to hush the exasperating voices of its more strident members. Instead, he relied on money raised through the exploitation of ancient kingly privileges and customs. These were thought by many to be abuses of power and an erosion of the people's civil liberties.

Religion added to the frictions. While many in the House of Commons were Presbyterian or Puritan, Charles was believed to be a Catholic sympathiser – a suspicion that was fuelled by the evident Roman Catholicism of his French wife, Henrietta Maria. The King was an intensely devout man who believed in an ecclesiastical structure in which bishops were not only the commanding pediment, but also the crucial cornerstone. A weak ruler generally, he insisted on the imposition of his strict religious views. Some Puritans, meanwhile, headed overseas to escape Charles's persecution, many of them gravitating to the new colonies in America.

In 1639 and 1640 the Scots invaded England in protest at Charles's attempts to inflict his High Anglican creed upon their Presbyterian churchmen. The King was obliged to summon Parliament in order to fund a defensive army. This left him vulnerable to the built-up resentments of members of the House of Commons arriving in Westminster, who demanded lasting and meaningful concessions. A key one of these was to make Parliament's summoning a regular occurrence, rather than remaining dependent on the whim of the Crown. Even in the face of foreign invasion, many MPs were unwilling to give the King what he wanted until they had been satisfied. Although Charles tried to regain control, he could not.

In August 1642, after further frustrations and humiliations, he raised his standard at Nottingham in a call to arms. That autumn the Royalist and Parliamentary armies stumbled into each other while heading towards London. At the ensuing battle of Edgehill, shockingly for both sides, many hundreds of Englishmen were killed by their compatriots.

The following year the war seemed to be going in the King's favour, but Parliament's control of London and the navy, its superior supply chain, and its subsequent alliance with the Scots, gave it an increasingly clear advantage. 1644 saw the Royalists lose control of the north of England, when Scottish and Parliamentary soldiers destroyed the King's forces at Marston Moor. The following year Parliament debuted its imposing, professional, fighting machine – the New Model Army – which triumphed at the battle of Naseby and captured Bristol, England's second city. By the spring of 1646 Charles's military forces were beaten, and the First Civil War was effectively over. The Crown's diverse enemies had been brought together by fear and suspicion of a monarch who seemed to threaten their civil and religious liberties. The question for them now was: what to do with the defeated King?

Chapter 1

Man of Blood

We have been by Providence put upon strange things, such as the ancientest here doth scarce remember. The Army acting to these ends, Providence hath been with us, and yet we have found little fruit with our endeavours. The kingdom and Army calls for expedition.

Edward Sexby, Parliamentary soldier, October 1647

The news that King Charles was being sent from Windsor for trial in Westminster was fresh – exhilarating to those who believed he must be held to account for the recent, rich bloodshed in his three kingdoms; deeply troubling to others who had either fought for his defeated cause, or who retained instinctive deference for God's anointed representative, in spite of his hand in the years of discord.

So when Mr Proctor, making the opposite journey from London towards Windsor, had almost reached the crossing of the Thames at Brentford – scene of a Royalist victory six years earlier – he quickly realised that the brisk rhythm of approaching cavalry was the King's escort, speeding the illustrious prisoner to the capital. It was a force powerful enough to see off a rescue attempt, numerous enough to make escape impossible.

The cavalrymen of the New Model Army – buff-coated, each armed with a pair of pistols and a sword, girded by chest armour and topped off with a lobster-tail helmet – began to pass him in disciplined formation. At the core of the column Proctor saw two men who he would clearly remember, under oath, a decade later: riding alone amongst the ranks of troopers was a tall, thin figure, who Proctor recognised as the charismatic firebrand preacher, Hugh Peters. Dynamic and lively, Peters triumphantly led his captive prize towards his interpretation of justice. Immediately behind Peters, sitting quite alone in the six-horse royal carriage, was the slight King – a reluctant passenger, on a winter road, the anguish in his heart triggered by the peril of his destination.

Proctor instinctively removed his hat, his eyes briefly locking with those of the King, who returned the courtesy shown him by his subject. Furious at this fawning, the soldiers nearest Proctor set their mounts at him, casting this eyewitness to history and his horse from the roadside, down into a ditch, 'where,' he recalled, 'I stayed till they passed by, and was glad I escaped so.'[1]

Charles's former progresses between London and Windsor had denoted a shuttling from one bastion of monarchical power to another. What Proctor had chanced upon was quite different: the taking of a King of England from a sprawling prison to a focused place of judgment. There, his life would be in play, in a forum where, for the first time in his quarter-century reign, he would be shorn of all power, and at the mercy of a body that absolutely denied the fundamental belief that was at the centre of his kingly philosophy: that he was answerable only to God.

Charles had made bids for freedom during the three years since the First Civil War had ended in his military defeat. In April 1646 he had slipped away from his beleaguered wartime headquarters of Oxford, in a party of three led by Dr Michael Hudson. The King valued Hudson as 'my plain-speaking chaplain', but he had useful secular functions too, having been the scoutmaster-general (intelligence chief) in the Royalist army of the North. This escape from Oxford was planned despite the disapproval of many of Charles's trusted followers, some of whom had called for him to accept a noble end in battle over the ignominy of being caught in disguise, while deserting his followers. The Parliamentarians, they said, would kill him either way.

But Charles was one for whom the last word of advice tended to weigh heaviest, and when his courtier and confidant John Ashburnham told him that a secret breakout from Oxford could succeed, Charles let his nephew, Prince Rupert, and his cousin, the Duke of Richmond, know his intention of immediate flight. By candlelight Ashburnham clipped at the King's hair and remodelled his beard, while providing him with a priest's cassock as a further disguise. The governor of Oxford, Sir Thomas Glemham, was now let in on the plan. Glemham retrieved the keys to the city, and just after the clock struck three in the morning, he led the King, the courtier and the priest over Magdalen Bridge, towards the East Gate, wishing them well as they slipped away. Glemham then rode back alone, locking the gates of Oxford to all for five days, as agreed with the King. It was hoped this would result in enough of a head start to give this desperate plan its best chance of success.

Charles's design was to leave England for another of his kingdoms, Scotland. The principal Scottish army was in league with his Parliamentary enemies, joined to them through a religious and military covenant. But Charles hoped to play on residual loyalty to his Stuart family roots: Charles's grandmother was Mary, Queen of Scots, while his father had been James VI of Scotland before succeeding Queen Elizabeth, in 1603, as ruler of England. Relying on the Scots was a risky strategy, but (after contemplating a bold appearance in London) Charles felt he had nowhere better to turn.

Hudson led his royal master through various dangers: outside one town they passed by Parliamentary dragoons without being challenged; at a checkpoint in a village they were stopped. On being asked, 'To whom do you belong?' Hudson replied, 'To the House of Commons.'[2] They were waved on.

The party of three eventually reached Norfolk, from where the prominent Parliamentarians Miles Corbet and Valentine Walton reported on the fugitive's progress to the Speaker of the Commons. The King, they said, had swapped his black coat for a grey one, dispensed with his long cassock, and acquired a new hat: 'Wherever they came, they were very private, and always writing,' Corbet and Walton noted. 'Hudson did enquire for a ship to go to the north, or Newcastle, but could get none.'[3]

The fugitives eventually succeeded in reaching Newark, where they knew the Scots were besieging one of the last remaining Royalist garrisons. The King and his two companions presented themselves to an astonished Scottish army, forcing its generals to face a startling conundrum: here was their ruler – their chief enemy – who had come to them for help, and in the process had made himself their prisoner. Hudson quickly realised the gamble had failed. He learnt that the Scots were considering two options, both of them disastrous for his master: selling Charles to Parliament; or using him at the head of one English army to attack and weaken the New Model Army, the force which had recently dealt the Royalists repeated heavy defeats and whose successes now made the Scots uneasy when they looked south.

Indignant that anyone might for a moment think they would let self-interest overcome their unswerving desire to do the right thing, the Scots wrote to Parliament in London: 'Trusting to our integrity we do persuade ourselves, that none will so far misconstrue us at that we intended to make use of this seeming advantage for promoting any other ends than are expressed in the covenant, and have been hitherto pursued by us with no less conscience than care.'[4] They then promptly sold the King to Parliament for a £100,000 down payment.

From the moment he was taken north from Newark and handed over in Newcastle, the King was treated with dutiful respect by a Parliament eager to explore options for peace. The Presbyterian majority in the Commons had grave reservations about the rampant power of the army. It wanted to find an accommodation with Charles that maintained the monarchy, while securing the regular summoning of Parliament, and blocking the King's ability to milk ancient, controversial powers and so circumvent it. If these goals were achieved, Parliament would be able to dismiss the troubling regiments that had given it victory over the Royalists, and live in peace with the much diminished Crown.

To the powerful Puritan element in the army, this conciliatory attitude was profoundly alarming. It signified a denial of the King's many and serious wrongdoings – something they believed God had made clear through administering Charles repeated defeats: in a superstitious age, battle was seen as an ordeal in which the righteous could expect to triumph. The level of success enjoyed by Parliament's New Model Army had been astonishing. Gone were many of the patrician senior officers who had fought their King with reservation and trepidation: their first lord general, the Earl of Essex, had embarked on his initial campaign with sufficient pessimism to take his coffin in tow; and another commander, the Earl of Manchester, had openly despaired, 'However many victories we win, there will still remain the King.'[5] This aristocratic high command had been replaced by a band of flinty colonels: hardbitten fighting men who had risen to regimental command, often from humble beginnings: they included a cobbler, a silversmith and a butcher's son. Many of them believed they were on a divine mission to establish God's will through force of arms. They had witnessed at first hand the slaughter of their men at battles and sieges, as well as the resulting suffering inflicted on the civilian population. They had honed their units into Christian powerhouses, where prayers were said morning and night, swearing was punished with the lash, blasphemy would see a man's tongue pierced through, and the striking of a civilian or the threatening of an officer would result in a sentence of death.

Meanwhile, an increasing number of soldiers wanted Charles to answer for what they saw as his personal crimes: no longer were they prepared to subscribe to the convention that the King was above wrongdoing, with any royal misdemeanour blamed rather on his advisers. This had reached absurd levels in the Civil War when Charles's enemies claimed to be fighting him in the name of 'the King and Parliament'.

The soldiers of the New Model Army had seen the Civil War up close, and believed the responsibility for its horrors lay firmly at Charles's feet. They feared that Parliament's determination to turn a blind eye to such a glaring and calamitous offence sent a dangerous message to the large swathes of the population that still held a super-stitious reverence for kingship. 'These things I say made the people ready to conclude,' wrote Edmund Ludlow, an MP and senior army officer, with a republican's hatred for the flummery of royalty,

> that though his designs had been wonderfully defeated, his armies beaten out of the field, and himself delivered into the hands of the Parliament, against whom he had made a long and bloody war; yet certainly he must be in the right: and that though he was guilty of the blood of many thousands, yet was still unaccountable, in a condition to give pardon, and not in need of receiving any: which made them flock from all parts to see him as he was brought from Newcastle to Holmby [Holdenby], falling down before him, and counting him as only able to restore to them their peace and settlement.[6]

Holdenby, where the King was now detained, was the enormous Northamptonshire mansion bought forty years earlier by his father, James I. Here, Charles was treated with such deference – his Parlia-mentary guardians decking out the Midland palace in freshly bought finery, and staffing it with royal minions – that tensions between Parliament and the army's rank and file escalated. Soldiers who had risked their lives in the Parliamentary cause, defending what they saw as the liberties of the people and God's true religion against a dangerous King who they believed harboured Catholic sympathies, were dismayed to see their defeated enemy easing back into a position of regal authority – one that he had not only exer-cised so calamitously in the recent past, but which threatened their wellbeing now. If the King were restored to anything approaching his former powers, he would inevitably seek vengeance against the men who had defeated his forces and slain his friends and followers. The sacrifices on the field would have brought no advantage; they would merely have demanded retribution.

Confident that they were in the ascendant, and that the soldiers that had won the war for their cause would soon be cashiered and put out to pasture, many in Parliament spoke openly of pricking the power of the army. Senior officers sitting in the Commons listened to increasingly strident attacks on the military with growing anger. 'These men,' the army's second-in-command, Oliver Cromwell, hissed to Ludlow, 'will never leave till the army pull them out by the ears.'[7] Some soldiers fought back in the hostile forum, bringing successive petitions to Parliament with three clear demands: they wanted the kingdom's affairs settled to their satisfaction; they insisted that they be given their outstanding wages; and they required that a pledge be made by MPs not to disband the army. Shocked by their impudence, Parliament instead threatened to treat any who repeated such petitions as traitors.

Certain that its enemies in Parliament were determined to settle with the King to its detriment, the army sent a force to Holdenby to remove Charles into its custody. During the succeeding year he was shuttled round various military centres of operations – Royston, Hatfield, Reading and Woburn. On his travels he was wooed by four parties keen to harness the prestige of the Crown for their own purposes: the army, Parliament, the Scots, and those championing the City of London's business interests. Sensing that Charles was feeling buoyed by the attentions of these powerful bodies, Henry Ireton, one of the leading figures in the New Model Army, warned: 'Sir, you have an intention to be arbitrator between the Parliament and us – and we mean to be so between you and the Parliament.'[8]

At Woburn the King was privately presented with proposals for a settlement that the army had approved, and intended to make public. Sir John Berkeley, one of Henrietta Maria's confidants, had acted for the King during the brokering of terms. This he did with a realistic understanding of the King's plight. Berkeley had felt compelled to concede various points: seven senior Royalists would be condemned for their role in the Civil War; none of the King's supporters would be allowed to stand for Parliament at the next election; the role of bishops – who were loathed by the Puritans as much as they were prized by the King – would be diminished. The army was confident that, if Charles agreed to these points, it could present them to Parliament with every chance that they would be accepted.

Surely, the King said, the army's leaders had no intention of reaching agreement with him, if this was what they thought to offer him? Berkeley forcefully disagreed, stating that the opposite was surely the case: if they had sought fewer advantages, then that would have proved that the enemy were not serious, 'there being no appearance, that men, who had through so many dangers and diffi-culties acquired such advantages, would content themselves with less than was contained in the said proposals; and that a crown so near lost was never recovered so easily as this would be, if things were adjusted upon these terms.'[9] The King was deaf to Berkeley's good sense, insisting petulantly that he would wait for the army to return to him with improved conditions.

When instead the army decided to announce its original proposals, Charles was indignant, repeatedly telling the officers present: 'You cannot be without me; you will fall to ruin, if I do not sustain you.' Even in defeat, and while being held in custody, the King felt sure he was indispensible. Berkeley, exasperated at his master's delusion, and embarrassed by his rudeness, reproached him: 'Sir, you speak as if you had some secret strength and power which I do not know of; and since you have concealed it from me, I wish you had done it from these men also.'[10]

Various key figures in the army now gave up all hope of striking a deal with Charles. Instead, they started to look to their own safety, and what they perceived to be the public good. To some, neither of these priorities required the King's wellbeing, or even his presence.

Charles was moved to Hampton Court Palace the next month, August 1647. This was a royal residence the King knew well: he had spent his honeymoon there, with his fifteen-year-old French bride, twenty-two years earlier. The wife of a Parliamentary colonel, Lucy

Hutchinson,* wrote with disgust that at Hampton Court, Charles 'lived rather in the condition of a guarded and attended prince than as a conquered and purchased captive'.[11] His courtiers reconvened there as his Privy Council, while representatives from Scotland had ready access to the King: they plotted privately with him, judging how best to use him against his Parliamentary captors.

Charles grew deeply anxious about his personal safety while at Hampton Court, hearing gossip of plans to assassinate him. A letter from Cromwell, conveyed by Colonel Edward Whalley, the King's custodian since early summer, only stoked these fears. Whalley, a hero of the Civil War and a first cousin of Cromwell, recalled: 'When I received the letter, I was much astonished, abhorring that such a thing should be done, or so much as thought of, by any that bear the name of Christians. When I had shown the letter to his majesty, I told him, "I was sent to safeguard, and not to murder him. I wished him to be confident no such thing should be done. I would first die at his foot in his defence." '[12]

Whalley's prime concern was not an attempt on the King's life, but the impossibility of keeping Charles at Hampton Court, should he choose to abscond: the King was not officially a prisoner, so had to be granted some privacy, as well as reasonable freedom of movement. But, as Whalley reminded his superiors, Hampton Court Palace 'is vast; hath fifteen hundred rooms ... and would require a troop of horse, upon perpetual duty, to guard all the out-goings'.[13] All Whalley felt able to do was show vigilance in the daytime, and appoint guards around the King's bedroom at night. It was, said Whalley, a 'careful and hazardous duty',[14] and one that he frequently asked to be relieved of because of its huge responsibility, made that much more onerous through the glaring inadequacy of his manpower.

---

* Born in the Tower of London, whilst her father Sir Allen Apsley was keeper there, Lucy Hutchinson was a formidable character, known for her intellect and her republicanism. A Latin scholar (then rare among women), she was the first person to translate the complete text of Lucretius's De Rerum Natura ('On the Nature of Things'), and later wrote poetry and many religious treaties. She was the mother of nine children, and her husband, John Hutchinson's, biographer after his death.

The King's routine was at least helpful to the colonel, because of its predictability. 'Mondays and Thursdays were the King's set days for his writing letters to be sent into foreign parts,' Whalley recalled. 'His usual time of coming out of his bedchamber, on those days, was betwixt five and six of the clock. Presently after he went to prayers. And, about half an hour after that, to supper: at which times I set guards about his bedchamber.'[15]

On a November evening, Whalley went to the anteroom that abutted the King's bedchamber and asked Charles's attendants if he could see their master. They said this was not possible: he was busy writing letters, and had left strict instructions not to be disturbed.

Whalley waited for an hour, with mounting anxiety. The courtiers persisted in their tale: the King was dealing with extraordinary business. When pushed further, they claimed he was writing a long letter to his eldest daughter Mary, the Princess of Orange. By seven o'clock, Whalley was deeply concerned. He suggested to a senior courtier that the King might be unwell and that he should look in on him. The courtier refused to disobey the King's instructions.

'I was then extreme restless in my thoughts,' recorded Whalley, 'looked oft in at the keyhole, to see whether I could perceive his majesty: but could not.'[16] Still stonewalled by the royal attendants, Whalley went to fetch Smitheby, the keeper of the privy lodgings, and with him approached the King's quarters from the other side, going up a stairway leading from the rear garden, before hurrying through the suite of rooms that culminated in the space adjacent to the King's bedroom. There, in the middle of the floor, lay Charles's crumpled cloak.

Circling back to the anteroom, Whalley insisted in the name of Parliament that the courtiers open the King's locked bedroom door. Realising that the colonel was no longer to be denied, one of them eventually agreed, went into the room, then reappeared. Confirming Whalley's fears, he simply reported that the King had gone.

It was found that Charles had left behind three letters, one of them containing a courteous acknowledgement of Whalley's good treatment of him.

The colonel sent soldiers on horseback to sweep the grounds, and on foot to scour the surrounding buildings. He also immediately reported the King's disappearance to his cousin, Cromwell, and to Sir Thomas Fairfax, the Parliamentary army's commander-in-chief. Then he dispatched men to John Ashburnham's house, a mile away, and learnt that he too was gone. The King and Ashburnham had embarked on another of their bids for freedom.

In the days leading up to his escape Charles had sent his trusted agent, Jane Whorwood – the striking, redheaded stepdaughter of one of his leading Scottish courtiers – to ask the astrologer William Lilly in which direction he should flee. Lilly was a known Parliamentarian: towards the end of the First Civil War he had urged the King to bow to the authority of Parliament, since to do otherwise would endanger his life. He had also berated Charles for having waged 'an uncivil and unnatural war against his own subjects'.[17] However, Lilly's reputation was such that Charles felt compelled to seek his advice: in his almanac for 1645, *Anglicus, Peace or no Peace*, Lilly had deduced from Mars's predicted alignment that June would be the most promising time to attack the King's forces – 'If now we fight, a Victory stealeth upon us.' The triumph of Naseby had duly occurred in the middle of that month. Both sides now looked keenly at Lilly's projections: his almanac for 1647 had sold 17,000 copies by the time Charles consulted him.

Lilly advised Jane Whorwood that the King's best hope lay in fleeing to Essex. But the King did not wait for Jane's return, and, headed south, instead of east intending to sail for France if he remained in danger. Through the bungling of a well-meaning courtier, Charles found himself compromised and in the hands of Colonel Robert Hammond – a cousin of Cromwell and the governor of the Isle of Wight. On arrival the King declared he had come to seek sanctuary on the island out of fear for his life, and claimed to be 'desiring to be somewhat secure till some happy accommodation may be made between me and my Parliament'.[18] He was housed in Carisbrooke Castle. While there, Charles was still treated as a respectfully detained king, staying in the comfort of the Constable's Lodgings. Some of the Parliamentary officers stationed there were openly hostile to the king, but the local population was largely Royalist. For several months Charles believed he would be able to leave at any time, the illusion of liberty completed by Hammond allowing him freedom to ride around the island.

Charles's former suitors soon gravitated towards the Isle of Wight, their honeyed words confirming his belief that he remained central in the framing of his subjects' future. Commissioners arrived from Parliament, eager to see if there was a way of negotiating a peaceful settlement of the nation, and at the same time achieving their aim of sidelining the army. Meanwhile Scottish emissaries appeared, intent on brokering what advantages they could for their people. They felt aggrieved that Parliament had failed to honour its side of their alliance, particularly in religious matters, and secretly plotted with the King: they talked of a march south by the Scottish army to overthrow the mutual enemy. This was clearly an exciting prospect for Charles, but he kept other options in play.

Charles consistently overestimated the strength of his hand and the patience of his enemies, as he played Parliament, the army and the Scots off against one another. He felt sure that none of these competing forces could achieve what they wanted without his support. At the same time, he felt no qualms of conscience about his many deceits: all was being extracted from him through duress, while he was in effect a prisoner. The King believed this negated his concessions: he fully intended to go back on any promises made, once his freedom was restored. He wrote as much, repeatedly, in letters that he intended for sympathisers on the mainland. Many were intercepted. As the conditions of his confinement became stricter, it began to dawn on Charles that Governor Hammond was not his protector, but his gaoler, and that he was under house arrest.

His most trusted intermediary, now shuttling between the Isle of Wight and London with secret messages, was Jane Whorwood, the intermediary who had consulted Lilly for the King. This 'tall, well-fashioned and well-languaged gentlewoman, with round visage ... exceedingly loyal, understanding and of good judgement', was, in the estimation of a Parliamentary spy, 'the most loyal to King Charles in his miseries of any woman in England'.[19] This was a reputation earned over several years. At the outbreak of the Civil War, Jane Whorwood's husband, Brome, had gone abroad rather than dare to fight for either cause. The abandoned wife remained in Holton House, Oxfordshire, with her two children. When the Royalists settled in Oxford, four miles from Holton, she utilised her family's trading connections and a network of sympathetic contacts to arrange a smuggling ring. In this way, during 1643 and 1644, she succeeded in getting 1,700lbs of gold from Royalist supporters into the King's hands, some of which was used to pay for the escape of Henrietta Maria and the Prince of Wales to France. Whorwood's principal role, though, was trafficking clandestine correspondence.

After the conclusion of the First Civil War, Whorwood remained an agent of the compromised Crown. She defrauded the Parliamentary revenue committee for Charles's benefit.

During Charles's detention on the Isle of Wight, Jane Whorwood tried twice to help him escape. During the first attempt, in March 1648, the King had become stuck between the bars of the window of his bedchamber. Charles had checked that his head would fit between the window bars, 'and he was sure, where that would pass, the body would follow'; but when he attempted to clamber out, 'His Majesty ... too late, found himself mistaken, he sticking fast between his breast and shoulders, and not able to get forwards or backwards ...' The second attempt, two months later, took place after Lilly had put Whorwood in contact with a locksmith who provided the King with the tools to escape: nitric acid and a file. The plan foundered after two guards, who had been bribed, betrayed him. Whorwood was left waiting in vain for weeks aboard a ship on which she planned to sail with the King to the Netherlands. The Royalist Marquess of Hertford concluded of the King's failure to escape, while acknowledging Jane's impeccable loyalty,

'Had the rest done their parts as carefully as Whorwood, the King would now have been at large.'[20]

Charles was now kept under closer guard in Carisbrooke, unable to receive visitors, his principal servants sent away. Increasingly frustrated by the King's obstinacy, and appalled by his lack of integrity, the feelings of those dealing with Charles hardened against him. There had been a vivid moment that onlookers saw as revealing Charles's true thinking, beneath the affably accommodating veneer. One day he was observed throwing a bone for his two spaniels, and taking inordinate pleasure in the ensuing tussle, as the dogs fought for the prize. Parliament's commissioners and the representatives from the Scots wondered if they, too, in seeking the King's cooperation, were ragging over a tossed bone in front of an amused monarch. They came to believe that his true intention was to keep them beholden to him, yet unfulfilled in their aims, until he was in a position powerful enough to turn and strike them down.

The opinion of the King from the army, in particular, was one of escalating contempt. In late October 1647, while Charles was ensconced seven miles away in Hampton Court Palace, a church next to the army headquarters in Putney became the venue for the start of a series of debates of a deeply radical hue. The General Council of the Army that convened there included not only senior officers, but also representatives of the New Model Army's regiments: highly politicised and articulate men from all ranks, who felt entitled through victory to have a say in the way their country should progress from this crossroads in its history.

Some were Levellers, an egalitarian movement that flowered briefly in the late 1640s. Strikingly modern in their aims, the Levellers wanted religious tolerance, manhood suffrage (the vote for all men), regular and accountable parliaments, and popular sovereignty, whereby those in power placed the public good ahead of their self-interest. Charles's example of kingship, insisting on privileges, assumptions and abuses rooted in the Middle Ages, was a lightning rod for their hatred.

The most senior officer openly advocating the Leveller position at Putney was Colonel Thomas Rainsborough, who had been a military commander on land and sea during the recent Civil War. Rainsborough's background was steeped in religious devotion and social liberalism. He was the son of an admiral who, as ambassador, had fought to end white slavery in Morocco. Rainsborough and his brother had both visited the colony of Providence Island, off the Central American Mosquito Coast, where English Puritans had tried to establish an independent utopian society, devoid of profanity, prostitutes, drunkenness and gambling – with a rather ill-matched sideline in piracy, directed against the nearby Spanish colonies.

When Rainsborough addressed the military assembly at Putney, he did so with broad vision and startling radicalism, championing the common man – the backbone of the army, as he pointed out – while highlighting the selfish tendencies of their social superiors, including those in Parliament. 'I would fain know what the soldier hath fought for all this while?' he asked; 'He hath fought to enslave himself, to give power to men of riches, men of estates, to make him a perpetual slave.'[21] The ordinary soldier had delivered victory. Now he deserved and demanded a stake in the fresh world he had created.

Among those listening to Rainsborough and the other impassioned debaters were two of the tightly meshed officer elite: Commissary General Henry Ireton, son-in-law to Oliver Cromwell; and Lieutenant Colonel William Goffe, son-in-law to Charles's former custodian, Colonel Whalley. An intensely religious man, Goffe took time to remind all present of God's omnipotence, and warned them of his appetite for severe retribution when his will was flouted. 'And I pray, let us consider this,' Goffe offered: 'God does seem evidently to be throwing down the glory of all flesh. The greatest powers in the kingdom have been shaken. God hath thrown down the glory of the King and that party . . . I do not say that God will throw us down – I hope better things – but he will have the glory.'[22]

Goffe warned that God met obstinacy with a rod of iron, and

that those who went away from his path would either be broken in pieces, or robbed of their glory. It was time, Goffe maintained, to listen to God, through a devout and humble prayer meeting. Otherwise, all may well be lost.

Ireton followed by paying tribute to Goffe's wisdom, eloquence, and godliness. The commissary general then confided that his own increasingly close relationship with God had given him confidence to ignore 'considerations of danger and difficulty . . . and perhaps to do some things that otherwise I should not have thought fit to have done'.[23] This was a statement pregnant with possibilities.

It became clear as the debates went into their second day that Goffe was in that growing group of soldiers convinced that the army and Parliament should cease trying to accommodate the King, and should instead call him to account for the bloodshed he had caused in the land. Goffe believed that these were very urgent considerations, for, through his fervent study of the Bible, and in particular the Book of Revelation, he was convinced he was living in the final days of human history: soon God would return, to judge all. There was no time to lose.

The army's wish for the King to be punished gained further traction in the spring and summer of 1648, when a series of Royalist risings flared up in a brief, twitching spasm that would be known as the Second Civil War.

In Wales, various Parliamentary troops switched their allegiance to the Crown. Colonel Thomas Horton, a bitter enemy of the Presbyterians in Parliament and a champion of the army's Puritan faction, was charged with striking them down. He was aided by Colonel John Okey, who commanded the New Model Army's one dedicated regiment of dragoons – mounted infantry. His men had fought with particular distinction at Naseby. Although his force was half the size of that of the Royalists, Horton's men were better trained, and had a significantly larger cavalry strength. They won a crushing victory at St Fagans, near Cardiff, in early May. Notable among the Parliamentary heroes that day was Captain Thomas Wogan, a Pembrokeshire man who shared Horton's firm attachment to the army's political interests. He was soon promoted to colonel.

A month later, Colonel Thomas Waite concluded the siege of Woodcroft House in Northamptonshire. The defending commander was Dr Hudson, Charles I's chaplain, who had guided him on the ill-fated escape from Oxford to the Scots. He was a Royalist who was particularly despised by the New Model Army. Hudson and his men were promised mercy on surrender. However, once the stronghold was secured, the victors poured in, and Hudson was pursued to the rooftop, where he clung from the edge by his fingertips. The Parliamentarians chopped off his hands, sending him plummeting into the moat below. Managing to flail his way to the bank, he was met with a flurry of blows and beaten to death. News of the fall of Woodcroft House, and the hated Hudson's end, secured Waite the thanks of Parliament.

The most significant Royalist forces in the south – Lord Goring's cavalry, Lord Capel's men from Hertfordshire, and Sir George Lisle's squadrons from Chelmsford – ended up after various reverses holed up together in Colchester. The Parliamentary commander-in-chief, Sir Thomas Fairfax, blocked sea access to the town, and settled into a determined siege. The Royalists' only hope of salvation rested with a large army coming south from Scotland, under Charles I's cousin, the Duke of Hamilton. This invasion was the consequence of the King's secret dealings with the Scottish commissioners on the Isle of Wight.

The Colchester garrison was poorly supplied, and was soon reduced to eating its horses, then the townspeople's dogs and cats, before feeding on soap and candles. After eleven weeks of resistance, the Royalists heard the besiegers' cannon fire in celebration. Kites drifted over the town's walls carrying the news that the Scottish army had been defeated in a three-day rolling battle at Preston, Lancashire. There could be no relief for Colchester, now. After the surrender, the Parliamentary council of war was in an unforgiving mood.

Its officers – who included Ireton, Whalley, Colonel John Bark-

stead and Colonel Isaac Ewer – sent the Royalist lords to be tried
by their peers in London. They also condemned two senior officers,
Sir Charles Lucas and Sir George Lisle, to face an immediate firing
squad in the courtyard of Colchester Castle. Lisle, a brave and
popular infantry general, witnessed a file of dragoons shoot Lucas.
He bent to kiss his slain comrade on the head, then rose to face his
executioners with bravado, beckoning them to come forward:
'Friends, I have been nearer you when you have missed me.'[24] They
made no mistake this time.

These executions shocked many, and brought home the determination of the New Model Army not to tolerate further Royalist
uprisings. It had lost several senior and respected figures in this
resumption of hostilities, which was a source of bitter resentment.
At Colchester, Colonel Simon Needham of the Tower Guards had
been killed early in the siege. His successor as colonel was William
Shambrook, who was in turn mortally wounded in early July. The
Parliamentary troops believed that both regimental commanders
had been shot with 'poisoned bullets' – musket balls chewed rough
and rolled in grit. Their use was a heinous breach of the prevailing
rules of warfare.

The Second Civil War produced many other fallen heroes of the
New Model Army. During the triumph at Preston, Colonel Francis
Thornaugh, charging dangerously ahead of his men, was run
through by a Royalist lancer. Propped up, his lifeblood ebbing
away, he presented a memorable deathbed tribute to the 'Good Old
Cause' of Parliament. As victory unfolded before him, his final
words were: 'I now rejoice to die, since God hath let me see the
overthrow of this perfidious enemy; I could not lose my life in a
better cause, and I have the favour from the Lord to see my blood
avenged.'[25]

Another notable Parliamentarian to fall was Thomas Rainsborough, who had impressed so many with his eloquence at the Putney
debates a year earlier. Rainsborough had achieved the rank of
vice-admiral in the Parliamentary fleet, but fellow naval officers
bridled at his Leveller views; they provoked a mutiny, and Rains-

borough was sent back to serve on land. Towards the end of the Second Civil War he was directed to command the siege of Pontefract Castle. Stopping in Doncaster en route, Rainsborough was surprised by a group of Royalist soldiers who, posing as friends, gained access to his bedchamber, intent on kidnapping him. When he resisted, they murdered him instead. Rainsborough's funeral in London was attended by thousands, wearing sprigs of rosemary in their hats and sea-green ribbons pinned to their clothes – symbols of Leveller support.

The soldiers had been at the sharp end of these bloodiest of conflicts: by their end the Civil Wars would, through battlefield casualties and war-borne disease, lead to the loss of an estimated 190,000 of the five million inhabitants of England and 60,000 of the one million Scots. (Figures for Ireland are less easy to establish but, during the same period, warfare, plague and exile reduced the 1.4 million population of Ireland by around 600,000.) Many believed Charles had caused the suffering, and they were now convinced that he would only add to it – for nothing would dissuade him from attempting to regain power, whatever the toll on his people.

Its patience at an end, the army held a three-day prayer meeting at its Windsor Castle headquarters, after which it resolved 'to call Charles Stuart, that Man of Blood, to an account for that blood he hath shed and the mischief he had done to his utmost, against the Lord's cause and people'.[26] Meanwhile, from August, representatives of the Lords and Commons intensified their negotiations with Charles on the Isle of Wight. The King was released from close guard after giving his word that there would be no further escape attempts, and celebrated his greater liberty by writing immediately to his 'Sweet Jane' (Whorwood) in code, inviting her to his quarters. She accepted, and the two became lovers.

Alongside her new role as royal mistress, Whorwood resumed her travels between the Isle of Wight and London, smuggling correspondence and gauging the mood in the capital towards the King. She found that the gulf between Charles's enemies in Parliament and the military was ever-widening. On 13 November she sent the

King an urgent dispatch, partly in code, telling him things looked so very dangerous for 'my dear friend' that, despite having given his word never to do so, he must escape immediately. If he did not, he would find himself at the mercy of the increasingly vengeful element in the army.

It was as if the New Model Army's repeated triumphs, built on soldiers' bravery and washed in their blood, were, to the politicians, an irrelevance. Whatever was achieved for the cause, the King would stand apart, treated with reverence – his powers only partially diminished – free to stir the embers of insurrection. Lieutenant General Edmund Ludlow shared such concerns with his commander, Fairfax. 'I told him,' Ludlow recalled, 'that a design was driving on to betray the cause in which so much of the people's blood had been shed; that the King being under a restraint, would not account himself obliged by anything he should promise under such circumstances.' He was also clear that those keenest to negotiate with Charles 'designed principally to use his authority and favour in order to destroy the army'.[27]

Edward Sexby, a soldier from Cromwell's regiment, had eloquently captured his comrades' feelings of vulnerability and frustration in victory with eloquent foresight during the Putney debates: 'The cause of our misery is upon two things. We sought to satisfy all men, and it was well; but in going about to do it we have dissatisfied all men. We have laboured to please a King and I think, except we go about to cut all our throats, we shall not please him; and we have gone to support an house which will prove rotten studs – I mean the Parliament, which consists of a company of rotten members.'[28]

There was now frantic activity as the army's restlessness grew ever more pronounced. Presbyterian Parliamentarians cast around desperately for a working compromise with the King. Their aim was to settle the nation, cease hostilities, and return a chastened but functioning monarchy that needed no standing army to police its conduct.

Meanwhile, a senior officer in the New Model Army arranged to consult secretly with the Royalist Sir John Berkeley. They met in a quiet space behind a pub in Windsor, the Garter Inn, where the anonymous soldier warned Berkeley, 'The way designed to ruin the King is, to send 800 of the most disaffected in the army to secure his person, and then to bring him to a trial; and I dare think no farther. This will be done in ten days; and therefore, if the King can escape, let him do it as he loves his life.'[29] All had changed, the officer explained, because of serious cracks appearing in the military: Cromwell, faced with the beginnings of a parade ground mutiny by troops sporting Leveller symbols, had ordered the twelve ring-leaders arrested, and had had one of the men face a firing squad.

Such frictions threatened to evolve into a split in the army's loyal-ties, with many regiments then likely to declare for Parliament. If this happened, those associated with the recent high-handedness of the New Model Army – Cromwell, Ireton and their closest associ-ates – would be vulnerable to severe retribution, which might cost them their lives. Out of self-preservation, these leaders now sided with those who were most vocal in calling for justice against the King, even if that made Charles's destruction all but inevitable.

On 1 December, Parliament's commissioners reported back from the Isle of Wight that the King had conceded on some of their most recent demands, in particular an admission that he had been 'guilty of the blood spilt in the late war, with the proviso, that if the agree-ment were not ratified by the House, then this concession should be of no force against him'.[30] The sticking points, as ever, remained the questions relating to bishops, and to the pardoning of key Royalists. On the same date Fairfax, nervous that Charles might be rescued from Carisbrooke, had the King moved across the Solent to Hurst Castle – a functional fortress, built on a shingle spit, that was devoid of frills. It was Charles's first taste of stark prison condi-tions. Meanwhile the Parliamentary commander-in-chief sent a force of 7,000 soldiers to occupy London.

Against this tense background, late into the night of 5 December, the House of Commons furiously debated the value of Charles's recent concessions to their demands. They concluded, by 129 to 83 votes, that there was enough in them to form the basis for settling with the King. Several of the MPs defeated in this motion – supporters of the army – demanded that their utter rejection of the majority decision be recorded in the House's book.

That same night, realising that time was running out, a subcommittee of six officers and MPs met to work out how best to bypass the will of the Presbyterian MPs. The next day Colonel Thomas Pride, a wealthy London brewer who had long been a vociferous champion of the army's cause, implemented this meeting's conclusions. It was effectively a military coup, known to posterity as 'Pride's Purge'. Sir Hardress Waller and his regiment stood in menacing support of Pride's men as young, ruddy-faced Lord Grey of Groby – republican son of the Earl of Stamford – pointed out which members could be relied upon, and so be admitted to the Commons, and which could not be trusted to implement the New Model Army's will. There were just seventy-five who passed muster; the rest were barred: some were arrested, while around 150 were denied access to the chamber. When one member, William Prynne, tried to push past the soldiers, he was manhandled and led away. As he went, he demanded that Pride and Waller explain who was authorising their aggression. In reply the two colonels pointed silently to their men, whose weapons were at the ready.

On 16 December, Fairfax sent soldiers to bring the King from Hurst Castle to London. They collected their prisoner three days later, and immediately headed back north.

Charles was now in the hands of Colonel Thomas Harrison, a most dangerous enemy. Harrison, a long-haired dandy, removed his hat on greeting the King, in feigned respect for a man he viewed with contempt. At the Putney debates, Harrison had been prominent among those calling for Charles to be punished for spilling his subjects' blood.

The son of a Staffordshire butcher, Harrison was a notorious and eye-catching scourge of the Royalists who had risen to prominence through merit, and through his closeness to Cromwell. Harrison's religious zeal also counted in his favour: at the battle of Langport, the final great victory of the First Civil War, he was heard to cheer at the sight of the fleeing enemy, and 'with a loud voice break forth into the praises of God with fluent expressions, as if he had been in a rapture'.[31]

The King had a particular terror of Harrison: he had heard that the colonel had been entrusted with his murder. Charles knew of Harrison's reputation for ruthlessness and brutality. One of the most obstinate pockets of Royalist resistance in the south had been Basing House, home of the Roman Catholic Marquess of Winchester. As an English stronghold, it was second only to Windsor Castle in size, and successfully withstood two sieges in 1643 and 1644. Conditions were so dire for Basing's defenders at one stage that the marquess's brother secretly plotted with some dispirited comrades to let the Parliamentarians take the place. When the scheme was discovered, this aristocrat's life was spared, but his punishment was severe: he was forced to hang his fellow conspirators.

Basing became a self-regarding bastion of Catholicism, and consequently a place of particular revulsion to Puritans. In 1645 the marquess insisted that all Protestants leave his property, and met the third siege of Basing, from late August, with just 300 Catholic troops. His estate's gamekeepers acted as snipers, while women and children assisted in the forlorn defence. The New Model Army experimented with poisoned gas, lighting wet hay bales doused in arsenic and brimstone, which the wind carried towards Basing's defenders. Meanwhile the sprawling mansion was pummelled with artillery fire. Cromwell's heavy guns rolled into position in October, under the command of Richard Deane. Deane's cannon-royal fired a 60lb shot that no wall could withstand, supported by 30lb cannonballs from two other mighty pieces. Discouraged by his priests from surrendering, Winchester invited disaster. A frontal assault by the 7,000-strong Parliamentary force followed, and slaughter ensued, in which women and children fell and priests were hanged. Harrison took part in it all with enthusiasm. He dispatched two of the senior Catholic officers: the Royalists claimed that one of these,

Major Robinson (from a family of prominent actors), was shot by Harrison in cold blood after surrendering.

Charles was right to be worried about Harrison. He was in cahoots with the Levellers, listening to their hopes of fundamental reform while remaining focused on his core belief: that the 'carnal' government of man in all its forms should be jettisoned in favour of the rule of God. Harrison did not want to scare his prisoner, so treated him with clipped politeness. But he wanted the King to be punished before he could be reconciled to the Presbyterian majority in Parliament. Such a rapprochement would inevitably involve the disbanding of the army, and that would quickly be followed by revenge against its leaders. Harrison was aware that his notoriety must place him high on the list of those to receive Royalist retribution. Twelve years later Harrison recalled: 'There was a little discourse between the King and myself. The King had told me, that he had heard, that I should come privately to the Isle of Wight, to offer some injury to him. But I told him I abhorred the thoughts of it.'[32] Harrison advised his prisoner that, 'Parliament had too much honour and justice to cherish so foul an intention; and assured him that whatever the Parliament resolved to do would be very public, and in a way of justice, to which the world should be witness, and would never endure a thought of secret violence.'[33]

In his determination to deliver Charles safely and speedily for trial, Harrison had those officers with the fastest horses ride alongside the King, with a hundred others in close attendance with pistols drawn. The colonel was suspicious when Charles insisted that they break their journey eleven miles south of Windsor, with dinner at Bagshot Park, a favourite royal hunting lodge where, Clarendon recorded, the King 'had used to take much pleasure'.[34] There they would be guests of a couple of Royalist stalwarts, Lord and Lady Newburgh: in 1643, Lady Newburgh had narrowly escaped execution for her active role in a plot to turn London over to the Crown; and both the Newburghs had helped convey letters between Charles and his wife during his time at Hampton Court Palace.

Lord Newburgh had got word to Charles during his detention in Carisbrooke Castle. The plan was that he should, when approaching Bagshot, pretend his horse was falling lame. Newburgh would provide the replacement from his stables: one of his own racehorses, allegedly the fastest in England. The King should then wait until he was being taken through Windsor Forest, whose wilder tracks he knew well, and then gallop away to freedom.

At Bagshot, though, Charles's hosts greeted him with devastating news: the champion mount had been kicked hard by a stable mate the previous day, and was itself lame; the escape plan was stillborn. Harrison tightened his grip on Charles at Bagshot Park, insisting he was guarded by at least six soldiers at a time, stationing sentries at every doorway and banning anyone from talking to the king in low or whispered voices. It ended up being a visit that was both brief and fraught, the Newburghs saying farewell to the King in tears, convinced they would never see him again.

On 23 December, Harrison delivered Charles to Windsor Castle. That same day a committee was appointed to consider 'how to proceed in a way of Justice against the King, and other Capital Offenders [the captured Royalist generals from the Second Civil War]'.[35] Five days later the reading took place of 'An Ordinance for Trial of the King'. Charles could now make sense of Harrison's words to him: he was going to be tried in public.

Soon he was in his coach, heading across London for St James's. At first the captured King had been treated with deference, accorded many of the trappings of kingship; but gradually he was deprived of his comforts, and his retinue; his dinners became increasingly modest, and eventually he chose to eat alone in his room. 'There is nothing more contemptible,' he is said to have uttered, coming to terms with his new lot, 'than a despised prince.'[36]

Chapter 2

A King on Trial

*And if the Parliament and Military Council do what they do
without precedent, if it appear their duty, it argues the more
wisdom, virtue, and magnanimity, that they know themselves
able to be a precedent to others.*

John Milton, 'The Tenure of Kings and Magistrates', 1649

The army and their hand-sorted Members of Parliament, known
as the Rump, had opted for the high-risk option of a public
trial; but no King of England had been tried in open court before.*
Indeed, procedure in legal cases had the accused being challenged in
the name of the Crown. To prevent a descent into confusion and
farce, it was essential that the legality of the proceedings be established, as best it could. The format, the charge, the dignity of the
court – all needed to be respectable. Crucially, his accusers needed
to show on what basis they were entitled to hold a king to account.

This was a many-pieced jigsaw that took shape, day by day,
during the first three weeks of January 1649. On New Year's Day,
the Rump declared that it was treason for the King of England to
wage war against Parliament and the kingdom. The House of Lords
unanimously rejected this impeachment on 2 January, at the same
time rebuffing the ordinance for the King's trial. The Lords thought

---

* Richard II (1367–1400) had lost his throne after resigning it before the House of
Lords, rather than through a public trial.

they could delay matters by adjourning for a week, but the Rump was not to be detained. When the Lords returned to their chamber, they found its doors padlocked: given their stance, they would not be allowed to be part of this delicate and unprecedented process.

The Rump reasserted its aims in the Commons on 3 January, and was pleased the next day to hear from Augustine Garland, one of the many lawyers in the House, the name of the body that was to sit in judgment of Charles: 'the High Court of Justice for Trial of the King'. It had a weighty ring to it, given added ballast by the bold assertion that, 'The Commons of England assembled in Parliament declare that the people under God are the origin of all just power. They do likewise declare that the Commons of England assembled in Parliament, being chosen by and representing the people, have the supreme authority of this nation.'[1]

The actual definition of 'Parliament' was the trinity of Crown, Lords and Commons. This declaration of unilateral power by one House – the first of its kind in English history – made it clear that the Rump was prepared to stand as the sole law-making body. The King, the Lords and the excluded members of the Commons were placed to one side, impotent and irrelevant.

On 6 January, the Rump passed an Act for Charles's trial, claiming that:

> Charles Stuart, the now King of England ... had a wicked design totally to subvert the ancient and fundamental laws and liberties of his nation, and, in their place, to introduce an arbitrary and tyrannical government; and that, besides all other evil ways and means to bring this design to pass, he hath prosecuted it with fire and sword, levied and maintained a cruel war in the land against the Parliament and Kingdom, whereby the country hath been miserably wasted, the public treasure exhausted, and infinite other mischiefs committed.[2]

One hundred and thirty-five commissioners were appointed to the High Court of Justice that day. 'All the chief officers of the army were named, and accepted the office,' the Royalist Earl of

Clarendon later wrote, 'and such aldermen and citizens of London as had been most violent against peace, and some few country gentlemen whose zeal had been taken notice of for the cause, and who were like to take such a preferment as a testimony of the Parliament's confidence in them, and would thereupon embrace it.'[3] Only twenty of these men needed to be present at any one time for the court to function, which was helpful since its work had to be completed quickly: the ordinance declared that this High Court of Justice should enjoy its powers for just one month.

The commissioners were instructed to meet in the Painted Chamber of the Palace of Westminster on 8 January, the first of sixteen such meetings that were held there for the preparation and management of the trial. Throughout this time of tension and fear, the vaults beneath the Painted Chamber were frequently searched for explosives.

There proved to be a dearth of leading lawyers prepared to lead the revolutionary court. Several of the most eminent, whether dissatisfied with the legality of the process, frightened of future retribution, or with an eye to both concerns, decided to make themselves scarce. John Selden and Bulstrode Whitelocke retired from London. Meanwhile Lord Chief Baron Wilde, Chief Justice Henry Rolle and Chief Justice Oliver St John refused to serve in the High Court of Justice.

On 10 January the commissioners chose as their lord president – the officer who would act as their spokesman, questioning witnesses and controlling the King's proposals – John Bradshaw, a man not in the first flight of lawyers. Bradshaw had initially declined the position. He only made himself available after braving a tirade from his wife, who was furious that he would think of accepting a role that would invite danger into his and their family's lives.

Bradshaw had a reputation for competence, for efficiency, for pleasing litigious clients who visited his Gray's Inn chamber – and for being incorruptible. The poet John Milton, ever vocal against the Crown, was proud to call Bradshaw a friend, and a brave one at that, given that the position he agreed to take 'was great and fearful, almost surpassing all example, marked out as he was by the daggers and threats of so many ruffians'.[4] Bradshaw was provided with a sizeable bodyguard, not only for his protection, but to enhance his status – it was essential to inflate his apparent importance, since he was to sit and judge a king. His official residence became the dean's house at Westminster. He was called 'lord president' outside the courtroom, as well as in it.

The High Court of Justice had already chosen its counsel for the prosecution, Attorney General Anthony Steel. Alongside him they ran Solicitor General John Cook. Clarendon, himself a lawyer at the time, characterised this pair as 'eminent for nothing but their obscurity, and . . . they were men scarce known or heard of in the profession'.[5] There was some truth in Clarendon's haughty remarks. Cook was the son of a Leicestershire farmer. He had studied theology in Switzerland, cared deeply about the plight of the poor, and had served Charles's most unpopular lieutenant, the Earl of Strafford. But he was by now no friend to the King: in 1647 he wrote of his belief that only the army could implement the changes necessary for England to find a peaceful post-war settlement.

Friends and colleagues tried to make Cook rethink his prominent involvement in such a singular and fraught business. James Nutley, a young student in the Temple, remembered going to Cook at this time: 'I desired him to consider the dangerous consequences of such a proceeding; I may say I did with tears in my eyes, for I had a very good respect to the Gentleman for his profession's sake, being learned therein: truly my lord he did answer me thus, "I acknowledge it is a very base business but they put it upon me, I cannot avoid it, you see they put it upon me." '[6] Nutley was adamant that, at this early stage, Cook said the King's life was in no danger, and that the High Court of Justice simply wanted Charles to submit to Parliament.

On 10 January, the commissioners instructed their legal team to prepare the charge. John Aske and Isaac Dorislaus were to assist the attorney general, as junior counsel. Aske was a relative of Lord Fairfax, the commanding officer of the New Model Army.

Dorislaus was a Dutchman, born to a deeply Calvinist father: his two brothers were named Abraham and Jacob.

Dorislaus came to England as the first lecturer in History at Cambridge University. His inaugural lecture caused a sensation. He took as his theme 'The Power of the People under the Kings', and claimed that it was possible for kings to be subject to the law and that they must only exercise legitimate authority. This he followed with a speech declaring that the good citizen was he who resisted the tyrant, basing his argument largely on the writings of the Roman historian Tacitus. Serious questions were asked about this dangerous rhetoric. Matthew Wren, the Master of Peterhouse, was particularly concerned that Dorislaus seemed to be making the case for republicanism and regicide (the killing of a king), which, he dared fancy, were 'appliable [sic] to the exasperations of these villainous times'.[7] Aghast at Dorislaus's politics, Wren ensured that the university delayed his appointment to the doctorate that was his entitlement, for four years.

During the First Civil War, Dorislaus had served as Advocate of the Army. He was active in the suppression of conspiracies that aided the Crown, and had tried to introduce martial law to facilitate his dealings with suspects. The Second Civil War saw him appointed Judge of the Admiralty. He was also sent to his native Netherlands to see if he could persuade his compatriots to join with Parliamentary England in a Protestant alliance against Charles. Dorislaus was highly regarded by Oliver Cromwell, and it was he who approved the Dutchman being brought in to help frame the charges against the King.

Meanwhile perhaps Anthony Steel had received similar warnings to those urged on Cook; for, two days before the case began, the attorney general suddenly claimed grave illness and insisted he was incapable of discharging his duties. With Steel's withdrawal from the case, it was decided that Dorislaus would lead the prosecution, once the King had – as was anticipated – pleaded not guilty.

MPs now busied themselves in laying the foundations for this unique legal enterprise. A committee of eight was appointed, any two of whom could act together to oversee the preparation and management of the trial. The lawyer Augustine Garland, who had presented the ordinance for the 'Erecting of a High Court of Justice', acted as the committee's chairman until Bradshaw's appointment as lord president came into effect.

Another significant figure in the framing of the trial was Nicholas Love. He was a son of the headmaster of Winchester College and a protégé of William Lenthall, the Speaker of the House of Commons. Love, a lawyer of Lincoln's Inn, would be included in four of the committees that prepared the ground for the trial. He believed, before proceedings got under way, that they would inevitably end in Charles's favour, the charge being 'nothing, but what he knew the K[ing] could clearly acquit himself of'.[8]

Also on the committee was Sir John Danvers, a sixty-five-year-old veteran of Parliament. As a younger man he had been so physically beautiful that, when he was touring France and Italy, 'people would come after him in the street to admire him'.[9] Danvers returned to England with an equal appreciation of continental aesthetics, particularly in the area of landscaping. ''Twas Sir John Danvers of Chelsea,' a grateful contemporary recorded, 'who first taught us that way of Italian gardens.'[10]

Insatiably extravagant, Danvers had taken as his first wife a wealthy widow twice his age, who was the mother of ten children. His family had suffered mixed fortunes through its dealings with the Crown. His oldest brother had been beheaded at the instruction of Elizabeth I, after taking part in the Earl of Essex's rebellion. Another brother had been created Earl of Danby, early in Charles's reign, and remained something of a royal favourite. Sir John had also enjoyed the King's esteem, serving as a senior courtier. However, when civil war broke out he sided with Parliament, serving in its army as a colonel.

The Puritan Sir Henry Mildmay had been a loud critic of the King during his last, ultimately doomed, negotiations with Parliament, warning that Charles was 'no more to be trusted than a lion that hath been caged, and let loose again at his liberty'.[11] A courtier with particular responsibility for the royal jewels, Mildmay was able to deliver up the Sword of State for the King's trial. Borne in front of Bradshaw, it gave proceedings added solemnity, and an air of authenticity.

John Lisle also sat on this key committee. They said he was 'bred to the law'.[12] An experienced legislator in the Commons, he was also a proven ally of Cromwell. His hostility to the King had reached new heights when the contents of the royal baggage train had been read after their capture at the battle of Naseby. The correspondence proved Charles's willingness to bring foreign troops to his aid in the Civil War. While Parliament felt justified in seeking Scottish support, it deemed the Crown's recruitment of men from overseas, to kill Englishmen, to be a grievous betrayal. Lisle would go on to be Bradshaw's busy assistant in the trial of the King, sitting next to him so he could communicate legal points to the lord president as the case progressed.

The committee was completed by a trio of highly intelligent men whose colourful private lives scandalised their straitlaced colleagues with behaviour more generally associated with the despised enemy Cavaliers. Gilbert Millington, a barrister, had an appetite for committee work, mainly in his native Nottinghamshire. He possessed a reputation for professional thoroughness, and also for personal laxness: he frequented taverns and brothels, and further shocked contemporaries when, on the death of his wife, he married a sixteen-year-old barmaid.

Similarly, Thomas Chaloner was, according to the contemporary academic, John Selden, 'as far from a Puritan as the East from the West'.[13] Chaloner was a hard-drinking womaniser, who counted among his lighter weaknesses a delight in practical jokes. One of his favourites was to go early to Westminster Hall and drop a ridiculous tidbit into conversation, before returning later the same morning to see how far his piece of nonsense had spread. He enjoyed hearing how much it had gained in the retelling.

Well-travelled, well-mannered and well-read, Chaloner's famed sense of humour did not extend to his view of the King. The Crown

had reneged on promised payments to the Chaloners on acquiring
the family's alum mines. Charles aggravated this shabby treatment
by passing the benefit of the mines to his courtiers at a further
profit. This, Chaloner could never forgive.

Chaloner's partner in flamboyant loose-living was Henry Marten,
the republican son of a judge, whose quick wit brightened debates
in the Commons. The King found Marten altogether less amusing:
indeed, Charles and Marten held one another in mutual contempt.
The King was, one of his close circle recalled, 'so great an example
of conjugal affection, that they who did not imitate him in that
particular did not brag of their liberty'.[14] Meanwhile a contemporary recorded what everyone knew: Marten was 'a great lover of
pretty girls'.[15] This moral mismatch reached its defining moment
before the Civil Wars, when both men were attending horse races in
London's Hyde Park. Spotting Marten nearby, Charles ordered:
'Let that ugly rascal be gone out of the park, that whoremaster, or
else I will not see the sport.'[16]

Marten quit the royal presence, but he never forgot nor forgave
such a crushing humiliation. The King had made a lifelong enemy
of this fiercely intelligent and charismatic politician, one of the first
to write public tracts in the mid-1640s in which Charles was
removed from his royal pedestal and addressed as a common man
– one who deserved to be put to death, like any other, if found
guilty of murder. During the Second Civil War, Marten raised a
regiment of irregulars, many of them republican Levellers, who
marched under the uncompromising banner, 'For the People's
Freedom against all tyrants whatsoever'.[17]

Marten had a knack for coining pithy phrases. Charles's Great
Seal – effectively, his badge of office – showed him sitting in
wisdom and splendour on his throne on one side, while on the
reverse he was charging bravely into battle. His God-given kingship and his defence of Protestantism were proclaimed on both
sides. On 4 January a committee was formed to design a fresh
Great Seal, to lend heft to the new status quo. Millington helped,
but it was Marten who, contemporaries recorded, did most of the

work. He it was who composed the winning construct: *Exit Tyrannus Regum ultimus* – 'The last tyrant of kings has gone'. When the assembled commissioners and their lawyers were ensconced in the Painted Chamber, trying to establish in whose name the charge against the King should be made, it was Marten who stood up, with the winning line, 'In the name of the Commons and Parliament assembled, and all the good people of England.'[18] It was the final call to arms before the commissioners rose to begin the judgment of their King.

While Marten thrilled at the prospect of a republic being established, there were others among the commissioners, even those with republican leanings, who believed that public trial by part of Parliament was not the correct way to deal with the King. The young MP Algernon Sidney, a hero of the victory on Marston Moor (where he was wounded) and the governor of Dover Castle, recalled the sharp exchange he had with Oliver Cromwell over the legal soundness of the High Court of Justice. 'First,' he told Cromwell, 'the King could be tried by no court; secondly . . . no man could be tried by that court.' Cromwell would have none of it: 'I tell you,' he replied, 'we will cut off his head with the Crown upon it!'[19] Sidney departed, refusing to have anything to do with a process he viewed as being flawed constitutionally, and in point of law.

By 20 January, Cook, Dorislaus, Aske and their helpers had compiled the charge, the preamble probably owing much to the Dutchman, since its themes resonate so closely with the declaration of independence all of his educated compatriots knew so well. This was the Act of Abjuration submitted by the Netherlands against their hated Spanish ruler, Philip II, in 1581, which opened with:

> As it is apparent to all that a prince is constituted by God to be ruler of a people, to defend them from oppression and violence as the shepherd his sheep; and whereas God did not create the people slaves to their prince, to obey his commands, whether right or wrong, but rather the prince for the sake of the subjects (without which he could be no prince), to govern them according to equity, to love and support

them as a father his children or a shepherd his flock, and even at the hazard of life to defend and preserve them. And when he does not behave thus, but, on the contrary, oppresses them, seeking opportunities to infringe their ancient customs and privileges, exacting from them slavish compliance, then he is no longer a prince, but a tyrant, and the subjects are to consider him in no other view.[20]

The charge against Charles began:

That the said Charles Stuart, being admitted King of England, and therein trusted with a limited power to govern by and according to the laws of the land, and not otherwise; and by his trust, oath, and office, being obliged to use the power committed to him for the good and benefit of the people, and for the preservation of their rights and liberties; yet, nevertheless, out of a wicked design to erect and uphold in himself an unlimited and tyrannical power to rule according to his will, and to overthrow the rights and liberties of the people, yea, to take away and make void the foundations thereof, and of all redress and remedy of misgovernment, which by the fundamental constitutions of this kingdom were reserved on the people's behalf in the right and power of frequent and successive Parliaments, or national meetings in Council; he, the said Charles Stuart, for accomplishment of such his designs, and for the protecting of himself and his adherents in his and their wicked practices, to the same ends hath traitorously and maliciously levied war against the present Parliament, and the people therein represented . . .[21]

The assertion that government was a contract, in which the people surrender some of their rights to a sovereign unless or until that sovereign breaches their trust, was at loggerheads with Charles's sincere and unshakeable view that he was God's anointed – that he therefore could not be answerable to anyone but God. Believers in this philosophy, the Divine Right of Kings, pointed to the passage in the Old Testament in which King David erred by lusting after the beautiful Bathsheba, and consequently arranged the death in battle of her husband, so he could have her for himself. David, in Psalm 51, admitted his shameful guilt, but he was in no doubt where any judgment could come from, or to where any apology was due: 'Against thee, thee only, have I sinned,' he told the Lord.

The duel between these contrary views was to take place in a setting chosen by the King's former custodians, Colonels Whalley and Harrison, in consultation with Sir Hardress Waller, Pride's collaborator in the purge; Colonel Deane, whose artillery had pounded Basing House before its fall; Robert Tichborne, a republican linen-draper from the City who had long wanted Charles brought to trial; as well as Cromwell, whose influence was everywhere at this time.

Ironically, their chosen venue had been built to advertise that magnificent power of the Crown that the commissioners were now determined to deny. Westminster Hall had been constructed by William II in the final years of the eleventh century. It was the most impressive public room in England – some said in Europe. Its walls were six foot thick, enclosing an interior of 17,000 square feet. This was where kings and queens were crowned. The centrepiece of the ceremonial space was the King's Table, a mark of the continuity of monarchy, a symbol of royal might, and the setting for the celebration banquets that followed coronations. Charles had hosted embassies and receptions here, in the days before civil warfare overwhelmed his reign. Its associations had always been historic. Now it was to be the setting of something truly momentous.

The areas used by the King's Bench and the Chancery Courts, at the upper west end of Westminster Hall, were cleared for the trial. A barrier was set up in the middle of the court arena to hold back the crowds who would flock to witness the proceedings. At the centre of the ranks of scarlet benches and seats reserved for the judging commissioners was Bradshaw's chair, situated behind a desk on which a cushion rested. Both the chair and the cushion were swathed in crimson velvet.

The King was carried in a closed sedan chair from St James's to

Whitehall, then transported by barge along the Thames, accompanied by a strong guard under his custodian, Colonel Matthew Tomlinson. Charles's holding pen while awaiting the lord president's summons to appear before him would be the home of the late Sir Robert Cotton, near Westminster's Old Palace Yard. This had a garden that led up from the river, and a library of rare books (which included two original copies of Magna Carta) that had provided scholarly support to Cotton when he had written tracts attacking arbitrary royal power. Charles had imprisoned Cotton, and confiscated his books, as a result of these criticisms: although released in an amnesty celebrating the birth of the King's eldest son, Cotton was never reunited with his library – a decision that blighted his final years. Now the King was the prisoner, a degraded and unwilling guest in his old adversary's home.

Royalists were still, at this stage, unsure what the enemy was planning to do with the King. Purbeck Temple, a gentleman of Surrey, had been charged by friends sympathetic to the Crown with trying to find out. On what would be the first day of the trial, he bribed an officer to let him into the corridors outside the Painted Chamber. Here he found a nook where there was a hole in the wall, through which he witnessed the commissioners arrive to finalise their plans for the day. 'When their prayer was over,' he recalled, 'there came news that the King was landing at Sir Robert Cotton's Stairs, at which Cromwell ran to a window, looking on the King as he came up the Garden, he turned white as the wall, returning to the board he speaks to Bradshaw and Sir Henry Mildmay, how they and Sir William Brereton had concluded on such a business, then turning to the board, said thus, "My Masters, he is come, he is come, and now we are doing the great work, that the whole Nation will be full of." '[22]

The lord president entered his courtroom, behind sixteen halberdiers, the bearer of the Sword of State, and the sergeant-at-arms who carried Parliament's mace. In his wake strode sixty-seven of his fellow commissioners and their legal officers. The gates of the hall were opened, and the public flowed in until there was room for no more. Silence was ordered, and the King sent for.

He arrived fifteen minutes later, with a twenty-strong guard under the command of Colonel Francis Hacker – a distinguished New Model Army officer from an otherwise Royalist family, who had twice refused enticements to switch to the King's side during the Civil Wars. A handful of royal attendants found seats near their master, but not next to him: Bradshaw had insisted that, rather than being placed to one side, as was customary for a defendant, the King must sit alone in a chair in the centre of the courtroom, directly opposite the scores of men who had come to judge him.

Charles looked slowly around, taking in the spectacle, spotting the few familiar faces among the commissioners. It was evident that he was coming to terms with the forum he found himself in, and the fight he faced. He looked calm to his supporters, stern to some recording the proceedings, and arrogant to his foes. Edmund Ludlow, one of the main forces behind Pride's Purge, wrote of the King that, 'He looked with as impudent a face as if he had not been guilty of the blood that hath been shed in this war.'[23] Charles sat down, before rising to his feet again to turn and look at the public in the gallery. He would have seen that they were divided into two bodies by a line of soldiers, the better to keep control. More troops stood on either side of the commissioners, and along the newly built barrier. Others guarded the entrance of each door to the hall.

The prisoner had not been informed of the charges he would face. Neither had he been granted access to legal counsel. However, Charles had thought hard about what was likely to be put to him, and had taken what advice he could, before entering this cockpit: his twin defence would be an insistence on the inability of his subjects to try their King, and the impossibility of one house of Parliament (let alone one fraction of a house, whose election had taken place more than eight years earlier) sitting as a place of judgment at all. His defiance was immediately obvious in his refusal to remove his hat: to do so would be to show respect for his accusers, and acknowledgement of the court they had concocted. Similarly, the judges sat with their hats on, making it clear that deference towards his royal status had no place in this setting: he was simply the prisoner at the bar.

After the Act of Parliament for the trying of the King was delivered, the names were read out of the commissioners present. Bradshaw's was first: he rose to confirm his presence. Next came the name of Lord Fairfax. There was no answer. It was repeated, to renewed silence. As all present began to appreciate the astonishing fact that Parliament's military commander had absented himself from the trial, a lady's voice rang out from a box in the gallery that extended high above the hall: 'He had more wit than to be here!'[24] Fairfax had ordered Charles's removal from the Isle of Wight to London, and had sat in meetings preliminary to the trial, but he would take no part in the court proceedings once he realised the commissioners would be pushing for much more than Charles's exile.

Bradshaw now presented a preliminary distillation of the charge to the prisoner:

Charles Stuart, King of England, the Commons of England assembled in Parliament being deeply sensible of the calamities that have been brought upon this nation, which is fixed upon you as the principal author of it, have resolved to make inquisition for blood; and according to that debt and duty they owe to justice, to God, the kingdom, and themselves, and according to the fundamental power that rests in themselves, they have resolved to bring you to Trial and Judgment; and for that purpose have constituted this High Court of Justice, before which you are brought.[25]

Bradshaw then looked to Cook to proceed. The solicitor general was standing to the right of the King, and as he started to speak Charles tapped him two or three times on the shoulder with his cane, in an effort to stop him so he could speak instead. Bradshaw instructed Cook to ignore these distractions, and proceed.

'My Lord,' said Cook, 'I am commanded to charge Charles

Stuart, King of England, in the name of the Commons of England, with Treason and High Misdemeanours; I desire the said charge may be read.'[26]

As Andrew Broughton, clerk of the court, delivered the charge, Charles interjected: 'I am not entrusted by the people, they are mine by inheritance.'[27]

When Broughton referred to him as 'a Tyrant and Traitor', the King's stern demeanour disintegrated into laughter. Ominously, during the reading of the charge, it was noted that the head of Charles's cane broke off and fell to the floor. He paused – perhaps in the expectation that somebody would pick it up for him – but was eventually forced to bend and retrieve it for himself.

When the charge claimed to be presented in the name of 'all the good people of England', the female voice that had jeered in appreciation of Fairfax's absence chimed in again: 'Not half the people; it is false!' it cried. 'Where are they or their consents?'[28]

This was a raucous disruption of the dignity of the court, as well as a grave challenge to its validity. Colonel Daniel Axtell, in charge of the troops in the hall, was enraged, pointing to the offending box and shouting at his men: 'Down with the whores! Shoot them!'[29] It was fortunate that they disobeyed, for although they could not have missed their target, they would have shot Lady Fairfax, the wife of the army's lord general, who was guilty of both interruptions.

After the charge was completed, Bradshaw directed Charles to respond to it. 'I would know by what power I am called hither,' the King countered: 'I was not long ago in the Isle of Wight; how I came there is a longer story than I think it fit at this present time for me to speak of; but there I entered into a Treaty with both houses of Parliament, with as much public faith as it is possible to be had of any number of honourable lords and gentlemen, and treated honestly and uprightly; I cannot say but they did very nobly with me, we were upon the conclusion of the Treaty.' It was noticeable throughout his trial that Charles spoke with fluency, his customary stammer never in evidence.

Charles demanded to know the basis of his accusers' power: 'I would know by what authority I was brought from thence, and carried from place to place, and I know not what: and when I know what lawful authority [that is], I shall answer.' He then warned those daring to sit in judgment of him: 'Remember I am your King, your lawful King, and what sins you bring upon your heads, and the judgment of God upon this land; think well upon it, I say, think well upon it, before you go further from one sin to a greater.' Next, he drew up the defensive lines from which he would not budge throughout the remainder of the proceedings: 'I shall not betray my trust; I have a trust committed to me by God, by old and lawful descent; I will not betray it, to answer to a new unlawful authority.' He again asked for the authority of the court to be justified.

Bradshaw was undaunted. 'If you had been pleased to have observed what was hinted to you by the Court,' he replied, 'you would have known by what authority; which authority requires you, in the name of the People of England, of which you are elected King, to answer them.'

Charles bridled at this startling assertion: 'England was never an elective kingdom, but an hereditary kingdom for nearly these thousand years ... I do stand more for the liberty of my people, than any here that come to be my pretended judges.'

Asking Charles if he had any further reply to make before he order the court into recess so the judges could consider the best way forward, Bradshaw prompted the King's most defiant response yet:

Sir, I desire that you would give me, and all the world, satisfaction in this: let me tell you, it is not a slight thing you are about. I am sworn to keep the peace, by that duty I owe to God and my country, and I will do it to the last breath of my body: and therefore ye shall do well to satisfy first God, and then the country, by what authority you do it: if you do it by an usurped authority, you cannot answer. There is a God in Heaven, that will call you, and all that give you power, to account.

It was Saturday afternoon. The court was adjourned until Monday. As the King left Westminster Hall, Colonel Axtell cajoled some of his men to call out: 'Justice! Justice!' Eyewitnesses recalled Axtell beating those soldiers who were slow to pick up the refrain. Others in the hall shouted out: 'God save the King!'[30]

Before the Monday session the commissioners met in the Painted Chamber. They applauded Bradshaw's conduct on the first day of the trial, and confirmed that Charles must not be allowed to question the jurisdiction of the High Court of Justice. The second session opened with Cook's demand: 'That the prisoner may be directed to make a positive answer, either by way of confession, or negation; which if he shall refuse to do, that the matter of the charge may be taken *pro confesso* [in place of a confession], and the Court may proceed according to justice.'

The King and the lord president locked horns again, both of them stubborn in defence and aggressive in attack, the creeds that had helped fuel a war reverberating round the packed amphitheatre. Bradshaw was clear in confirming the commissioners' absolute confidence in their authority, which he said came from 'the Commons of England – and all your predecessors, and you, are responsible to them'. When Charles continued his challenge, Bradshaw lost patience: 'Sir, you are not to be permitted to go on in that speech and these discourses.' The King persisted, presenting himself as the defender of 'the liberty and freedom of all his subjects'.

'Sir,' admonished Bradshaw, 'you are not to have the liberty to use this language: how great a friend you have been to the laws and liberties of the people, let all England and the world judge.'

The lord president declared the session closed. Charles was escorted back to Sir Robert Cotton's house, indignant at being treated as a common prisoner, perplexed that he was being overruled by one of his subjects.

Charles was remanded once more, and told to return to the court for a third day, on 23 January. The stalemate recurred, and Bradshaw barked his anger at the King's continued defiance: 'Sir, this is the third time you have publicly disowned this court and put an

affront to it . . . For truly, sir, men's intentions are used to show by
their actions. You have written your meaning in bloody characters
throughout the whole kingdom . . . Clerk, record the default! And,
gentlemen, you that brought the prisoner, take him back again.'

The next morning was spent in examining witnesses against the
king, in the Painted Chamber. There were more than thirty of these,
all male, from Charles's three kingdoms. They ranged from
Londoner Arthur Young, a twenty-nine-year-old barber and
surgeon, to George Cornwall, a fifty-year-old ferryman from
Herefordshire. Many of them were Royalists, obliged to recount
episodes when they had seen Charles rallying or leading his troops
during the Civil Wars, in order to establish the King's direct involvement in the bloodshed of his people.

Their testimony was laced with other damning evidence,
including a dramatic presentation by Thomas Chaloner of some of
the King's captured letters. This reminder of Charles's double-
dealing, even extending to employing foreign troops in the war
against his subjects, was devastating. Edmund Ludlow, sitting as a
commissioner, recalled 'that it was obvious to all men, the King
himself had proved, by the duplicity of his dealing with the Parliament; which manifestly appeared in his own papers taken at the
battle of Naseby, and elsewhere'.[31] As the case progressed, some of
those opposed to the King found their anger turn into contempt.
Astonished onlookers observed one man spit in Charles's face. The
King reached for his handkerchief and silently wiped himself clean.

Meanwhile, Ludlow and others of the God-fearing judges
looked for divine guidance as to how to proceed. A passage from
the Book of Numbers began to resonate with them in their deliberations. It was a well-known verse, which had been deployed a
few years before by Parliament in the trial for high treason of an
Irish lord: 'That blood defileth the land, and the land cannot be
cleansed of the blood that is shed therein, but by the blood of him
that shed it.'[32] It seemed to speak of the need to make the King pay
in person for the loss of life that had ensued, since he had raised
his royal standard as a military rallying point in the summer of

1642. 'And therefore I could not consent to the counsels of those who were contented to leave the guilt of so much blood upon the nation,' Ludlow concluded, 'and thereby to draw down the just vengeance of God upon us all; when it was most evident that the war had been occasioned by the invasion of our rights, and open breach of our laws and constitution on the King's part.'[33] If England were to return to divine favour, Charles's life would need to be offered up in sacrifice.

The King's attitude throughout the trial made the contemplation of spilling royal blood more palatable: it was clear that, if the possibility ever arose, Charles would seek full vengeance against his enemies. 'The gentlemen that were appointed his judges,' wrote Lucy Hutchinson, whose husband was one of the commissioners, 'and divers others, saw in him a disposition so bent to the ruin of all that had opposed him and all of the righteous and just things they had contended for, that it was upon the consciences of many of them that if they did not execute justice upon him, God would require at their hands all the blood and desolation which should ensue by their suffering him to escape, when God hath brought him into their hands.'[34]

Many of the commissioners had assembled to try the King in the expectation that he would either be excused the charges, or be punished in a way that did not extend to the ending of his life. However, they now all agreed to proceed to the death sentence on the basis that Charles was 'a tyrant, traitor, murderer, and public enemy to the Commonwealth'.[35] The majority of the judges seem to have been motivated by a sincere belief that they were doing what needed to be done, rather than acting out of a hatred for the King himself. 'Concerning myself,' recorded Edmund Ludlow, 'I bear no [more] malice to the man's person, than I do to my dear father; but I hate that cursed principle of tyranny that has so long lodged and harboured within him, which has turned our waters of law into blood.'[36]

Preparation of the precise terms of the warrant was left to Harrison, Ireton, Marten, Lisle, Love, Say and the Parliamentary spymaster Thomas Scott, with the manner of execution left blank for now. Eager to share responsibility for this act of regicide, the commissioners in Westminster sent urgent instructions to all their absent colleagues to join them immediately.

On the morning of Saturday 27 January, the commissioners assembled in the Painted Chamber to agree the final version of the sentence. Once formulated, it would be sent for publication in key points of the capital. It was agreed that all that could have been done, had been done: that the King had been given ample opportunity to defend himself against the charge. Once condemned, he must not be allowed by Bradshaw to speak, for he would be 'dead in law'. To demonstrate the unanimity of the judges, they would all stand once the sentence had been read.

On his final appearance, that afternoon, Charles once more refused to acknowledge the court. He seems to have appreciated that judgment against him was imminent, and asked if he might make a proposal in front of a combined assembly of the Lords and Commons; it would, he promised, reconcile all parties, and return peace to the three kingdoms. Ludlow, one of the better-informed commissioners, heard rumours that the King would have offered his abdication in favour of his eldest son, Charles, Prince of Wales, upon terms to be agreed.

The King had not realised that his trial would be ended quite so abruptly. When he made to speak he was silenced by Bradshaw. One of the judges, John Downes, protested that this was too heartless, and urged that the accused must be heard. He was determined and loud enough to force a recess.

The judges withdrew to the Inner Court of Wards to consider the King's proposal, and Cromwell now turned on Downes, attacking him for his ill-timed intervention. Downes was reduced to tears by this dressing-down. The commissioners considered the King's proposed meeting of both Houses of Parliament for half an hour, but decided it was too late for anything positive to come of it: they would press on. They returned to the courtroom, and the sentence was pronounced. After recapping, at length, the charge, the judges' definition of kingship, the evidence and the King's obstructive attitude throughout the trial, it concluded: 'For all which treasons and crimes this Court doth adjudge that he, the said Charles Stuart, as a tyrant, traitor, murderer, and public enemy to the good people of this nation, shall be put to death by the severing of his head from his body.'[37]

After standing up in acknowledgement of their unanimous support of the sentence, the commissioners adjourned to the Painted Chamber. They chose five of their regimental commanders – Waller, Harrison, Dean, Okey and Ireton – to find a suitable and secure place of execution, and to advise when this should take place. They concluded that the King should be executed on a scaffold in front of Whitehall on Tuesday 30 January, and that the officers to oversee the execution would be Colonel Francis Hacker, Colonel Hercules Huncks and Lieutenant Colonel Robert Phare. To these three officers was addressed the death warrant:

> Whereas Charles Stuart, King of England, is and standeth convicted, attainted, and condemned of high treason and other high crimes, and sentence was pronounced against him by this Court, to be put to death by the severing of his head from his body, of which sentence execution yet remaineth to be done: These are therefore to will and require you to see the said sentence executed, in the open street before Whitehall, upon the morrow, being the thirtieth of this instant, month of January, between the hours of ten in the morning and five in the afternoon of the same day, with full effect. And for so doing, this shall be your sufficient warrant. And these are to require all officers and soldiers, and other good people of this nation of England, to be assisting unto this service. Given under our hands and seals.

There then followed seven columns of signatures, the first three those of Bradshaw, Lord Grey of Groby (the only titled nobleman present) and Cromwell. Also present among the fifty-nine signatories prepared to endorse the King's execution were Charles's former custodians, Whalley and Harrison; the organisers of the purge of the Commons, Pride and Waller; the arch-republicans Ludlow and Marten; the Civil War heroes Goffe, Barkstead and Okey; the spymaster Scott; and the Parliamentary stalwarts, Corbet and Carew. Next to their signatures they pressed their seals into hot melted wax. During the signings, Cromwell and Henry Marten were in such high spirits that they flicked ink at one another from their pens, like naughty schoolboys.

These fifty-nine were now fully signed-up regicides – a term that would be extended by the Royalists to include the officers of the court during Charles's trial, and those involved in the act of execution. In all, there would be around eighty men who were considered directly responsible for killing the King.

The officers in the Tower of London were ordered to deliver up the 'bright execution axe for the executing [of] malefactors', which would be used for the beheading. Lieutenant Colonel Goffe was told to furnish the King with suitable puritanical preachers, to prepare him for the afterlife. Charles chose instead to be tended by William Juxon, Bishop of London, who had previously served him as a royal chaplain, and as lord high treasurer of England.

The Royalist Clarendon maintained that, though not the best of kings, Charles I was 'the best husband, the best father and the best Christian that the age in which he lived had produced'.[38] It was a side of his character acknowledged by his enemies, Ludlow recalling Cromwell saying that 'he had lately seen the tenderest sight that ever his eyes beheld, which was, the interview between the King and his children; that he wept plentifully at the remembrance thereof'.[39] Three of the King's children, Charles, James and Mary, were safely out of Parliament's reach, overseas. The two younger ones – eight-year-old Henry, Duke of Gloucester, and thirteen-year-old Princess Elizabeth – were now brought to say their final farewell to their father. They burst into tears on seeing him. Elizabeth recalled much of the subsequent conversation clearly, writing soon afterwards:

> He bid us tell my mother that his thoughts had never strayed from her, and that his love would be the same to the last. Withal, he commanded me and my brother to be obedient to her; and bid me send his blessing to the rest of my brothers and sisters, with communications to all his friends. Then, taking my brother Gloucester on his knee, he said, 'Sweetheart, now they will cut off thy father's head.' And Gloucester looking very intently upon him, he said again, 'Heed, my child, what I say: they will cut off my head and perhaps make thee a King. But mark what I say. Thou must not be a King as long as thy brothers Charles and James do live; for they will cut off your brothers' heads when they can catch them, and cut off thy head too at the last, and therefore I charge you, do not be made a King by them.' At which my brother sighed deeply, and made answer: 'I will be torn in pieces first!'
>
> And these words, coming so unexpectedly from so young a child, rejoiced my father exceedingly. And his majesty spoke to him of the welfare of his soul, and to keep his religion, commanding him to fear God, and He would provide for him. Further, he commanded us all to forgive those people, but never to trust them; for they had been most false to him and those that gave them power, and he feared also to their own souls. And he desired me not to grieve for him, for he should die a martyr, and that he doubted not the Lord would settle his throne upon his son, and that we all should be happier than we could have expected to have been if he had lived; with many other things which at present I cannot remember.[40]

The King gave Elizabeth and Henry his remaining jewels, before the children were taken from their father. The deeply devout Charles countered the agony of their final parting with prayer.

The scaffold was erected outside the Banqueting House, a new doorway being knocked through the building's external wall to allow direct access to the place of execution. It was covered in black cloth, the block and the axe placed together at its centre. Elsewhere a coffin was prepared, trimmed with black velvet.

On the winter morning of his execution, so bitter that the Thames had frozen over, Charles is said to have chosen to wear two shirts beneath his doublet to counter the cold in case he shivered: he would not have his enemies say he had trembled in fear. At ten in the morning, Charles was escorted from St James's to Whitehall on foot, a New Model Army regiment in attendance, flags flying, drums beating, marching before and behind the condemned man. The King remained in conversation with Colonel Tomlinson, who had proved to be a kind and respectful custodian, while Bishop Juxon followed, offering Christian platitudes as comfort during his final ordeal.

Some reports have Jane Whorwood rushing into her lover's arms during this procession to the scaffold, though this is not certain. What is for sure is that, with customary ingenuity, she had managed to communicate with the King in the days between his death sentence being proclaimed and carried out.

Charles noted various figures in the crowd, including one of his servants, sobbing wildly as his master passed. Another, Parliamentary, man mocked the King as he went by.

In Whitehall, Charles remained composed. He spent time praying, declined to dine, but – as his wait extended – at around noon he picked at some bread and sipped on a glass of claret.

Two hours later the King was taken through to the scaffold, Juxon by his side. Charles looked around, seeing the enormous multitude that had come to witness his death. Between them and the scaffold were thick knots of soldiers, guarding against any last-minute rescue attempt or disruption. The King then focused on the scene directly in front of him. He was troubled by the height of the block where he would soon lay his head: it was only six inches high. When he asked Colonel Hacker, the senior officer present at the execution, if a higher one might be brought in its place, his request was politely brushed off. Around the block were four pins, with pulleys attached: these were to be used to secure the King if, when it came to it, he physically resisted his fate.

Charles had prepared notes on stubs of paper, to help him with his final speech. He soon realised that the crowd was too far away, beyond the soldiers, to hear his words, but insisted on speaking to those on the scaffold, rather than have his silence misinterpreted as an acceptance of guilt. The King directed the majority of his words directly at Tomlinson, perhaps because he thought him most likely to give an honest recollection of what had been said. Meanwhile, reporters stood behind the King and wrote down his last words.

Charles was determined to talk of his innocence, particularly on the greater charges against him: he insisted with disdain that he had not begun the war with Parliament, pointing instead to how his opponents had taken his militia from him; that had been, he said, the first act of the hostilities. He also insisted that he had not encroached upon Parliament's privileges: 'That is, so far as I have said, to show you that I am an innocent man.'

Charles now turned to those who were responsible for his imminent execution – his regicides: 'I have forgiven all the world, and even those in particular that have been the chief causes of my death. Who they are, God knows, I do not desire to know, God forgive them. But that is not all, my charity must go further. I wish that they may repent, for indeed they have committed a great sin in that particular. I pray God, with St Stephen, that this be not laid to their charge.' Instead, he urged these sinners to dedicate themselves to the peace of the kingdom.

His attention turned to the best way ahead for his people, in terms of government and religion. He broke off when he saw a man touching the axe, fearing he might dull the blade: 'Hurt not the axe, that may hurt me,' he implored. He was keen to avoid a terrible end such as that suffered by his grandmother, Mary, Queen of Scots, in 1587. She had had to endure three strokes of the axe, before her head was severed from her body: it was said her lips had twitched for fifteen minutes after the stubborn gristle was finally cut through.

Resuming his speech, Charles repeated his wish for the people to enjoy liberty and freedom. To the end, he was adamant that this could not be achieved through a share in kingly government. 'Sir, that is nothing pertaining to them. A subject and a sovereign are clean different things,' he maintained.

Charles was proud of the stand he had made, believing it correct, despite its fatal consequences for him: 'If I would have given way to an arbitrary way, for to have all laws changed according to the Power of the Sword, I needed not to have come here. And therefore I tell you, and I pray God it be not laid to your charge, that I am the martyr of the people.'

He thought that he had said all he wanted to, but Bishop Juxon prompted him to reaffirm his Christian faith. This he did, briefly, before addressing Colonel Hacker. 'Take care that they do not put me to pain,' he implored, 'and, sir, this, and it please you –' before breaking off again, having spied someone else toying with the axe. 'Take heed of the axe,' he repeated, 'pray, take heed of the axe.'

The King now dealt with the practicalities of preparing for execution. 'I shall say but very short prayers,' he told the axeman – the leader of the two masked executioners present: 'and when I thrust out my hands . . .' That would be the signal that he was ready to die. He asked Juxon for his nightcap, and pushed some of his hair up into it. 'Does my hair trouble you?' he asked the executioner. It did: he and the bishop tucked all of it up beneath the white satin, so the King's neck could be presented clean. 'I have a good cause,' Charles reassured himself, 'and a gracious God on my side.'

'There is but one stage more,' soothed Juxon. 'This stage is turbulent and troublesome; it is a short one. But you may consider, it will soon carry you a very great way. It will carry you from Earth to Heaven. And there you shall find a great deal of cordial joy and comfort.'

Charles persisted with this heartening thought: 'I go from a corruptible to an incorruptible crown; where no disturbance can be, no disturbance in the world.'

'You are exchanged from a temporal to an eternal crown,' the old bishop concurred, 'a good exchange.'

The King checked his hair once more, before turning to Juxon, pressing the George – the jewelled medal, symbolic of high and courtly honour – into his hand, and saying to him, forcefully: 'Remember!'[41] On the scaffold, they took this to be a reminder that the George be passed on to the Prince of Wales.

Charles took off his doublet, draped a cloak around his shoulders for warmth, and asked the executioner to set the block fast, before again asking for a higher one to be brought. The executioner was polite but clear: the block was fast, and it was of the necessary height.

After raising his arms and eyes to the skies, the King lay down in prayer, his head on the low block, the executioner tucking some unruly hair back under the nightcap.

Charles soon stretched out his arms in the agreed manner and the axe fell. Death was delivered in one powerful blow, the head severed at around the third/fourth vertebra. It was held high by the masked second executioner. The shock of the sight of the bloodied top of the freshly killed King drew a groan from many in the crowd, who could scarcely believe what they had seen. In a posthumous vindication of Charles's belief in the Divine Right of Kings, some rushed forward to dip their handkerchiefs in the royal blood, believing it to have sacred properties.

Immediately after Charles's execution, Colonel John Hewson, one of the signatories of the death warrant, rode through the centre of London from Charing Cross to the Royal Exchange. Clattering behind him went a squadron of cavalry, as he rushed to spread a clear and uncompromising message: anyone, he declared repeatedly, who so much as questioned the justice of Charles Stuart's death would in turn forfeit their own lives. For many Londoners this was a heavy-handed postscript to an already overwhelming day. The following week Bradshaw approved payment to the guards on the scaffold, for the care they had taken, and the cheerfulness they had shown while performing their duties.

Concerned that vengeance might appear in the shape of the dead

King's two older sons, in March it was declared that Charles, Prince of Wales, and James, Duke of York, should die without mercy, wherever they might be found.

In mid-December 1650, William Say passed the trial documents to clerks for safe storage, noting, 'That the persons instructed in that great service had discharged their trust with great courage and fidelity.'[42] They were filed away with customary efficiency by the Parliament bureaucrats, nobody realising that they gave a forensic account of proceedings that, under another regime, and through other eyes, might be viewed as the embodiment of that most heinous of charges – high treason.

Chapter 3

The Republic

And whereas by the abolition of the kingly office provided for in this Act, a most happy way is made for this nation (if God see it good) to return to its just and ancient right, of being governed by its own Representatives or national meetings in council, from time to time chosen and entrusted for that purpose by the people.

Act of Parliament, 17 March 1649

Weeks after Charles's death, the Rump declared that, 'The office of a King in a nation, and to have power thereof in a single person, was unnecessary, burdensome, and dangerous to the liberty, safety, and public interest of the people, and therefore ought to be abolished.'[1] England, for the first time in many hundreds of years, was a republic. It was named the Commonwealth.

This change was celebrated by the Crown's bitterest enemies, but left others feeling distinctly nervous about what would happen next. John Evelyn, a conservative Royalist, heard about the execution from his brother George, who had been one of its thousands of eyewitnesses. Evelyn wrote in his diary: 'The villainy of the Rebels proceeding now so far as to try, condemn, and murder our excellent King, the 30th of this month, struck me with such horror that I kept the day of his martyrdom a fast, and would not be present, at that execrable wickedness.'[2]

The trial and execution had taken place (not surprisingly, given the profession of many of those sitting in judgment) with military

efficiency and ruthlessness. Among those who felt the loss of the
King most deeply, there was now a rush to give him the aura of
Christ-like suffering: parallels were found in both figures having
been mocked by soldiers during their torment, and having behaved
with humble submission at their end. Clarendon would write of
Charles's 'saint-like behaviour, and his Christian courage and
patience at his death'.[3] A beautifully written book, *Eikon Basilike*
('Image of the King'), appeared after the execution, which many at
the time believed to be the King's own work. It added to the image
of a gentle and spiritual man having been cruelly put to death for his
principles, on behalf of his people. Within a year of Charles's death,
fifty editions of it had appeared in a variety of languages.

When further incarnations of the High Court of Justice sentenced
prominent Royalist leaders from the Second Civil War to execution, the Duke of Hamilton – leader of the force from Scotland,
defeated at Preston – asked the executioner if the axe he saw awaiting
him was the one that had dispatched the King. Informed that it was,
the duke kissed it in homage, before presenting his neck to the same
blade.

The execution of the King had removed the man the army felt to
be dangerous, and knew to be untrustworthy. It could not, though,
bring harmony to a deeply divided nation. Nor could it dictate how
other countries would react. The Scots were particularly appalled at
the death of their King: Parliament had guaranteed it would not
allow him to be put to death, when he was sold to them. The Scots
now used 'high language and invective against the late proceedings
in England',[4] and proclaimed the Prince of Wales as the new 'King
of Scotland'. The Commonwealth heard reports, 'that in Scotland
are many English officers and soldiers, who expect employment
when their new King cometh'.[5]

Meanwhile much of Continental Europe joined in the outrage at
the royal beheading. A dangerous attack on those responsible for
the killing came in a much-read Latin treatise, *Defensio Regia pro
Carlo Primo* ('The Royal Defence of Charles I'), whose rapid
dissemination around Europe caused huge concern among the new

rulers of England. For those still struggling to make sense of such a shocking episode as the execution of a king, in what was regarded as the most exemplary of monarchies, this fiery tract provided plausible answers. It also dissuaded the Commonwealth's neighbours from engaging with the new English republic, in terms of trade or diplomacy.

The perpetrators of the 'miserable and amazing marvellous murder' were, the anonymous author said, 'savage, sternly steeled and stony-hearted'. He railed against the regicides as 'sons of the soil, persons scarce of the nobility at home, scarce known to their own countrymen', who had taken it upon themselves to judge, then execute, a king. 'But with those judges that were chosen from the lower House were joined even judges from the army; soldiers never, though, had a right to sit in judgment upon a citizen.' The author gave an emotive and one-sided account of Charles's final two or three years: 'They put him to several sorts of torments ... They removed him from prison to prison, often changing his guards. Sometimes they gave him hopes of liberty – sometimes even of restoring him to his crown upon articles of agreement.' In the end, after enduring 'buffetings and kicks that were given by common soldiers', 'he suffered death as a robber, as a murderer, as a parricide, as a traitor, as a tyrant'. This was the crime of these cruel and despicable men, who had the gall to 'toss kings' heads like balls, play hoop with crowns, and make no more of imperial sceptres than of fools' bauble-sticks with heads atop'.

This published assault gained further appeal when the anonymity of its author was penetrated, and it was established that it was the work of one of the most respected professors teaching in the Dutch academic hothouse of Leiden. Claude Salmasius, a Burgundian, was of a Protestant creed that was closer to the Presbyterians than to the Puritans of England. Given the acclaim *Defensio Regio* received, and Salmasius's eminence (Queen Christina of Sweden invited him to be a guest at her court, where he was deluged with honours), a rebuttal was required to justify the King's death.

The regicides' champion was the poet John Milton, who in the two weeks before the King's execution had written the *Tenure of Kings and Magistrates*, a justification for the calling to account, and even the execution, of a tyrant. Two months after the King's beheading, Milton was given the post of Secretary of Foreign Tongues, on behalf of the freshly hatched republic. Installed in an official apartment in Whitehall, his rooms hung with pictures he had selected from the confiscated royal collection, his duties ranged from the translation of documents received from overseas, to writing propaganda against the Irish – whom he condemned as the most savage of barbarians, undeserving of mercy.

His prime responsibility now became the rebuttal of written attacks against those responsible for Charles's death. Milton was, he said, happy 'to render this never-to-be-regretted assistance to the valiant liberators of my country'. He dissected the arguments that had swayed the well-read of a continent, determined to expose them as lies, while defending the regicides in terms of motive, justification and background.

First, he claimed that Charles Stuart had abdicated his right to be viewed as a King, 'For a tyrant is no real King; he is but a player-King, the mere mask and spectre of a King.' This, Milton claimed, explained why, 'The whole army and a great part of the people from almost every county in the kingdom cried out with one voice for justice against the King as the very author of all their calamities.' Charles, he continued, 'had been taken a prisoner of war, and found incurable'. As a result, 'Can anyone fail to see that the preservation of any one man to the destruction of all others is utterly contrary to nature?'

Salmasius may have looked down on the bloodlines of the men who judged the tyrant-King, but Milton pointed to the distinguished ancestry of some, while 'others, being as it were their own ancestors, tread the path to true nobility by way of industry and personal worth, and are comparable with any of the noblest soever'. Merit, he claimed, could trump the showiest of family trees.

Above all, Milton applauded the regicides as heroes. 'No men ever undertook with a loftier courage,' he wrote, 'and, as our adversaries themselves confess, with a more tranquil mind, an action so distinguished, so worthy of heroic ages – an action whereby they ennobled not only law and its enforcement, which thenceforth seem restored to all men equitably, but Justice's very self, and rendered her after so signal a judgment more glorious, more august, than ever she had been before.'

The clash of creeds championed by Salmasius and Milton demonstrated the passion and the division of the times. Those responsible for the death of the King – those who had presented the case against him; those who had found him guilty and applied their signatures and seals to his death warrant; or those who had stood on the scaffold supervising the moment of death – were all aware that their actions attracted horror, as well as praise. Salmasius had announced in his tract the need for retribution, writing, 'These men's injustice, impiety, perfidy, cruelty, I will cry out unto heaven and earth; themselves the perpetrators I will turn over to posterity convicted, and transfix the culprits.'

In fact, the vengeance had already begun.

Dr Isaac Dorislaus, the Dutch junior counsel, had, in the end, not been called upon to take a prominent role in the great trial. Joseph Herne, present at the High Court of Justice on the hearing's second day, recalled seeing Solicitor General Cook deep in conversation with Dorislaus even after Charles was seated in readiness for proceedings. Lord President Bradshaw had had to interrupt their legal tête-à-tête, to enquire what Cook required of the court. Dorislaus otherwise remained in the shadows, poised to cross-question the King if he had pleaded not guilty, busying himself with notes and advice, eager to see the tyrant condemned.

After the trial Dorislaus told friends that the King's fatal error had been a refusal to plead: if he had done so, the doctor calculated, Charles might well have survived, for he might then have drawn out proceedings indefinitely – until the conclusion of the single month that constituted the High Court's permitted lifespan. Such a delay could have left the judgment incomplete. In addition, this extra time would have given supporters of the Crown time to galvanise, and come to the King's aid. Charles's curt and absolute rebuttal of his judges had played into the hands of those who wanted him rapidly dealt with.

Friendless and isolated, the new republic in England was keen to establish alliances abroad: it was feeling vulnerable, particularly to the threat of a further Scottish invasion, while Ireland was seething with enemies too. France was sheltering Henrietta Maria, one of its own princesses, and the widow of the beheaded King. The Commonwealth would need to look elsewhere for political acceptance and profitable trade.

The Prince of Wales and his younger brother James had found sanctuary with their sister Mary and brother-in-law William, the Princess and Prince of Orange, at The Hague, in the Netherlands. The Orange family was the leading Dutch dynasty, but it lacked the supreme power enjoyed by many of Continental Europe's monarchies, and faced strong and established political opponents. Some of these were hostile to the support shown to the beleaguered Stuart princes. Noting this, as well as the shared Protestantism of England and the Netherlands, and relying on the Dutch reputation for putting trade before all else, the new English republic explored possible diplomatic and commercial ties.

First to be approached as ambassador was Bulstrode Whitelocke, a Puritan lawyer who was a friend of Cromwell. However, Whitelocke was one who preferred discretion to valour, as had been shown by his refusal to engage in the prosecution of the King. He was aware that many displaced Royalists had followed their exiled leader across the North Sea to the Netherlands. Rather than become vulnerable to them, he turned down the diplomatic post.

Dr Dorislaus was less concerned about threats to his safety, having positive memories of his previous mission to the Dutch provinces. The States-General, the federal representatives that helped govern the seven Dutch provinces, had received him in the summer of 1648. For several months he had assisted Walter Strickland, Parliament's ambassador general to the Dutch since the outbreak of the Civil War. Dorislaus spent much of his time spying on the rogue squadron that had broken away from the Parliamentary navy to form a Royalist fleet under Charles's nephew, Prince Rupert of the Rhine.

Dorislaus had returned to England that winter, working on the case against the King, before turning his attention the next month to the prosecution of other prominent Royalists. This had resulted in the execution of Lord Capel, the Duke of Hamilton and the Earl of Holland, despite the last two having surrendered on guarantees that their lives would be spared. (The Earl of Holland had perhaps exhausted all reasonable expectation of mercy, having, over the previous decade, fought in turn for Parliament, the King, then Parliament again, before his final, fatal, dabble with Royalism.)

When asked by the new governing body in London, the Council of State, to return to his native land on its behalf, Dorislaus agreed to do so, despite the dangers. His request in return was that, after he had completed his spell as Resident of Parliament at The Hague, he might be allowed to retreat to academic backwaters, and be appointed Keeper of the Library of St James, which, a contemporary boasted, contained 'choice books and manuscripts ... and there were not the like to them, except only in the Vatican, in any other library in Christendom'.[6] This was, therefore, to be his last mission, before a gentle semi-retirement in scholastic heaven.

Dorislaus arrived in the fishing port of Scheveningen, near The Hague, on 29 April, taking lodgings at an inn, *De Swaen*, which was run by friends. One of his first visitors was Strickland, who urged him to come to stay with him and his family, where he could be better protected. So nervous was Strickland about his own security that he had publicly pretended that his mission was concluded: he was now in the Netherlands, he claimed, in an unofficial capacity, owing to his Dutch wife wanting to spend time with her family. Dorislaus declined Strickland's invitation, staying on at the inn with a small retinue of armed guards.

Soon afterwards a man arrived posing as a member of Strickland's staff, bearing instructions for Dorislaus to follow him to a meeting.

Dorislaus suspected a trap and refused to go. This was fortunate because, as Strickland reported to London, 'diverse rogues were ready to have killed him had he come out'.

The next night a friend warned Dorislaus of the rumour that he, Dorislaus, had been one of the two masked men who performed the King's execution, either the one who had wielded the axe, or his assistant who had held the King's severed head aloft. And now the Royalists wanted him dead.

Dorislaus found it laughable that he, a bookish academic, might have been involved in something as brutally physical as the beheading. He told his companions not to worry: even if he was attacked, he was confident in his bodyguards' protection.

In the spring of 1649, Walter Whitford, a colonel in the King's defeated army, found himself among the many Royalists sheltering in the Netherlands. Whitford's father had been Bishop of Brechin before his support for Charles I's religious beliefs had seen him expelled from Scotland. Charles had found him a parish in Northamptonshire as compensation, but Whitford senior had remained open in his sympathies for the Crown. This had made his last years ones of hardship at the hands of Parliament: they had expelled him from his living a year before his death, in 1647.

Colonel Whitford was one of many seeking to avenge the King's death, and no doubt to strike a blow on behalf of his father. Brought up in a religious household, he went to seek guidance from the English priest acting as Catholic confessor to the Portuguese ambassador: was it a sin, he asked, to slay a man who had killed your King? What happened next gives us a clue as to the probable answer.

Late one evening, Whitford led eleven men to *De Swaen*. One of the Royalist gang knocked at the door, pretending that he wanted to buy some wine; when the inn staff admitted him, Whitford and his men poured in behind, snuffing out the lights in the entrance, then fanning out to hunt down Dorislaus. The Dutchman's body-guards rushed forward to block the intruders while the startled group dining with Dorislaus urged him to run to a prearranged secure room.

Dorislaus's servants swore afterwards that their master never managed to find the door. The Dutch authorities, who made their own investigations, concluded that Dorislaus reached it, but for some reason failed to open it – maybe through terror, or perhaps because it was locked. Either way, Dorislaus's guards were over-whelmed, with two of them seriously wounded in the scuffle. Whitford and his main force surged forward, informing all in the inn to calm down: they were only there for the King's murderer. One of the guests, a man called van Valkenstein, made a sudden start, and, momentarily mistaken for Dorislaus, received a serious wound that led to a lingering death.

Now the assassins found Dorislaus, hiding under a chimney. He tried to keep his attackers at bay with a chair, but it was hope-less: his head was spliced by Whitford's broadsword, before another slash ripped him open, the wound running from heart to liver. One of the attackers shouted, 'Thus dies one of the King's judges!'[7]

Accounts of the murder were trumpeted everywhere, their details sometimes changing in the retelling. Clement Walker – an MP who had been expelled in Pride's Purge, and whose continued resistance to the Commonwealth would lead to his death, without trial, in the Tower of London – wrote, 'about 18 Scotsmen (friends to [the Duke of] Hamilton) repairing to [Dorislaus's] lodging, 6 of them made good the stair-foot, where expostulating with him concerning the unjust condemnation and execution of the duke, they stabbed him to death, and escaped'.[8] Bulstrode Whitelocke reported, with more accuracy: 'Letters from the Hague, that twelve English Cava-liers in disguise came into a room where Dr Dorislaus, who was a public minister there for the Parliament, was with others at supper, that they murdered him by stabbing him in several places, and cut his throat.'[9] The particulars may have varied, but the horror among Parliamentarians was uniform.

Royalists viewed the killing as justified retribution for the death of the King. Sir Edward Nicholas, who had served as one of Charles's most measured and trusted advisers, had been living in impoverished exile since the fall of Oxford in 1646. He allowed his customary reserve to slip, writing triumphantly of Dorislaus's end being 'the deserved execution of that bloody villain'.[10]

The consternation among the Commonwealth's heavyweights was great. The King had only been dead for a little more than three months, but already one of the key figures in his trial had been slain in an act of brutal vengeance. In London, as a warning that such acts against the regicides would not be tolerated, Parliament decided to execute a prominent Royalist prisoner in return; but Sir Lewes Dyves, selected as the sacrifice, managed to escape.

The dismay at Dorislaus's slaying quickly turned to anger and suspicion. It was noted with concern by the Council of State that the killers had got away, the Dutch being seen as either unable or unwilling to help in tracking them down. (In fact, Whitford had slipped over to the Spanish Netherlands, part of present-day Belgium, thanks to the help of the Portuguese ambassador, which would have made his apprehension extremely difficult.) The regicide, Edmund Ludlow, commented: 'Though this action was so infamous and contrary to the right of nations, yet the Dutch were not very forward to find out the criminals, in order to bring them to justice.'[11] The Commonwealth urged the Dutch now to make doubly sure of Strickland's safety.

Dorislaus's naked body was laid out on a table in his lodgings. The corpse attracted huge, ghoulish interest, a constant stream of people passing through *De Swaen*. But nobody provided help in tracking down or even identifying Whitford* and his men, despite a huge reward of 1,000 guilders for information, and a threat of death for any who harboured the fugitives. This would remain a

* Whitford's identity as the killer of Dr Dorislaus would remain secret until the following May, when he was on the way to his execution with other defeated Royalists, and declared who he was, and what he had done. The Scots then declined to execute him. Whitford was from that point on hunted by the Commonwealth, but always remained a step ahead of them.

diplomatic grievance between the two nations, as relations deteriorated through the following years, a period of mutual distrust that eventually led to warfare.

The new English republic was determined to honour one who had been murdered for his part in bringing a tyrant to justice. Dorislaus's body was returned to London, embalmed, then lay in state in Worcester House, one of a series of grand mansions on the Strand overlooking the Thames. The perpetrators of the 'Horrid Murder' might not be known by name, but the Council of State concluded the culprits clearly came from 'that party from whom all the troubles of this nation have formerly sprung'[12] – the Royalists. In compensation for their loss, £500 was awarded to each of Dorislaus's daughters, while an annual pension of £200 was granted to his son.

Dorislaus was given a lavish funeral, before burial in Westminster Abbey. John Evelyn noted: 'This night was buried with great pomp Dorislaus, slain at The Hague, the villain who managed the trial against his Sacred Majesty.'[13] A Royalist balladeer – mindful that Charles had been granted the most modest of funerals, having been quietly transported to Windsor for a simple interment, in the presence of a handful of loyal supporters – gloated at the grief of the distinguished mourners at Dorislaus's committal:

> Now pray observe the Pomp, the Persons, State
> That did attend This Alien Reprobate:
> Here, went Lieutenant General Crocodile,
> And's Cubs, bred of the Slime of our Rich Nile:
> Who weep before they kill, and whose False Tears
> Trickle from Blood-shed eyes of Murderers . . .[14]

Behind the tears – crocodile or otherwise – was genuine fear. The Parliamentary army officers who had sent Sir George Lisle and Sir Charles Lucas to die in front of a firing squad, after the siege of Colchester, had reprieved a third Royalist, Sir Bernard Gascoigne, when they discovered that Gascoigne was a Tuscan. It had been immediately agreed that adding such a man to the list of the condemned could place the Parliamentarians and their families at risk when travelling abroad. He was spared.

This same sense of self-preservation was foremost in the mind of Anthony Ascham. An Eton and Cambridge Scholar, Ascham had been tutor to the King's second son, James, during the boy's time in Parliament's custody. After the young duke's escape from London to Holland, disguised as a woman, Ascham had published an influential treatise justifying the political supremacy of the army during a time of confusion and revolution.[15] He then became a diplomat, serving the Commonwealth in Hamburg, before, as the State Papers for 16 January 1650 record, 'Anthony Ascham [was] approved to go as resident to the King of Spain and to have notice to go in the fleet going southward.'[16] He left on this mission, extremely concerned about the murderous intent of Royalist exiles.

Arriving in the southern Spanish town of Puerto Santa Maria in late May, Ascham was 'in so much alarm for his safety that he would not stir from the port . . . until he had a Maestro di Campo [senior regimental officer] and three or four soldiers to guard and accompany him.'[17] Next to his chest he wore an oval-shaped lucky talisman, engraved with the image of regicide: a sword thrusting downwards through a crown. Within a day of his arrival in Madrid, though, the charm had failed, and Ascham had followed Dorislaus as the victim of a gang of sword-wielding Royalists. This time, the perpetrators were arrested. Although contemporary accounts vary, it seems likely that they had stumbled upon Ascham by chance, and had wrongly identified him as John Aske, the barrister assisting Cook and Dorislaus at the King's trial.

John Milton, the regicides' propagandist-in-chief, recalled the King's last word to Juxon on the scaffold: the bishop had been interrogated so as to establish what Charles's final instruction to him – 'Remember!' – had meant. The browbeaten Juxon had eventually revealed: 'The King ordered me, if I could ever get to his son, to carry him this last command of a dying father, that, should he ever be restored to his kingdom and his power, he would pardon you the authors of his death: this is what the King charged me again and again to remember.'[18] Milton publicly berated the Prince of Wales for his failure to honour this, his father's final wish: 'But in what manner has he paid obedience to it, when either by his order or by his authority, two of our ambassadors, one in Holland, the other in Spain, have been murdered; the latter without even the slightest suspicion of being accessory to the King's death?'[19] This shrill outrage revealed the level of Parliamentary anxiety at the murder of their vulnerable diplomats.

It was not just the regicides that were under threat; it was also their families, exactly as John Bradshaw's wife had warned him would be the case when he had accepted the lord presidency – against her strongest advice. Indeed, one of their near relatives was targeted for royal revenge.

In December 1652, Richard Bradshaw, nephew of the lord president, was sent from his regular ambassadorial posting in Hamburg on a special mission to Denmark. The Danish royal family was closely linked to the Stuarts: Princess Anne of Denmark had been wife to James I and mother to Charles I. The current ruler of Denmark, Frederick III, was therefore first cousin to the executed English King. After the beheading, the Danes had joined with the Swedes in working on the Dutch government 'to join with them in assisting the King of Scots to gain his birthright'.[20]

Richard Bradshaw was 'a bold fellow',[21] who had served as a quartermaster general during the civil war. His brief now was to gain an audience with Frederick, with the aim of securing the release of twenty-two English merchant ships that had been impounded in Copenhagen. The vessels carried valuable naval provisions, including large quantities of hemp, used in the manufacture of rope.

The Danish King was in no hurry to meet the favourite nephew of the man who had judged and condemned his cousin. He sent word that he would not receive Richard Bradshaw's mission until Christmas had been celebrated.

Thomas Whyte, one of the King of Denmark's naval lieutenants, was in Norway when he learnt that Bradshaw would soon be arriving in Copenhagen. According to an anonymous Commonwealth spy, Whyte declared Richard Bradshaw a rebel, and vowed that he would 'shoot a brace of bullets into him'.[22] The informant reported to Parliament that he had been unsure at that stage whether Whyte was being serious or not, so pretended to agree with this plan in order to find out more. Whyte then started to plan the killing in earnest, saying he would gather a group of men to help him see it through.

On the night of Tuesday 4 January, 1653, Whyte arrived in the Danish port of Elsinore, where foreign shipping had to pay toll money for passing through the straits between Denmark and Sweden. Having established that Bradshaw's nephew was also in Elsinore, Whyte shared his plan with his companion – who he had no idea was a Commonwealth spy. London soon learnt the structure of the plot: to 'have the said resident killed in his own lodging, upon a Sunday night, as he sat at supper. At which time the said Whyte said, there were no lights abroad. And that the nature of the people at Copenhagen was such, that, when any quarrel happened at such a time, the people would shut their doors.'[23] The Danes' reluctance to get involved in unexpected drama would, Whyte hoped, assist in the assassins' escape.

Whyte decided that the murder would not, after all, involve the blast of the 'brace of bullets' originally envisaged. Instead he and his companions would rely on silent weapons: axes. What could be more suitable for the near relative of the man who had ordered the late King's beheading? The would-be killers travelled by wagon from Elsinore to Copenhagen, arriving there late on 6 January, intending to strike quickly. Meanwhile the Commonwealth spy slipped off to warn Richard Bradshaw of the plan against his life. When he learnt about it, Bradshaw encouraged the informant to urge Whyte on: he would be ready, when he came for him.

Whyte, meanwhile, appears to have been so excited by his mission that he became torn about which method of assassination would work best. The plan involving the axe was now left to one side, as he vacillated between shooting Bradshaw with a musket through the windows of his lodgings, and slaying him face to face with a pistol. One day he was going to kill his man in Denmark; the next he was planning to wait till he had returned to Hamburg. Whyte shared every, shifting, detail with the man he thought was his friend, but who was in fact reporting all to London – even down to how Whyte planned to cut off the dead man's fingers and steal his valuable rings. Meanwhile, throughout January, nothing happened.

Early in February, Whyte presented his latest plans to one of Frederick III's heralds, who reported 'that the King of Denmark would be glad this business were done, to wit, the killing of Lord Resident Bradshaw; but was unwilling to have it done in his land'.[24] So it was that Richard Bradshaw escaped assassination – partly because of Whyte's procrastination, and partly because of this royal request not to have the murder committed on his soil. However, when reports of Whyte's plots reached the remaining regicides in England, they were reconfirmed in their fear that, one day, they might suffer death at the hand of Charles I's avengers.

Those who had been most openly engaged in the trial and execution of Charles were soon adapting to life under a republic, where the army remained a formidable force. Having been infrequently paid for a long time, the soldiers now demanded that Parliament make good its debts. This it attempted through the sale of land and chattels belonging to the late King and his Royalist supporters.

Although one of the intentions of killing the King had been to stop further risings in favour of the Crown, the execution made the Prince of Wales the new focus of opposition. The Marquess of Ormonde, the leading Irish Royalist, proclaimed Charles Stuart 'the King of Ireland, Scotland and England'. Meanwhile, the Scots – for so long divided by Charles I's uncompromising religious convictions – began to unify after the King's death and explore ways of uniting behind his heir. The Commonwealth, England's new republic, geared itself up for further action in the Third Civil War.

Cromwell took command of the Commonwealth forces headed for Ireland, a country known to be a grim place to wage war, with its uncompromising enemy, thick mud and disease-ridden bogs. Some English soldiers had mutinied at being sent there in 1647, and they would do so again now. Meanwhile the Parliamentarians who had been fighting against Royalists and Catholics in Ireland since the beginning of the decade were low in morale, supplies and funds: Sir Charles Coote, leading Parliamentary troops in the north of Ireland, reported that the men of his six regiments 'have had but eight months' pay in eight years, and a peck [2 gallons] of oatmeal a week'.[25]

The New Model Army had twenty-eight regiments. It was decided that eight of these – four regiments of foot and four of cavalry – would suffice for the invasion. The choice as to who would be sent on this bleak campaign was decided, after prayer, by lot: 'Ten blanks and four papers with "Ireland" writ in them were put into a hat, and, being all shuffled together, were drawn out by a child, who gave to an officer of each regiment in the lot the lot of that regiment; and being [done] in this impartial and inoffensive way, no regiment could take exception at it.'[26]

Six of the eight regiments were commanded by regicides: Henry Ireton, Richard Deane, John Hewson, Thomas Horton, Isaac Ewer and Adrian Scroope (Scroope who had captured the Earl of Holland during the Second Civil War, then helped organise security in Westminster Hall during the King's trial). They departed in the knowledge that this would be a dangerous assignment: learning he would be crossing the Irish Sea to fight, Isaac Ewer wrote his will, 'not knowing,' as he said, 'whether God may ever bring me back'.[27] He would be one of several men closely involved in Charles's execution destined to die in Ireland. Indeed, Colonel Horton, hero of St Fagans, died of dysentery very soon after landing there. Colonel John Moore, a former governor of Liverpool who had helped to sign the King's life away, would follow soon after, from fever.

The English invaders headed for a land that had been at war since 1641, when Irish Catholics rose against Protestant settlers from

England and Scotland. Parliamentary pamphlets claimed that 200,000 Protestants were massacred then, although the actual figure was perhaps 4,000, with another 8,000 perishing from cold and disease after being driven from their homes in winter. This black propaganda, stoked by the tracts of John Milton and the sermons of their Puritan preachers, combined to form a black hatred of the Irish Catholics, and their Royalist cause, in the hearts of Cromwell's soldiers. Colonel Hewson, a signatory of Charles's death warrant, spoke for his fellows when he said that, if the Irish failed to surrender, 'the Lord by his power shall break them in pieces like a potter's vessel'.[28] The New Model Army, with its uncompromising professionalism, reinforced by religious passion, was just the tool for this job.

In the meantime, the force it faced lacked training and harmony. It was made up of Anglo-Irish Royalists, Catholic Confederates, Munster Protestants and Ulster Scots. The Confederates had come into being in 1642, and comprised two-thirds of the population. Led by native Catholic noblemen, clergy and army officers, they resented being expected to serve under the Marquess of Ormonde, who was a general of modest abilities, a Protestant convert, and their former enemy commander. The Confederates reluctantly provided him with troops because, in return, he, with equal reluctance, promised toleration for Irish Catholics. The other forces under Ormonde joined him with similarly grave misgivings.

Given its natural divisions, credit should go to Ormonde's diplomacy in holding this dysfunctional military force together. However, militarily, he failed: he oversaw the loss of Ireland to Cromwell in just nine months. His strategy and tactics were flawed from the start. Ormonde had surrendered Dublin to the Parliamentarians during the summer of 1647, preferring then for his English enemies to have the city than for the Irish Catholics to gain it. He now failed in his attempt to recapture the city. Not only that, but the besieged garrison boldly seized the initiative, attacking Ormonde's lines at Rathmines on 2 August 1649 with great success. The marquess's troops were scattered, and his artillery captured. Thirteen days later, Cromwell was able to land near Dublin, unopposed.

Ormonde now went on the defensive, ordering his forces to hold fast in a string of key towns, hoping the invaders would succumb to hunger and sickness during protracted sieges. But the New Model Army set about cracking the strongholds, one by one, with a speed that made Ormonde's plans irrelevant.

The first to receive Cromwell's lethal attention, in early September 1649, was Drogheda. Thirty miles north of Dublin, the town guarded the coastward march up into Ulster. Its defending commander, Sir Arthur Aston, had boasted that it would be easier to capture Hell than Drogheda, but the high, thin walls he so admired were suited to an earlier period of warfare. They were no match for Cromwell's eleven 48lb siege guns. Drogheda held out for just eight days.

Cromwell had offered terms of surrender to the garrison, which had been scorned. Angered by the casualties his forces had subsequently endured, and seeking vengeance for the Catholic massacre of Protestants in 1641, he stormed the town with 12,000 men, ordering that none of the defending troops should be spared. Two of those who had signed the King's death warrant were among the four regimental commanders to distinguish themselves in this, the bloodiest of assaults: Colonel John Hewson and Colonel Isaac Ewer.

Hewson – a former cobbler who had fought for Parliament since the outbreak of hostilities in 1642, and whose bravery had been rewarded with speedy promotions – was in his element. He had played an important part in the Second Civil War, leading his regiment with determination during the storming of Maidstone in Kent. A fellow regicide, Major General Edmund Ludlow, recalled of that engagement: 'The dispute growing hot, he [Hewson] was knocked down with a musket; but recovering himself, he pressed the enemy so hard, that they were forced to retreat to their main guard.'[29] Hewson was just the sort of gritty officer the New Model Army prospered by. His famed toughness unsettled the enemy and made him feared by civilians: it was Hewson who, in the immediate aftermath of the King's execution, had ridden through London, forbidding any to mourn Charles, on pain of death.

Ewer had been on the council of war that had ordered the summary execution of Lisle and Lucas after the fall of Colchester. Known for his outstanding loyalty to the cause, he had subsequently been sent to oversee the removal of Charles from vulnerable Carisbrooke Castle on the Isle of Wight to the solid security of Hurst Castle: there had been doubts about Charles's custodian, Colonel Hammond, at that time, but there were never doubts about Ewer. He had attended every day of the King's trial and was an enthusiastic regicide. Now, aware that Ireland might well be his graveyard, he showed similar fervour in battle.

Around 2,000 of the 2,800 defenders of Drogheda were killed, along with an estimated 750 civilians. Cromwell ordered that any priests or friars found in the town should be treated as combatants, and must be 'knocked on the head' – that is, be bludgeoned to death. This was also the fate of Aston, the Royalist commander. He had surrendered Millmount Fort, a small but doughty defence, to Colonel Axtell, on the promise that he and his men would be spared. This was the same Daniel Axtell who had been in charge of troops in Westminster Hall during the King's trial, ordering his men to fire on the loudly intrusive Lady Fairfax, and forcing them to bay for justice, then for execution, at the height of the proceedings.

Axtell had the Royalist prisoners disarmed, then led to a mill, where, within the hour, they were murdered in cold blood. Aston was beaten to death with his wooden leg, which his killers then split open: there had been a rumour that this was where he stored gold coins. This gossip proved to be false.

It was a bloody day all round. When a hundred Royalist soldiers sought sanctuary in the Church of St Peter, Cromwell ordered Hewson to flush them out with fire: thirty were burnt to death, while fifty were killed as they fled the flames.

Cromwell sent news of his blood-drenched success to John Bradshaw, who was in nominal charge of the Commonwealth's executive: John Evelyn wrote of him being, in that summer of 1649, 'then in great power'.[30] Cromwell passed to Bradshaw an unashamed account of his ruthlessness. 'It hath pleased God to bless our endeavours at Treda [Drogheda] . . . I believe we put to the sword the whole number of the defendants. I do not think thirty of the whole number escaped with their lives.'[31] The few survivors were transported to Barbados, to work the plantations in a state akin to slavery.

The Irish campaign continued to be bloody, and one-sided. Three weeks after Drogheda, the New Model Army sacked the town of Wexford while terms for surrender were being negotiated. Again, artillery played an important role, siege guns being brought along the coast for Cromwell by the ships of Richard Deane, who had bombarded Basing House four years earlier, before judging, and signing the death warrant of the King. Deane was now a general-at-sea – an admiral – in the Commonwealth navy.

Hundreds of women and children were put to death, or drowned in the River Slaney, while attempting to flee the indiscriminate massacre of the Wexford garrison. Again, Cromwell felt little compassion, justifying this suffering as fair vengeance for the shedding of Protestant blood at the start of the decade, and pointing to the loss of just twenty Commonwealth troops as proof of God's continuing favour.

The seasons were now changing ominously: Wexford was so badly mangled by the attack that it could not serve as the English winter quarters. Illness was rife in the cold, the mud and the effluence of the makeshift military camps. But with spring came further triumphs, the capture of Kilkenny and Clonmel effectively ending the campaign. Leaving Ireton to hold down Ireland, with Ludlow his second-in-command, Cromwell was now urgently called back to England.

Ireland had been a running sore for years; but now, for the first time, the various factions in Scotland were ready to unite behind the Prince of Wales. Charles Stuart would need to make compromises of conscience that his father had rejected to the end. However, this he eventually agreed to do, urged on by his mother and the French court to settle with the Scots on any terms, since they presented the only hope of recovering his father's throne. Charles therefore promised to support the imposition of Presbyterianism in England, once his southern crown had been reclaimed.

To ensure Scottish support, the Prince even allowed the ill use and sacrifice of some of his family's most loyal supporters. Its bravest general in the north, the charismatic and brilliant Duke of Montrose, who had resurrected his campaigns in Scotland to avenge the death of Charles I, was now betrayed after defeat and – testimony to the hurt his previous successes had caused his enemies – was denied the nobleman's customary death of beheading. Instead, in May 1650, he was led in an open cart through the streets of Edinburgh, his hands tied fast so he could not shield himself from the crowd's missiles. Montrose conducted himself with a dignity so remarkable at his end, that it was said to have been of more use to the Royalist cause than all his years of military gains. He was hanged, before his body was mutilated – his head stuck on a high spike, his limbs sent off to four important Scottish cities as a warning to others. The same month, twenty-one-year-old Charles Stuart was formally proclaimed King of Scotland.

Cromwell's army was half the size of that of his enemy, but his men were united and disciplined, while the Scots' loyalties were pulled in many directions, many of their men reluctant to serve. Lord Fairfax, an isolated and unhappy figure since Charles's execution, now stood down from command of the army, claiming he could not in good conscience invade Scotland, whose people had been his allies in the First Civil War.

Fairfax was replaced by Cromwell, fresh from Ireland. He gathered his forces, then headed towards Berwick-on-Tweed. Thomas Harrison, the Puritan dandy who had escorted Charles from the Isle of Wight towards his trial, and had been promoted major general, was left in charge of military forces throughout the rest of England.

The able Scottish commander, General David Leslie, had the

better of two skirmishes near Edinburgh, but his plans were then hampered by interference from the Kirk party – radical Presbyterians who were nicknamed 'Whigs'. With Cromwell's men within striking distance, the Kirk suddenly ordered a three-day pause in hostilities so it could purge the army of the 'ungodly'. Eighty officers and 3,000 troops were replaced by religiously correct, but militarily inferior, men. On 3 September 1650, confident in supreme command, and focused on the task in hand, Cromwell pulled off perhaps his finest victory, at the battle of Dunbar. The New Model Army annihilated the Scots, despite being outnumbered two to one.

Cromwell, repeatedly succumbing to serious illness – perhaps malaria contracted in Ireland – spent the next eleven months manoeuvring to capture Leslie's strongholds. Deciding to strike at Perth at the end of July 1651, Cromwell warned Harrison to stand ready in defence, in case the Scots took this opportunity to march south into England. This they did, King Charles of Scotland at the head of thirty regiments, confident he could reclaim his primary throne, and eager to hold to account those who had put his father to death. He and his men covered 150 miles in their first week.

The Scottish invasion caused terror in the south. There was particular consternation in the Council of State, many of whose members had royal blood on their hands. 'Bradshaw himself,' wrote Lucy Hutchinson, 'as stout-hearted as he was, privately could not conceal his fear; some raged and uttered sad discontents against Cromwell.'[32] Panic even made them question the new lord general's loyalty.

Cromwell quickly took Perth, and then wheeled south, sending some of his cavalry under the outstanding young major general, John Lambert, to harry the Scottish force from the rear. Meanwhile Harrison had defused many of those in England who might rise in support of a Stuart restoration. There were raids on suspects' homes, when their private armouries were confiscated, and the more worrisome among them were taken into custody. Harrison marched slowly back southwards, his retreating footsteps mirroring those of the advancing Royalists, watching them closely while refusing to be brought to battle.

Colonel Robert Lilburne, a Baptist Leveller who had been the forty-seventh of the fifty-nine to sign Charles's death warrant, brought about the first major reverse of Charles's invasion. He defeated the Royalist Earl of Derby at the Battle of Wigan Lane in Lancashire, in late August. The main Stuart army was now out on a limb, its northern wing defeated, the hoped-for support for the Crown not materialising.

On 3 September 1651, the first anniversary of his triumph at Dunbar, Cromwell struck. At the battle of Worcester he led 31,000 men of the New Model Army against the 16,000 men in Charles Stuart's predominantly Scottish army. Cromwell lost only 200 men that day, while killing 3,000 and capturing 10,000 of the enemy. The Royalist military cause was shattered, and the Third (and final) Civil War was over. Victory rescued the Commonwealth. It also saved the necks of the regicides – for now.

Chapter 4

A New Monarchy

The hand of God was mightily seen in prospering and preserving
the Parliament, till Cromwell's ambition unhappily interrupted
them.

Lucy Hutchinson, wife of the regicide Colonel Hutchinson

To those who knew him well, Cromwell was different after the battle of Worcester. Hugh Peters – who had ridden before the King's carriage on its final journey from Windsor to London – was a chaplain to Cromwell, and his intimate confidant. In 1649, Peters had been on the Irish campaign, combining his ministry with command of an infantry regiment.

He was aware that Cromwell was prone to moments of intense euphoria, but Peters would recall that his leader had been particularly 'elevated' (as Peters politely termed it), as soon as the scale of victory at Worcester became clear. It was enough of a concern to him, Peters later confided to Edmund Ludlow, that he 'told a friend with whom he [Peters] then quartered in his return to London, that he was inclined to believe Cromwell would endeavour to make himself King'.[1] It was as if the consecutive 3 September victories, Dunbar and Worcester, had taken Cromwell over the threshold, from a belief that he was leading troops in a godly cause, to a personal conviction that he had been marked out by God for a special duty.

There were many with a hand in the death of the King who

watched with horror and concern, as their suspicions about Cromwell's limitless ambition seemed set to become reality: horror, because they had not ended one man's life and absolute rule to see another govern as an autocrat in his place; concern, because they feared this character flaw in one man might leave them all vulnerable to a Royalist resurgence.

Colonel John Hutchinson, who sat as one of the King's judges, had been quick to identify Cromwell's self-serving streak. Even before the Third Civil War he had noticed Cromwell subtly begin to bend the army to his personal cause, replacing officers and soldiers 'with rascally turn-coat Cavaliers and pitiful sottish beats of his own alliances and others such as would swallow all things, and make no questions for conscience's sake'.[2] After the campaign in Scotland and the triumph at Worcester, Lucy Hutchinson recalled that her husband 'was confirmed that [Cromwell] and his confederates in the army were carrying on designs of private ambition, and resolved that none should share with them in the commands of the army or forts of the nation but such as would be beasts and ridden upon by the proud chiefs'.[3] Men such as Hutchinson, who had fought for civil liberty at huge personal risk and financial cost, felt shoddily treated and excluded.

Cromwell was supported by an army in which his two key subordinates held sway. One was John Lambert, who had risen to the rank of major general in his twenties. A brave and brilliant cavalry commander, Lambert had contributed significantly to the victories that ended the Second and the Third Civil Wars, Preston and Worcester. The other was Thomas Harrison. Cromwell had spotted Harrison's potential when the Staffordshire butcher's son was just a captain, and since then he had been Cromwell's protégé. Now the lord general had supreme control, Harrison continued his heady ascent: he would be regarded by many as the second most powerful man in the kingdom.

Harrison was a Fifth Monarchist. He believed that he was living in the prelude to the fifth empire of the world (the previous four had been those of Babylon, Persia, Greece and Rome), when the

Messiah would reappear to judge all, as envisaged in the apocalyptic Book of Daniel. The Fifth Monarchists even knew the year in which this Judgment Day would fall: 1666, for that year incorporated the dreadful number 666. This figure belonged to the Beast of the Sea, which, the Book of Revelation confirmed, would 'rise up out of the sea, having seven heads and ten horns, and upon his horns ten crowns, and upon his heads the name of blasphemy'.[4]

Fifth Monarchy was not a creed for the faint-hearted, and Harrison was a sufficiently rabid believer to become one of its leaders. He believed his role was to help make England godlier, before taking the crusade abroad, helping to prepare the way for the imminent Second Coming.

Cromwell, with customary pragmatism, harnessed Harrison's fanaticism for his own purposes. Aiming to bring to heel one of the heartlands of Royalism in the first two Civil Wars, he appointed Harrison president of the Commission for the Propagation of the Gospel in Wales: this involved the turning out of 'scandalous' (that is, Royalist) priests from the principality. While fulfilling his religious brief, it was inevitable that Harrison would at the same time root out any remaining support for the Crown.

Harrison was a complex character. His sincere and profound religious devotion was of a brand normally associated with those of a dour disposition. However, the major general was, according to a contemporary, 'of a sanguine complexion, naturally of such a vivacity, hilarity and alacrity as another man hath when he hath drunken a cup too much. But naturally also so far from humble thoughts of himself that it was his ruin.'[5]

Such was advertised by Harrison's peacock apparel. The first foreign ambassador to come to Westminster in recognition of the new republic was that of Spain. This was an important validation for the Commonwealth, albeit from a Catholic power. The day before the audience, Harrison spied several members in a cluster, and took it upon himself to tell them how they must appear the next day: he stressed, one of those present recalled, that they should aim to shine through 'wisdom, piety, righteousness and justice, and not in gold and silver and worldly bravery, which did not become saints'.[6] Tomorrow, he advised, the order of the day would be one of restraint: their dress should therefore be sober, and dignified.

Surprised by this unsolicited advice, the members nevertheless took care to appear in smart but staid clothes – muted colours, silver buttons and a modest touch of gold in the trim. However, to their astonishment, Harrison entered the chamber in altogether different attire: 'In a scarlet coat and cloak, both laden with gold and silver lace, and the coat so covered with clinquant [glitter] that scarcely could one discern the ground, and in this glittering habit set himself just under the Speaker's chair; which the other gentlemen thought that his godly speeches, the day before were but made that he alone might appear in the eyes of strangers.'[7]

Such finery came at a cost, and Harrison was one of the busier regicides when it came to building up stockpiles of personal wealth. The Rump soon discovered that finding money to pay its army was an impossible task. Instead, it offered soldiers certificates of credit. These Harrison amassed with such effectiveness, buying them at reduced rates from subordinates desperate for cash, that he was able to buy a slew of confiscated royal and Church properties around London and in his home county of Staffordshire. He became a very wealthy, and much resented, figure.

There were members of the Rump Parliament who feared Harrison. They heard rumours that he was secretly building up what amounted to a vast army in Wales, and decided to conclude his Propagation of the Gospel there. At the same time, members wanted to curtail the size, power and expense of the army. This was a threat that Cromwell could not tolerate, since it would reduce the basis of his power. Meanwhile Cromwell was frustrated that Parliament was making no discernible progress in the great undertakings of the day, including the drafting of a new constitution.

In April 1653, Cromwell and Harrison were in the Chamber of the House of Commons, listening to other members in fruitless discussion. Cromwell could take no more. He whispered to Harrison, 'This is the time I must do it',[8] got to his feet, and launched a tirade at the uselessness of the House, before taking personal aim at some of his fellow regicides. He chastised them for their lack of morals. Marten he called a whoremaster, and Chaloner a drunkard.

Cromwell then told Harrison to call in his men, and two dozen soldiers entered the chamber. While they began clearing the members, Harrison asked William Lenthall – styled by the Commonwealth as 'Speaker of the Parliament of England' – to vacate his chair. When Lenthall refused, Harrison grabbed the Speaker by his gown, and hauled him to his feet.

This violent ending of the Rump Parliament caused lasting consternation and division among those who had striven for the removal, then agreed to the execution, of the King. Three years later Edmund Ludlow asked his fellow regicide, Harrison, if he regretted what he had done: helping to expel an elected assembly at Cromwell's bidding. Harrison deflected responsibility, saying his heart had been 'upright and sincere' when the rumpus took place. Ludlow would have none of Harrison's evasiveness, replying, 'That I conceived it not to be sufficient in matters of so great importance to mankind, to have only good intentions and designs, unless there be also probable means of attaining those ends by the methods we enter upon.'[9]

Ludlow felt that the Rump had deserved more time to find its bearings in uncharted waters. He was also furious at the open door that Parliament's dissolution now presented to Cromwell's ambitions. 'It could not but be manifest,' he told Harrison, 'to every man who observed the state of our affairs, that upon the suppression of the civil authority, the power would immediately devolve upon that person who had the greatest interest in the army.'[10]

Cromwell and his Council of Officers considered the best way forward for the government of the nation. Lambert was for a committee of a dozen men, to control all. But Cromwell and the army representatives instead approved Harrison's proposal to commit the government of the nation to a council of religious men, who would contemplate God's will, and express it through legislature. This body became known as Barebone's Parliament after one of its members, Praise-God Barebone, a leather merchant of Fleet Street and a 'man of great piety, understanding and weight'. It proved to be rather better at prayer and contemplation than government, and it soon became clear that Harrison had recommended it to Cromwell as a prelude to the Second Coming, in accordance with his apocalyptic beliefs, rather than as a practical political entity. Fifth Monarchists believed that good men were needed to prepare the way, before the victory over the Anti-Christ could be made complete.

Harrison also wanted a continuation of the war that the Commonwealth had provoked with the Netherlands. This began in July 1652 because, as George Monck, serving as one of England's generals-at-sea, stated, 'The Dutch have too much trade, and the English are resolved to take it from them.'[11] The war was a naval one, involving terrible casualties on both sides. One who was lost was Richard Deane, the New Model Army's artillery supremo, who had been twenty-first out of the fifty-nine signatories on Charles I's death warrant. Deane was cut in two by a Dutch cannonball at the start of a 200-ship engagement, the Battle of the Gabbard, in June 1653. Monck threw a cloak over his fellow commander's steaming remains, so the sight of his mutilation would not demoralise the crew. The corpse was afforded a more dignified end later, being interred with great pomp at Westminster Abbey.

Harrison saw the war with the Dutch not as a matter of commercial practicality, but as a rebuff to the Netherlands, on behalf of God, for having allowed financial greed to distract them from their religious duty. Once the Dutch were defeated, Harrison and his fellow radicals very much hoped that the war would be continued, its ultimate goal the conquest of Rome. When, in 1654, Cromwell pushed through a peace treaty with the Netherlands (he had never been happy fighting a Protestant nation) his rift with Harrison was complete.

Barebone's Parliament was an experiment that imploded within a few months, because of indecision and infighting. Its final act, to the dismay of the Fifth Monarchists, was to surrender its sovereignty to Cromwell. Recognising his pre-eminence in the land, the Instrument of Government of 1653 proclaimed, 'Oliver Cromwell, Captain-General of the forces of England, Scotland and Ireland, shall be, and is hereby declared to be, Lord Protector of the Commonwealth of England, Scotland and Ireland, and the dominions thereto belonging, for his life.' The next phase of England's republican decade was to be Cromwell's Protectorate.

After the shattering defeats of the Civil Wars, Royalist sympathisers retained negligible armed strength, and lacked coordination. With little hope of a turning tide, and with the Prince of Wales in an exile that, after the rout at Worcester, looked as though it might be eternal, his supporters looked to any signs of hope. John Evelyn wrote of a violent summer storm, the likes of which nobody could remember, that ended a four-month drought: 'The hail being in some places 4 and 5 inches about, brake all the glass about London: especially at Deptford, and more at Greenwich, where Sir Thomas Stafford, vice-chamberlain to the Queen, affirmed some had the shape of crowns.'[12] In desperate circumstances, this was viewed as a rare positive omen.

Cromwell did all he could to ensure that hopes of a Stuart restoration remained a fanciful prospect. However, his brutal single-mindedness added to the unpopularity of his regime. Some who had loyally supported the Parliamentarian cause, including the regicide Colonel Hutchinson, watched in dismay as Cromwell played into the hands of the enemy. Lucy Hutchinson recorded that her husband and his allies recognised that 'while Cromwell reduced all by the exercise of tyrannical power under another name, there was a door open for the restoring of their (the Royalists') party'.[13]

Cromwell's chief intelligence officer had been the regicide Thomas Scott. However, under his Protectorate, Cromwell passed this responsibility on to John Thurloe, his family's lawyer. Thurloe combined censorship with espionage, to quash Royalist plots before they took root. As postmaster general, he had access to all mail, whether to foreign governments, or between Stuart sympathisers. He brought together a team of codebreakers, one of them the son of the slain Dr Dorislaus.

In 1655 there was a ripple of seemingly disjointed Royalist rebellions across England. It was Thurloe and his network of agents that thwarted these efforts, having prior knowledge of the conspirators' plans after infiltrating their ranks, and reading their correspondence. Such failures crushed the morale of other potential plotters, and dissuaded foreign powers from becoming embroiled in the luckless intrigues of the exiled Prince of Wales.

Despite his successes, the Lord Protector asserted ever tighter control over England, dividing it into ten military governorships. Each was under the control of a major general, answerable only to him. Those chosen by Cromwell included two fellow regicides: William Goffe in Berkshire, Hampshire and Sussex; and Edward Whalley controlling five Eastern and Midlands counties, from Lincolnshire to Warwickshire. A third signatory to the King's death warrant, John Barkstead, was appointed deputy to the major general of Middlesex. Barkstead performed the day-to-day duties, commanding the Tower of London, administering the key area that included the City of London and Westminster, and overseeing everything from the rounding up of hundreds of prostitutes to the suppression of Shrove Tuesday celebrations.

Cromwell relied on the major generals to preserve peace, and also to enforce his will: Harrison and Ludlow, despite their impressive military records, were considered too independent for posts that demanded obedience to the Protector. One of the major generals' tasks was to extract the Decimation Tax, a fine of one-tenth of their property, payable by defeated Royalists. This was a particularly galling levy, since its proceeds went to fund local militias whose prime role was the policing of the Royalists. This cycle of heavy taxation and suffocating security created a self-feeding monster, whose master was Cromwell.

Ludlow detested the rule of the major generals, claiming that they frequently acted outside the law, threatening those who failed to obey them with transportation to the plantations of the West Indies. 'And it was a misery to be bewailed in those days,' agreed Lucy Hutchinson, 'that many of the Parliamentary party exercised cruelty, injustice, and oppression to their conquered enemies.'[14] She thought the major generals 'silly, mean fellows ... who ruled according to their wills, by no law but what seemed good in their own eyes.'[15]

Further anger greeted Cromwell's hope, partly implemented through his major generals, to improve the nation's morality. Swearing, drunkenness and blasphemy were harshly punished; theatres were closed, and the horses of those riding on Sundays were confiscated. Horse races, bull-baiting and cock-fighting were banned: the seventeenth-century stomach for animal-based enter-tainment was strong, and its forced suppression was widely resented. In 1655, Colonel Pride sent a file of musketeers into the Bear Gardens at Bankside, London, where bear- and bull-baiting had been popular on Tuesdays and Thursdays since early Tudor times: Elizabeth I had taken the Spanish ambassador there, subtly probing him for secret intelligence during the entertainments. Now, it was decreed, such sport had to end, because it degraded the godly Commonwealth.

Pride had the bears tied by the nose and shot by firing squad, sparing just one white cub. He had the mastiffs that had been the bears' tormentors sent to the plantations of Jamaica.[16] Soon after-wards Thomas Walker, a petticoat-maker from Cannon Street, bought the area and built tenement buildings in place of the redun-dant amphitheatre. This was, to many, a Commonwealth subterfuge: their traditional enjoyment had been removed in the name of morality; but, it was strongly suspected, the true motive had been profit.

Religion was the root of much controversy. In the late 1640s and early 1650s the Quaker Movement spread south from northern England. Its central tenets were suited to the instability of the times: Quakers questioned the authority of Church and state, and believed that every human was blessed with a divine 'Inner Light'. William

Goffe, the major general who had shone at the Putney debates before sitting in judgment on the King, condemned the Quakers as 'doing much work for the Devil and deluding many simple souls'.[17]

James Nayler was a prominent Quaker. He had served with Parliament during the Civil Wars, most recently under Cromwell at Dunbar, returning to life as a farmer in the West Riding. A vision summoned him from his life in the fields to a ministry spreading his religious beliefs. Nayler was famed for his eloquence, which he used to attack slavery. But it was his actions, rather than his words, that provoked the greatest uproar.

During a rainstorm he rode his horse into the city of Bristol, with his followers in attendance, proclaiming 'Holy, holy, holy'. He later claimed that his aim had been to highlight every person's possession of the Inner Light, but this failed to convince. Puritans were outraged at his impersonation of Jesus. They also condemned as blasphemous his assertion that mankind could be considered spiritually equal to the Son of God.

Nayler was brought to trial in London. There, another of Cromwell's major generals, William Butler, called for Nayler to suffer the penalty prescribed by the Old Testament book of Leviticus: 'Bring forth him that hath cursed without the camp; and let all that heard him lay their hands upon his head, and let all the congregation stone him.'[18] Goffe joined in the call for Nayler to be killed, with the inflammatory accusation that Quakers 'would tear the flesh off the bones of all that profess Christ'.[19]

Cromwell favoured leniency for Nayler, but he had to concede to the demands for serious punishment. Nayler was placed in a pillory, where he was viciously pelted by the crowd, before being made to walk through the streets, being whipped as he went. His forehead was branded with a 'B' – a permanent reminder of his blasphemy – while his tongue was pierced with a hot iron. Nayler was then returned to Bristol, where he was forced to re-enter the city – this time, to show his unworthiness, facing his horse's rear. He was flogged again, before being sentenced to two years of imprisonment so hard that he never recovered. Assaulted on his way back home to

Yorkshire in 1660, he died soon afterwards aged forty-two.

If Cromwell was occasionally forced to bend his policy to the prejudices of his lieutenants, he was also powerful enough to build up bastions of influence that owed him unquestioning and total loyalty.

Ireland became almost a family fiefdom: Cromwell's son-in-law Henry Ireton took control of it, when the lord general was called away to fight the Scots. Ireton continued his father-in-law's ruthless ways, before succumbing to grave illness. This leading regicide died in agony in Limerick at the end of 1651, his last words allegedly a call for fresh blood to flush out the fiery fever that had consumed his body. Ireton, like Dorislaus and Deane before him, was buried in a magnificent ceremony at Westminster Abbey.

Cromwell's eldest daughter Bridget endured a short widowhood, marrying Charles Fleetwood just six months after Ireton's death. Fleetwood, another senior officer in her father's service, was now sent as commander-in-chief to Ireland, where he continued the brutal crushing of resistance, persecuting Catholics, and favouring Puritans over Presbyterians.

When Fleetwood was transferred to an English major-generalship in 1655, Ireland largely became the responsibility of Cromwell's intelligent twenty-seven-year-old son Henry, who already had five years' experience there. During his time in charge of its armed forces, then its government, he had become a popular figure, demonstrating a sense of fairness and compassion notably absent in his three predecessors. Offered £1,500-worth of Irish property as a reward for his services, he turned it down, saying Ireland was too poor a country to bear such a gift.

The Cromwell children were intriguing to contemporaries, filling the void left by the exile and imprisonment of the Stuart princes and princesses. Once their father became Lord Protector, from which point he was addressed as 'Your Highness', the offspring were treated as quasi-royal. Bridget was viewed as down to earth but, Lucy Hutchinson believed, 'the rest were insolent fools'.[20] The eldest surviving son – the two senior ones had died of sickness while, respectively, a student and a Parliamentary army officer – was Richard, a disappointment to his father because he preferred to indulge a passion for country sports to serving the Protectorate. Lucy Hutchinson considered Richard 'a peasant in his nature, yet gentle and virtuous; but [he] became not greatness'.[21]

Elizabeth Claypole was Cromwell's favourite daughter. Captain Silius Titus, a Royalist, wrote to the Prince of Wales's court in exile with a delectable tale of her snobbery. Elizabeth was attending a wedding, where the wives of the major generals were surprisingly nowhere to be seen. 'The feast wanting much of its grace by the absence of those ladies, it was asked by one there where they were,' recorded Titus: 'Mrs Claypole answered, "I'll warrant you washing their dishes at home as they used to do." This hath been extremely ill taken, and now the women do all they can with their husbands to hinder Mrs Claypole from being a princess.'[22]

The great question of Cromwell's latter years was whether he would become King or not. It was an exquisitely fraught issue, since many who had signed the death warrant of one king had done so with no thought that another would ever take his place. Others, such as Lord Broghill – an ally in Ireland, who had ably assisted Cromwell and Ireton in their campaigns – urged kingship on Cromwell as the only security against the return of the Stuarts.

When Cromwell recalled Parliament in 1656, the republican Ludlow suspected that the prime reason for the summons was to have the Lord Protector proclaimed King. Cromwell closely controlled the elections for that assembly. He was particularly troubled that two of the most prominent of his fellow regicides – Lord President Bradshaw, and Ludlow himself – might cause problems, since they had made clear their absolute opposition to the return of kingship. Cromwell ordered a letter to be read aloud, in Bradshaw's constituency of Chester. It made clear that the Lord Protector would be extremely displeased if Bradshaw were returned as a Member of Parliament. Meanwhile, in Wiltshire, voters were fed the lie that Ludlow was a prisoner in the Tower of London. He was not; but belief that he was meant that he could not be considered for election.

Even those who were elected required Cromwell's endorsement. Using a clause in the Instrument of Government that excluded anyone from standing if they had questionable integrity or sincerity, ninety newly elected members of the House of Commons, including the regicide Thomas Scott, were barred from taking their seats. They appealed to their fellow members to help them overcome Cromwell's ban, but the Lord Protector was too powerful to resist.

January 1657 saw the first open suggestion that Cromwell should become King. A Colonel Jephson, who pushed for him to be crowned, was teasingly told by the Lord Protector, 'Get thee gone for a mad fellow, as thou art.'[23] This was a 'madness' that was quickly rewarded by the secretly delighted Cromwell: the colonel and his son received rich rewards, including military promotions, and an ambassadorship to Sweden.

Jephson proved to be a rarity in the army: the majority of senior officers would not countenance a return to crowned rule and, as the possibility of a 'King Oliver' grew, they bared their teeth.

Lieutenant Generals Fleetwood and Lambert and Colonel Desborough – rated 'the three great men'[24] of the land by the Commonwealth's spymaster John Thurloe – warned Cromwell, 'that those who put him upon it were no enemies to Charles Stuart; and that if he accepted of it, he would infallibly draw ruin on himself and his friends'.[25] Desborough went further, claiming that if Cromwell became King, he would betray the cause they had fought for, and be the ruin of his family. Colonel Pride also warned the Lord Protector against reaching for the Crown.

Cromwell was on the point of ignoring all of these warnings when a lieutenant colonel presented a petition on behalf of thirty-three brother officers which declared:

That they had hazarded their lives against monarchy, and were still ready to do so, in defence of the liberties of the nation: that having observed in some men great endeavours to bring the nation again under their old servitude, by pressing the General to take upon him the title and government of a King, in order to destroy him, and weaken the hands of those who were faithful to the public; they therefore humbly desired that they would discountenance all such persons and endeavours, and continue steadfast to the old cause.[26]

After months of agonising, Cromwell finally refused the crown on 8 May 1657. He consoled himself, soon afterwards, with the passing of the Humble Petition and Advice. This legislation, which gave him the right to appoint his successor as Lord Protector, was deeply unpopular with republicans and with many in the military. However, it was approved by the majority of civilian Members of Parliament, who had been unsettled by various recent attempts on Cromwell's life, which were linked to seditious cells and to Royalists, 'it being a received principle amongst them', Parliament noted,

that no order being settled in your lifetime for the succession in the Government, nothing is wanting to bring us into blood and confusion, and them to their desired ends, but the destruction of your person; and in case things should thus remain at your death, we are not able to express what calamities would in all human probability ensue thereupon, which we trust your Highness (as well as we) do hold yourself obliged to provide against, and not to leave a people, whose common peace and interest you are entrusted with, in such a condition as may hazard both . . .[27]

There was a duty to protect the cause into the next generation and beyond. Otherwise the Stuarts might return, with vengeance their inevitable companion.

When the second term of this Parliament opened in January 1658, the ninety members excluded from the opening session were at last admitted. It was an opportunity for the republican regicides to justify their actions nine years earlier, and to attack Cromwell for not remaining true to their aims at that time.

The former spymaster Thomas Scott was quick to speak: 'Shall I, that sat in a Parliament that brought a King to the bar, and to the block, not speak my mind freely here?'[28] he challenged.

Scott was particularly incensed that the Lord Protector had formed a new House of Lords, given the Rump's decision – immediately after Charles I's head was cut off – to dispense with the Upper House. 'The Lords would not join in the trial of the King,' he reminded the Commons. 'We must lay things bare and naked. We were either to lay all that blood of ten years war upon ourselves, or upon some other object. We called the King of England to our bar, and arraigned him. He was for his obstinacy and guilt condemned and executed; and so let all the enemies of God perish. The House of Commons had a good conscience in it.'[29]

On 3 September 1658, Cromwell died unexpectedly, aged fifty-nine. He had suffered from malaria and urinary infections for some time, and it seems likely that complications to these conditions led to septicaemia. Certainly, incompetent doctors hurried the death along. Equally, Cromwell's spirit had been broken by the recent death of his favourite daughter, Elizabeth, at the age of twenty-nine. As he neared the end, Cromwell bequeathed the Lord Protectorship to his eldest surviving son, Richard.

Oliver Cromwell's funeral was based on that of James I, father of the man in whose execution he had played so prominent a role. The cortege processed from Somerset House to Westminster Abbey, for interment in Henry VII's Chapel. The route was strewn with sand, to muffle the clatter of hooves and wheels on the cobbles, and so set a suitably sombre tone. Rails were put in place to hold back the crowds. Soldiers looked on, their banners bound in a cypress mourning veil. Six horses drew the coffin, set on a bed of state bedecked in black velvet, to the burial place of England's kings.

John Evelyn was among the onlookers. He noticed that 'The Pall [was] held up by his new Lords: Oliver lying in effigy in royal robes, and crowned with a crown, sceptre, and mund, like a King: the Pendants and Guidons were carried by the Officers of the Army, the Imperial banners, Achievements etc. by the Heralds in their Coats ...' It was a magnificent procession. Cromwell's generals, lords, courtiers and family were joined by the ambassadors of Holland, France and Portugal, 'many thousands of people,' it was recorded, 'being spectators in the windows, and upon the scaffolds all along the way as it passed'.[30]

'But,' John Evelyn noted in his diary, 'it was the joyfullest funeral that ever I saw, for there was none that cried, but dogs, which the soldiers hooted away with a barbarous noise; drinking, and taking tobacco in the street as they went.'[31]

Richard Cromwell, the new Lord Protector, had neither the resolve nor the ruthlessness to make a success of his inheritance. His quiet personal authority won over some of the senior army officers loyal to his father's legacy, including the regicides Colonel Ingoldsby and Major Generals Goffe and Whalley, each of them related to the Cromwells by blood or marriage. These three were among the new Lord Protector's closest followers. However, Richard was unable to control the army as a whole: his father had been its brilliant general and had earned its loyalty – successes Richard had neither attempted nor achieved. At the same time, with Oliver dead, the many Parliamentary enemies of the Protectorship felt able to speak freely.

These dangerous stirrings were noted by Colonel Thomas Pride, who was among those to sign Richard Cromwell's proclamation as the new Protector. Pride, in failing health, felt pessimistic about the future for England, Scotland and Ireland. His last words, from his deathbed in October 1658, were, 'that he was very sorry for these three nations, whom he saw in a most sad and deplorable condition'.[32] Richard stood down in May 1659, after fewer than nine months' rule. The Rump Parliament, dispersed by Cromwell and his henchman Harrison six years earlier, now reconvened, promising to maintain a Commonwealth with no King, no Lord Protector and no House of Lords. It also formed a Council of State of twenty-one men, seven of whom had signed Charles I's death warrant: those responsible for the King's death were still grimly holding on to power. But life in the absence of the charismatic and commanding Oliver Cromwell was difficult for those who had loved or loathed him: his followers found themselves leaderless, while his enemies discovered they really had very little in common, other than a hatred for the deceased.

The army was now divided, with Fleetwood and Lambert each keen to gain control of it and the nation. Yet both generals were now alienated from many of their junior officers and men, who resented their commanders taking advantage of rank and file poverty to enrich themselves: like Harrison, they had profited from their men's desperation and bought their credit notes for wages owed by Parliament at bargain rates. Vavasor Powell, a Fifth Monarchist from Wales, spoke for many when he claimed of the newly wealthy generals that 'Their great parks and new houses and gallant wives had choked them up.'[33]

Tension between the army and Parliament was taken to a higher pitch when, on 12 October 1659, MPs voted to be rid of the seven-man committee and take greater military control for itself. Lambert, with Fleetwood's connivance, descended on the Palace of Westminster with two regiments, surrounding it, and having its doors locked and guarded. Lambert replaced Parliament's authority with a twenty-three-man Committee of Safety, with himself and Fleetwood as its military men.

John Bradshaw, the lord president during Charles I's trial, now stepped forward. He had lost his posts during the mid-1650s as a result of his breach with Oliver Cromwell. Richard Cromwell had called Bradshaw back to high office during his brief rule, but by then Bradshaw was seriously ill – probably with malaria. In October he insisted on being taken from his Whitehall sickbed to Parliament to denounce the military's intimidation of the Rump. At the end of the month, by now on his deathbed, Bradshaw's final words were defiant: if a judge had been needed to try Charles I once more, he declared, he would have been 'the first man to do it'.

Parliament now called for loyal officers to come to its aid. Oliver Cromwell's commander in Scotland for the previous five

years, George Monck – who had served as an admiral in the
Anglo-Dutch War, casting his cloak over Deane's mangled remains
– resolved to see through a promise he had earlier made in print:
to protect Parliament and to champion political stability, whatever the personal danger to himself. He looked for an alliance
with Colonel John Jones and Sir Hardress Waller, two of the regicides commanding forces in Ireland, but they refused to join him,
fearing a fatal division in the army if they did. Monck nevertheless
felt strong enough to act alone. He had discarded those likely to
sympathise with Lambert and Fleetwood from his northern army.
More importantly, he had ensured his men were fully paid: a
decade earlier, when serving in Ireland as a colonel, 500 out of his
700 men 'ran away to the enemy, because they ha[d] money
there'.[34] He would not allow such a situation to arise again. Monck
prepared to march south with a unified, disciplined and well-fur-
nished force.

In November 1659, Lambert led an army north to Newcastle, to
meet Monck. He was not seeking battle, but rather for Monck and
his men to unite with him: together they could block the ambitions
of the common enemy, the Royalists. Lambert wrote to the
Commissioners of the Army of Scotland: 'My soul longs for such
an accommodation betwixt the armies as may tend to the glory of
God, the peace of these Nations, and preservation of that interest
which God has owned as his own, and from which I shall (the Lord
enabling me) never part.'[35]

But Monck had no need for, or trust in, Lambert. He delayed
negotiations, knowing that Lambert's forces were poorly supplied,
unpaid, and were already beginning to desert. Meanwhile in
London, on 24 December, the Committee of Safety fell. Two days
later Parliament gave Monck, in Clarendon's words, 'the office and
power of general of all the forces in the three kingdoms . . . as absolutely as ever they had given it to Cromwell'.[36]

Although some officers rode north now, to encourage Lambert
to bring Monck to battle, it was too late: Lambert's forces had all
but evaporated. He rode south with just fifty men, most of them

officers. He was scooped up and committed to the Tower of London.

On 2 January, Monck entered England, crossing the border at Coldstream with a force of 5,000 infantry and 2,000 cavalry. He received support from many quarters, including the retired lord general, Thomas Fairfax. Monck sent men ahead to have London cleared of other forces, so his men, trusted veterans, could be quartered there on their arrival. Parliament made their dependence on Monck clear once more by preparing his lodgings in a grand suite of rooms in Whitehall.

Monck had fought for the King in the Civil War, before being taken prisoner. He had then chosen to serve Parliament, rising to high rank on land and sea. Nobody could tell how he would use his great power now.

Chapter 5

The Word of a King

The cursed Presbyterian crew
Was then put to the flight,
Some did fly by day,
And others run by night.
In barns and stables they did cant,
And every place they could,
He made them remember,
The spilling royal blood.
'King Charles the Second's Restoration,
                    29 May' – a ballad, 1660

The Prince of Wales had learnt of Cromwell's death with disbelief. In the mid-1650s, Charles Stuart's existence had diminished to one of impoverished despair. Cromwell had successfully insisted, by the terms of a treaty with France, that the family of Charles I be exiled from French territory. The Prince had moved for two years to Cologne, 'whilst,' one of his companions recalled, 'all the princes of Europe seemed to contend amongst themselves who should most eminently forget and neglect him'.[1] He was in the countryside of what is now Belgium when his father's nemesis died. He moved immediately to Brussels, eagerly awaiting possibilities.

In 1655 a false report of Cromwell's death, and his replacement by Major General Lambert, had reached the Royalists in exile. Secretary Nicholas had written at the time: 'If Cromwell should be dead, and Lambert chosen in his place, he or any other who had not actually a hand in the murder of the late King may be treated with and pardoned, so as to restore the King on good conditions, which is the only hope I expect from such a change.'[2] Now, with Oliver Cromwell's death confirmed, it was welcome news that Monck had become the most powerful man in the country: he had played no part in Charles I's execution. It was possible to negotiate with such a man.

At first, the Royalists received no word from Monck. Indeed, his early actions were discouraging for Charles, and reassuring to those who wanted to perpetuate the Commonwealth. Monck stated his intention was to serve Parliament, and its members were happy to take him at his word, and use him as their sword arm. When the City of London refused to grant desperately needed funds until a free Parliament was called, the members asked Monck to intervene. He took his troops into the City and, to the consternation of the Royalists, arrested the ringleaders there. Monck then broke the gates that marked, and the portcullises that symbolised, the City's independence. When the Prince of Wales heard this, his confidant Clarendon recalled, 'All the little remainder of his hope was extinguished, and he had nothing left before his eyes but a perpetual exile.'[3]

The following day Praise-God Barebone attacked the Stuarts in Parliament, his petition insisting that only those who took an oath rejecting the line of Charles I should be allowed to hold public office. Even to mention restoration, Barebone urged, should result in a charge of high treason. Monck realised that he would be among the first called upon to make this oath of renunciation. He would very soon be forced to declare his hand.

Meanwhile Monck made quiet contact with Sir Charles Coote, Lord President of Connaught, the western province of Ireland. Like Monck, Coote had been a Royalist officer who had switched allegiance during the First Civil War to fight for Parliament. Coote appreciated that the tide had suddenly and definitely turned in favour of the Stuarts. He was desperate not to be punished for his treachery, or for his actions as a Parliamentary commander. Coote was keen to capture Edmund Ludlow, one of the most prominent regicides in Ireland, so he could deliver him up to Charles as a demonstration of his rediscovered loyalty to the Crown. This, he hoped, would result in his being pardoned. Ludlow was too wary to be trapped, though, so Coote next settled on catching John Cook, the lead prosecutor at Charles I's trial.

Coote invited Cook to come from his home in Waterford, to a meeting in Dublin. The lawyer and his wife were troubled by this summons, and considered fleeing to the American colonies. But Cook eventually decided to accept, and headed towards Dublin. He was picked up en route by Coote's men, and thrown in prison.

Coote now rounded up a handful of others involved in Charles I's death: Colonel John Jones, Cromwell's brother-in-law; Sir Hardress Waller, who had been so pivotal in the success of Pride's Purge; Colonel Matthew Tomlinson, who had guarded the King in his final days; and Colonel Hercules Huncks and Lieutenant Colonel Robert Phare, two of the officers who had been on duty on the scaffold when the execution was carried out. As the possibility of Stuart restoration turned into likelihood, there was a scramble for redemption among Parliamentarians. The regicides were quickly identified as especially vulnerable pawns, to be bartered in return for forgiveness.

Fear at the consequences of a royal return became clear in the House of Commons by mid-March 1660, with dissolution looming, and the future unsure but threatening. Those who had stood against the late King wanted to lay down a clear marker between their conduct, and that of those who had been behind the judicial death of Charles I. John Crew, MP for Brackley during the Long Parliament, had been an eager opponent of the Royalists during the first two Civil Wars. However, he had been one of the members excluded by Pride's Purge, and now was his moment for revenge. He moved that, before this Parliament voted itself into extinction, it must bear witness against those responsible for the infamous execution, which prompted many members to declare their hands innocent of the King's blood.

The return to royal rule was not yet guaranteed. On 12 April there was a reigniting of republican hope with the news that John Lambert was free again: he had escaped the Tower of London with the help of his chambermaid, who took his place in his prison bed, wearing his nightcap and managing a gruff goodnight to the guards from behind the bed curtains. Lambert let himself down from his window by a rope made from bound sheets. On reaching the ground, six of his followers spirited him away by barge. When the gaoler unlocked the cell door the next morning, all he could say was, 'In the name of God, Joan, what makes you here?'[4]

Lambert wanted a return to the days when an irresistible Parliamentary army controlled the land. He planned a rendezvous, on Easter Day 1660, of like-minded nostalgics at Edgehill, Warwickshire – chosen because of its central geographical position, and also because this was where the first great battle of the Civil War had taken place. Ripples spread through the army, as they recalled the days of triumph. Parliament declared Lambert a rebel, offered £100 for his capture, and dispatched a force under Colonel Richard Ingoldsby to bring him in, dead or alive.

Among those riding with Lambert as he moved through Northamptonshire towards Warwickshire were Colonels Okey and Axtell, both of whom had had a hand in the king's death. Other regicides were slow to help – a matter for later regret. One of those who had organised Lambert's escape from the Tower went to see Lieutenant General Edmund Ludlow, imploring him to raise troops in the west, and bring them across as reinforcements. 'But,' Ludlow would later apologetically admit, 'I thought it not prudent to engage my friends in so public a manner, till I should see some possibility of making a stand.'[5]

A stand of sorts was made near Daventry but, with only 300 cavalry and forty infantry, Lambert's force was no match for Ingoldsby's. Lambert tried to escape, but his Berber horse was built for speed and agility, not the Northamptonshire plough. He surrendered to Ingoldsby, without resistance. Trying to find a way of keeping the cause afloat and himself at liberty, Lambert offered his services in the reinstatement of Ingoldsby's patron and cousin, Richard Cromwell. Ingoldsby made it clear that he was not there to negotiate, but merely to take Lambert prisoner. 'Pray, my lord,' said Lambert, 'let me escape; what good will my life, or perpetual imprisonment, do you?'[6]

Ingoldsby, like Coote in Ireland, knew the answer to that question. It seemed certain the Stuart line would soon be restored and he needed to accrue credit or be held to account for his past conduct. Although Ingoldsby had not sat in judgment of the King, his signature was on the death warrant, and in the period between the conclusion of the First Civil War and Charles I's execution his regiment had been one of the most radical, demanding the King be judged for shedding the blood of his people. Ingoldsby returned Lambert to London, and the Tower. It was not immediately obvious, but with Lambert's renewed incarceration went the last hope of the regicides to halt the tide towards Royalism. Ingoldsby was pleased to accept the thanks of Parliament for his 'late great and eminent services to this Nation'.[7] He hoped that this gratitude would manifest itself in redemption and pardon.

All the surviving regicides now focused on their likely fates, as the reign of another Charles Stuart beckoned. During Lambert's time on the loose, Colonel Hutchinson sought advice from his friend Sir Anthony Ashley Cooper, who had disagreed so forcefully with Oliver Cromwell over the ability of a king to be judged at all, let alone by a legal entity as contentious as the High Court of Justice, and had refused to take part in the trial.

Hutchinson knew Cooper was an intimate of Monck's, and asked him what his all-powerful friend's aims were. It was a crucial enquiry, wrote Lucy Hutchinson, in order that 'both he and others might consider their safety, who were likely to be given up for a public sacrifice. Whereupon Cooper denied to the death any intention besides a commonwealth. "But," said he, with the greatest semblance of reality that can be put on, "if the violence of the people should bring the King upon us, let me be damned, body and soul, if ever I see a hair of any man's head touched, or a penny of any man's estate, upon this quarrel." '⁸ Colonel Hutchinson passed this reassuring message on to several of his fellows. However, it was quickly clear that things would not be as Cooper had claimed.

Parliament was dismissed in mid-April 1660. Some of the sitting regicides were not prepared to go quietly. 'Upon the last day of our sitting,' Major General Browne, the lord mayor elect, recalled later, 'Mr Scott seeing the House must break, said, "Their heads must be laid to the block if there were a new Parliament, for I confess I had a hand in the putting the King to death, and I desire all the world may take notice of it, and I desire when I die it may be written on my tomb. I do not repent of any thing I have done; if it were to do, I could do it again." ' When it became clear that these appeals had been ignored, and that this Parliament would cease to be, Thomas Scott added, 'Being it is your pleasure to have it so, I know not how to hinder it; but when that is done, I know not where to hide this hated head of mine.'⁹ Hearing of plans to assassinate him, Scott fled abroad, in disguise.

There was widespread joy at the Long Parliament's eventual passing, and excitement that a new order would emerge in its place. Army officers who had committed all to the cause looked with disgruntled distaste at public celebrations marking the change. Some involved bonfires on which, with simple symbolism, rumps of beef were burnt. At the same time insults were directed at an overbearing military, finally brought low.

Colonel Hacker, who had been the commanding officer on the scaffold at Charles's execution, was at this point stationed with his regiment in Nottingham. The taunting his troops received from the young men of the town, who beat drums and paraded in a mock military manner, tipped over into aggression when Hacker's troops moved to confiscate their instruments and banners. Forty of Hacker's men were hurt in the resulting hail of thrown stones. His troops opened fire, killing two onlookers: one was an ageing academic, the other a respected munitions officer from Nottingham Castle's wartime garrison. The violent clash between the army and the local people had claimed the life of a man who had risked all for Parliament – slain by his former comrades-in-arms.

In the face of this chaos, Nottingham's Presbyterian preachers now openly called for the restoration of the Stuart royal line: it at least promised a return to stability. When Hacker learnt of this, he led his men in a plundering spree against those he considered disloyal. It was only the intervention of the regicide Colonel Hutchinson, whose family had strong local interests, that prevented Hacker turning his raid into a bloodbath.

Augustine Garland, who had also sat in judgment of the King, would later refer to this time as one 'when the Government was . . . tossed, and turned, and tumbled, and I know not what'.[10] As anarchy threatened the nation, Monck began to communicate in earnest with the Prince of Wales. He advised Charles to move from the Spanish Netherlands to Dutch territory, since communications from an enemy Catholic land would not endear him to politicians in London. Monck also highlighted the key issues that the Prince needed to address if a royal restoration was to become palatable. Charles had expected that he would need to agree to severe limitations on his royal powers, such as his father had faced during his final negotiations on the Isle of Wight, but he instead found Monck preoccupied less by concessions and more by the need for reassurances.

In April 1660, Charles addressed these points from his Dutch quarters, in letters that were edited into the Declaration of Breda. This was a proclamation skilfully constructed by Charles's key advisers, promising religious toleration, recognition of property rights and pay for the military. More specifically, 'a liberty to tender consciences' was reserved for those whose faith did not disturb the peace. Meanwhile any who had materially benefited under the Commonwealth would keep possession of estates accumulated during and since the Civil Wars. Equally importantly, there was a commitment to meet arrears for those soldiers who acknowledged Monck's command. The Declaration was, essentially, an acknowledgement that retribution was impossible, when so many people had stood against the Crown during the previous two decades:

> And to the end that fear of punishment may not engage any, conscious to themselves of what is past, to a perseverance in guilt for the future, by opposing the quiet and happiness of their country, in the restoration of King, Peers and people to their just, ancient and fundamental rights, we do, by these presents, declare, that we do grant a free and general pardon, which we are ready, upon demand, to pass under our Great Seal of England, to all our subjects, of what degree or quality so ever, who, within forty days after the publishing hereof, shall lay hold upon this our grace and favour, and shall, by any public act, declare their doing so, and that they return to the loyalty and obedience of good subjects . . .

The next words in the declaration were less straightforward:

> . . . excepting only such persons as shall hereafter be excepted by Parliament, those only to be excepted.

Then, the Declaration returned to tones of comforting clemency:

> Let all our subjects, how faulty so ever, rely upon the word of a King, solemnly given by this present declaration, that no crime whatsoever, committed against us or our royal father before the publication of this, shall ever rise in judgment, or be brought in question, against any of them, to the least endamagement of them, either in their lives, liberties or estates or (as far forth as lies in our power) so much as to the prejudice of their reputations, by any reproach or term of distinction from the rest of our best subjects; we desiring and ordaining that henceforth all notes of discord, separation and difference of parties be utterly abolished among all our subjects, whom we invite and conjure to a perfect union among

themselves, under our protection, for the resettlement of our just rights and theirs in a free Parliament, by which, upon the word of a King, we will be advised.[11]

It was a general reconciliation, with problematic passages for those involved in Charles I's trial and execution: in particular the ominous words 'as far forth as lies in our power', and 'a free Parliament . . . by which . . . we will be advised'. The Prince of Wales was guaranteeing his kingly forgiveness, emblazoned with the Great Seal of England; yet he was quietly making it clear that a new Parliament would of course have its own views on matters, which he would be forced to listen to, and act on. While the majority of those who had acted against the Crown, and profited from its fall, could rest easy, there remained scope for Royalist revenge against the most extreme Parliamentarians – clearly, though they were not named, those responsible for the late King's beheading. For these, forgiveness was intimated, rather than guaranteed.

Three weeks after the declaration was made, a 'free' Parliament was formed, one that was not called by the King (for there was none), but was rather summoned by the will of the people. It was known as the Convention Parliament, and it immediately accepted Charles's reassurances, even declaring that he had been King since the moment of his father's execution.

The ruthlessness that Cromwell had exhibited in Ireland, and to a lesser extent in Scotland, had rarely been glimpsed during his rule of England. One of the new King's greatest confidants, Clarendon, conceded that the Lord Protector

was not a man of blood, and totally declined Machiavelli's method, which prescribes upon any alteration of a government, as a thing absolutely necessary, to cut off all the heads of those, and extirpate their families, who are friends to the old. And it was confidently reported, that in the council of officers it was more than once proposed that there might be a general massacre of all the royal party, as the only expedient to secure the government, but Cromwell would never consent to it; it may be, out of too much contempt for his enemies.[12]

Whatever the reason, Cromwell had allowed a large body of Royalists to survive. The prince and his court were left to live unmolested in exile; prominent Royalists, courtiers and men of power had also been allowed to flee abroad. Cowed and humiliated by their banishment during his Protectorate, they were eager not only to restore the Stuart line but also to avenge the years of defeat, and the death of their King.

These men formed a clear majority in the Convention Parliament. They granted the new King generous sums of money, and invited him to return to England. Six days later the large bronze of Charles I was erected once more in the Guildhall, and the emblems of the Commonwealth were removed from public view. The City of London proclaimed its duty to Charles, as did the navy. Charles's courtiers dryly noted the large number of Englishmen arriving in Breda, falling over themselves to parade their loyalty to a man they had ignored for so long. Now came gifts of gold, with which Charles was able to pay his cash-starved retainers. There were also, Clarendon recalled, 'some being employed to procure pardons for those who thought themselves in danger'.[13] The Earl of Northampton spoke on behalf of Colonel Ingoldsby, Lambert's captor, passing on Ingoldsby's wish that: 'your pardon and forgiveness of his former errors are all that he aimed at'.[14]

Ingoldsby was clever to get in an early good word on his behalf. The Convention Parliament was quick to settle its gaze on the regicides, and made its view clear. On 14 May, with the King's return imminent, the Commons resolved, 'That all those Persons who sat in Judgment upon the late King's Majesty, when the Sentence was pronounced for his Condemnation, be forthwith secured.'[15]

When, at the end of May, Charles Stuart was conveyed back to England, it was not on the *Naseby*, the newly built flagship of the Commonwealth navy, but on the renamed HMS *Royal Charles*, the laurel-crowned figurehead of Oliver Cromwell having been removed before she set sail for the Dutch coast. As the King disembarked at Dover, he was accompanied, amongst others, by the diarist Pepys and the former Parliamentarian Sir Harbottle Grimston, who had signed the document asking Charles to return. England was, Charles and his retinue quickly appreciated, in a frenzy of Royalist fervour. The vast majority were determined to do anything they could to demonstrate their passionate loyalty to the Crown. It was an opportune time for vengeance. The King came first for the lawyers John Cook, Andrew Broughton, John Phelps and Edward Dendy, as well as for the two masked executioners, whose identity remained a mystery. At the same time, for completeness's sake, the Commons asked for a full list of all the King's judges.

Cook, the former solicitor general, was summoned from Ireland to answer for his actions. He set off under guard, accompanied by his wife Mary. Cook claimed he was happy to be leaving a country where the people were more interested in drinking and swearing than in religious devotion. However, he was shocked by his rough reception in England, where he estimated he was cursed a thousand times on his journey from Chester to London. On arriving in the capital, on 18 June, he was placed in an open cart along with three soldiers accused of high treason: two of the army officers who had overseen the royal beheading, and William Hewlet, who was suspected of wielding the axe. They were all committed to the Tower of London.

Meanwhile, four of those to be condemned for the late King's execution were named: Bradshaw, Oliver Cromwell, Ireton and Pride – a quartet of the dead. Major General Thomas Harrison was the first among the surviving regicides to be selected for punishment. He was readily linked with the King's death. At the same time many of the members would not forgive his helping Cromwell to turn them out of the Commons. Tales circulated, alleging that Harrison had treated the King with great rudeness on his final humiliating journey from the Isle of Wight to Windsor and London.

It was seven years since the peak of Harrison's power, when, at Cromwell's bidding, he had forced Speaker Lenthall from his chair. Harrison's uncompromising Fifth Monarchy beliefs, together with his disillusionment and clashes with Cromwell, had made the intervening years difficult: he had been imprisoned four times during the six years of the Protectorate.

By the spring of 1660, Harrison's life was a simple, pious, domestic one. He lived in Newcastle-under-Lyme, Staffordshire, with his wife Mary. Their three offspring had died in childhood. Harrison had not been called on by Lambert, during his failed rebellion. Neither, more surprisingly, had he followed General Charles Fleetwood: long ago he had served with distinction as a major in Fleetwood's regiment. Only forty-four years old now, Harrison's spells in prison, together with the many wounds he had received in battle, added to the agony of the loss of his children, left him an ailing, sidelined relic from the days of hot contest – military and political.

But Harrison remained as uncompromising as ever in his beliefs, refusing to apologise for his past, or to counter the ever-increasing likelihood that he would be forced to pay for them with his life and possessions. He stayed strong in his religious fervour, a pamphlet of the time recording his chief occupation as being, 'Looking for the immediate reign of our Saviour upon Earth.'[16] It was a lonely but heartfelt vigil.

Harrison was warned that he would soon be taken prisoner but, as Ludlow recorded, he refused 'to withdraw himself from his house, accounting such an action to be a desertion of the cause in which he had engaged'.[17] At the end of April they came for him, a body of militia under Colonel John Bowyer, an influential member of the Convention Parliament. They confiscated his weapons, sent his impounded horses to the Royal Mews in London, and took him into custody.

So important was news of the detention of this leading regicide, that it was the first piece of business for the Commons to consider after its opening prayers on 11 May 1660. The members resolved that Harrison 'be delivered by the Officers and Soldiers who have him in Custody to the Charge of such Person or Persons as shall be appointed by the lord general to receive him'.[18] He was sent to the Tower of London, where he was kept 'close prisoner', bound in leg irons and chains, forbidden from receiving visitors or legal advice, with guards in his cell at all times to prevent suicide or escape. He was attended by a solitary servant who had to share his master's misery.

The charge would be high treason, a capital offence. Harrison was not only certain he would be put to death, but – after it was swiftly confirmed that he would *not* be considered for mercy – seemed to relish the prospect. He felt sure he would be returning to Earth in 1666, serving God in his army of the Second Coming with the pious fidelity and courage he knew had been his trademark during his country's Civil Wars.

Throughout the spring and summer of 1660 the Commons heard almost daily reports of the regicides' actions as they faced the possibility of condemnation.

On 20 May a letter from the Earl of Winchelsea was read out, stating that he had captured one of the King's judges, Sir Henry Mildmay, as he and his servants tried to board a ship in the Channel port of Rye. Mildmay had been a prominent courtier to the previous Stuart kings, James and Charles I. His responsibilities to them included custody of the royal Jewel House, and he exploited his positions aggressively enough to set the foundation of a considerable fortune. However, his Puritanism put him at odds with Charles before the Civil War broke: Mildmay was a Congregationalist, who acted as patron to clerics of a similar creed, including Leonard Hoar, a president of Harvard College (where Mildmay's son was educated). During the fighting, Sir Henry assisted Thomas Scott's intelligence service. After its conclusion, Mildmay sat as a judge at the royal trial in 1649: he was a less than diligent attendee, but was involved with the preliminary committee work. For the capture of an unpopular turncoat, Lord Winchelsea was thanked, and his soldiers rewarded. Mildmay's progress to the coast led to a parliamentary order, 'to the end that none of those who are ordered to be apprehended, as having sat in Judgment upon the late King's Majesty, may make Escape beyond the Seas'.[19]

Gregory Clements had been a more conscientious judge of the late King, attending all four days of his trial, and entering his signature on the death warrant: it had been written in, apparently over an erased name. Clements had had a chequered life, mainly as a merchant, working in India as a young man (where he was dismissed from a good job for bad behaviour), before making a fortune trading with the American colonies. His business interests extended from new ventures in the Bahamas, to the accumulation of a large estate in Ireland. While in England he bought up a patchwork of confiscated Church and Royalist lands. 'He had no good elocution,' conceded Edmund Ludlow, a political ally, 'but his apprehension and judgment were not to be despised.'[20]

Clements had been dismissed from the Commons in May 1652, damned in the eyes of pious colleagues after being caught *in flagrante* with a maidservant – the sexual transgression was recorded as 'carriage offensive and scandalous to Parliament'.[21] For eight years he had cleverly tended his financial affairs, accumulating a fortune out of the public view. But when the Stuarts returned he knew his actions of eleven years earlier would be looked upon with a critical eye, and so he went into hiding. He settled in a 'mean house in Purple Lane near Gray's Inn'.[22] The Royalists learnt he was in that area, but did not know exactly where to find him. In the end, his expensive tastes betrayed him: when particularly fine food was seen being delivered to his modest address, the authorities surrounded the house, before forcing their way in to conduct a search.

The problem was, none of those present knew Clements by sight. They therefore took the suspicious man that they found in the house for interview by the militia's local commissioners. The one examining official there who recognised the suspect was an acquaintance of Clements, who wished him no harm. After a short interview this officer told his colleagues that he did not know who the man before them was, but he certainly was not Clements. 'But as he was about to withdraw,' it was recorded, 'it happn'd that a blind man who had crowded into the room, and was acquainted with the voice of Mr Clement [sic], which was very remarkable, desired he might be called in again; and demanded, if he was not Mr Gregory Clement.'[23] The commissioners insisted that he answer the blind man's question, at which Clements admitted his true identity. He was sent to the Tower.

The House of Commons was informed of this arrest on 26 May, along with the welcome news that a book had been discovered on Clements, detailing his possessions and business interests. Because those guilty of high treason forfeited all their worldly goods, as well as their lives, this was a significant find. Given the woeful finances of Parliament and the King, it made his hopes of pardon distinctly poor.

On 31 May, the House was told of the successful escape of another regicide: that of Miles Corbett, previously MP for Great Yarmouth, and one of the officials who had reported on Charles I when the King had been with his chaplain in Norfolk en route for the Scottish army after fleeing Oxford. Two local men, James Puckle and Thomas Ellis, were found to have rented Corbett 'a vessel, and otherwise, assisted in the conveying away, into the Parts beyond the Seas',[24] and were summoned to Parliament for interrogation.

In early June, a Cornish MP reported how John Carew, who was considered second only to Harrison in the Fifth Monarchy sect, had similarly slipped away by boat. A customs officer from the port of Looe, named Henry Chubb, admitted to having assisted in the escape unwittingly, despite the recent insistence that all ports be closed to fugitives. Chubb acknowledged that he had received the order, but claimed that Carew had said he had no intention to go overseas, before setting sail. Chubb also pointed out that the warrant relating to Carew had misspelt his name 'Carey'. Chubb joined the list of those heading to Parliament to explain himself, while attempts to locate Carew – wherever he might then be – were redoubled.

Parliament decided at this point that an orderly system needed to be established whereby the regicides would be brought in and dealt with. A draft proclamation was sent for the King's approval on 2 June, which he tinkered with, then issued from Whitehall four days later. It summoned those 'named who sat, gave judgment, and assisted in that horrid and detestable Murder of His Majesty's Royal Father of blessed memory, to appear and render themselves within fourteen days, under pain of being excepted from Pardon'. Forty-four regicides were then individually identified – most of them signatories to the death warrant, with a handful of the prosecution's legal officers added – who 'have out of the sense of their own guilt lately fled and obscured themselves, whereby they cannot be apprehended and brought to a personal and legal Trial for the said Treasons according to Law'. They were instructed to hand themselves in to the Speaker of either House of Parliament, to the lord mayor of London, or to a county sheriff. The decree ended with a sharp reminder: 'That no person or persons shall presume to harbour or conceal any of the persons aforesaid, under pain of Misprision of high Treason.'[25]

Meanwhile decisions were taken, established on the findings of recent interrogations. On the basis of the questioning of John Cook that had taken place in Dublin a month before, the Commons confirmed on 7 June that not only would he be tried for his life and estate, but so would his legal colleagues Andrew Broughton (who had read the charge against Charles at the opening of the trial) and Edward Dendy. The answers given by one Leonard Watson, on the frenzied question of the identity of the two executioners on the scaffold, resulted in the arrest being ordered of Hugh Peters, the charismatic preacher who had led the King from Windsor Castle to his judgment in London, and of Cornet Joyce, who had commanded the soldiers who had removed Charles from Parliament's custody at Holdenby, and taken him into the army's charge.

On 16 June, John Milton – who had passionately attacked Charles

I as a tyrant, and defended the actions of the regicides – was also placed on the list of those to be taken into custody. Milton, by now blind, had gone into hiding the previous month in the house of a friend in West Smithfield. While the Royalists hunted for him, a proclamation was made regarding his books. The public hangman incinerated them at the Old Bailey in late August. Later Milton would be imprisoned for a few weeks in the Tower, and lose his financial savings. Many felt him extremely lucky to escape with his life.

The net was cast ever wider, now. A committee of five members was established, to pore over all the records, and so determine who had sat as judges on each of the days of the trial: previous focus had been on 27 January, the day of the death sentence. It was decided that, apart from those already denied the possibility of pardon for their life and estate, a further twenty would suffer 'Pains, Penalties, and Forfeitures', but would not be in danger of losing their lives. This was put to a vote, and passed by the close majority of 153 votes to 135. The full list was presented to the House the following day, along with news that William Heveningham had been the first to surrender himself, under the terms of the recent proclamation. Heveningham, a Hampshire MP, had sat in judgment of the King, but had refused to sign his death warrant.

Fifty-two regicides who had signed it were now publicly 'excepted out of the General Act of Pardon and Oblivion, for, and in Respect only of such Pains, Penalties and Forfeitures, (not extending to Life) as shall be thought fit to be inflicted on them by another Act, intended to be hereafter passed for that Purpose'.[26] This declaration seemed clearly to promise that *all* who handed themselves in would be spared capital punishment. That was certainly how a dozen of the judges read it: Sir John Bourchier; Colonels Roe, Lilburne, George Fleetwood (brother of General Charles Fleetwood), Scroope, Harvey, Marten and Sir Hardress Waller; Aldermen Penington and Tichborne; as well as James Temple and Henry Smith. They surrendered to the authorities, expecting to be fined but to have their lives spared.

Others were unconvinced by the King's promises of amnesty. Colonel John Dixwell quietly sold part of his family estate and sent a message to the Speaker claiming that he had been unwell: he would be surrendering himself as soon as he was restored to health, he lied, for he was eager to benefit from the King's proclamation. He would not be able to turn himself in within the stated timeframe, he explained. The House granted Dixwell an extension, while he made plans to escape England at the earliest possible opportunity.

Colonel Richard Ingoldsby was keen to build on the credit he had accrued by capturing Lambert. His eagerness to extract a pardon from Parliament led him to lie to it. In a tearful speech to the Commons he claimed that his cousin Oliver Cromwell had physically bullied him into signing the death warrant. Ingoldsby said Cromwell was laughing as he forced the pen into his fingers, then held his hand tight as the signature was forcibly formed.

Nobody at the time had witnessed Ingoldsby being anything other than a willing signatory. His writing on the parchment was well defined, showing no sign of force. Next to it was the Ingoldsby family seal, neatly applied. But Ingoldsby hoped his recent achievement would make people overlook the evidence, and gain him mercy. His speech delivered, he withdrew from the chamber, distraught, to await the Commons's verdict on his plea.

Colonel Hutchinson arrived at Parliament while Ingoldsby was pleading his case for clemency. Immediately afterwards, another regicide started to appeal for his own forgiveness and a member leant over to suggest to Hutchinson that this would be a suitable time for him to follow suit.

Hutchinson gave a polished speech. He explained that any errors he had made should be put down to his youth and lack of judgment at the time (when he had been thirty-three). He was adamant that his actions were on behalf of the country, and were without malice towards the late King. That said, he offered himself as a sacrifice, if the House believed his death and the confiscation of his property useful. However, he pointed out that his family's estate lay in ruins, and nobody could accuse him of having acted for his own advancement or financial advantage. He reassured the House that his feelings about the King's death were those of an Englishman, a Christian and a gentleman.

When Hutchinson sat down, a member rose to say that it seemed that Hutchinson was more concerned about the personal consequences of what he had done, rather than being truly sorry for taking part in the most shocking of crimes. Another defended the colonel, reminding all present of the convention that when two interpretations of a man's words exist, a gentleman must select the one that reflects better on the speaker.

Hutchinson then joined Ingoldsby in an ante-room, to await the verdict. A red-eyed Ingoldsby embraced him and said, 'Oh, did I ever imagine we could be brought to this? Could I have suspected it, when I brought Lambert in the other day, this sword should have redeemed us from being dealt with as criminals by that people for whom we had so gloriously exposed ourselves.'[27] Hutchinson replied coolly that he had known since Cromwell had ejected the Rump Parliament in 1653, and enthroned himself, that their business could end no other way. However, Hutchinson told Ingoldsby that he had no regrets: he had acted throughout with integrity, and 'this made him as cheerfully ready to suffer as to triumph in a good cause'.[28]

These two regicides were suspended from Parliament that day. They then looked to Monck to speak on their behalf, as he had promised he would. But, in the face of the Convention's thirst for vengeance against the King's killers, Monck went back on his word and remained silent.

Up until this point, Lucy Hutchinson had reassured her husband that the restoration of the King would not threaten his life or property, or that of any of the regicides. However, she now judged the situation to be ever more perilous. She recognised at the same time that her husband was preparing to become a martyr to a cause that he felt had been betrayed by Cromwell, and which now, through the bewildering reversal that had thrown up a new Stuart King, was lost. Lucy Hutchinson's writings show that she considered herself an otherwise obedient wife; but this, she acknowledged, was the one occasion on which she deliberately flouted her husband's will. She insisted he leave home and stay quietly with friends until Parliament had settled on whom it would punish for the late King's execution. While he was in hiding, she made clear, he must prepare an escape plan in case it transpired that he was on the list of those who must suffer. Meanwhile, she busied herself by calling in favours and using her family connections.

Her brother, Sir Allen Apsley, was of the King's party, and proved particularly useful. Apsley had served as a Royalist cavalry colonel in the Civil War, where he saw action in several of the great battles and sieges, and also as governor of Barnstaple, in Devon. He managed to surrender the town on terms that spared his life, but left him liable for an extremely large fine. Colonel Hutchinson worked hard to have this reduced, pointing out that much of Apsley's property in fact belonged to his wife. In 1647, Apsley paid Parliament £434, a fraction of what had originally been demanded. Since then, in exile, Apsley had become one of the future Charles II's drinking friends. At the Restoration he was given a court role, Master of the King's Hawks, that provided a generous annual income of £1,200. He was also elected MP for Thetford, in Norfolk. This favoured and influential figure was in a good position to pay back his brother-in-law's great efforts on his behalf, now the two men's situations had been reversed.

For two months in the summer of 1660 the question of who would be punished for their part in Charles I's death was ever present. There would be an Act of 'Free and General Pardon, Indemnity and Oblivion', by which the lands of the Crown and the Anglican Church would be restored, and all but a few named men would be pardoned for their actions during the years 1638–60. At this, Colonel Henry Marten (who had been shamed and dismissed from the King's presence for his scandalous reputation and then been so active in the preparations for Charles's trial at the London horse races), wrote to his mistress: 'I shall now give some comfort to thy little heart, having lately perused the King's Speech and the Chancellor's, either I am very much mistaken in them, or they signify no great danger to us, whose faults are almost as old as our selves.'[29]

Parliament's first conclusion was that a few of the regicides must be held to account, while the rest could be treated with mercy. It decided that seven sacrifices would suffice: after the Civil War, Parliament had sought the same number of deaths from among the upper echelons of the King's supporters. Charles II, realising how unsettling it would be for all involved in his father's execution not to know if they were one of the seven, insisted that they should be quickly named. They were: Major-General Harrison; William Say, who had been one of the forces behind Charles's trial, but who managed to slip across to the Continent; Colonel John Jones, an ardent republican; Thomas Scott, the Civil War spymaster; John Lisle, one of the key lawyers at the trial; Cornelius Holland, the MP for New Windsor, who was believed to have been one of the main hands in drawing up the charges against Charles I; and – after much debate between contending factions – John Barkstead, despised by the Royalists for his cruelty and corruption when in charge of the Tower of London. Parliament then referred the King to his promise to listen to their thoughts on this matter, and Charles conceded: he allowed the lawyers John Cook, Andrew Broughton and Edward Dendy to be added to the list of those denied mercy. These names were revealed in early June. All others, the King said, must come in to seek their pardon, when their lives would be spared, and their property secured.

Many of the regicides had already taken flight. Dixwell was now safely across the Channel, and Thomas Scott had fled the country twice, in April 1660, having heard rumours that he was about to be assassinated. During the first attempt, pirates captured his ship and he was stripped of his possessions, before being discarded on the Hampshire coast. Friends helped to arrange his second escape, to Flanders. He lived there in disguise, before being recognised. Royalists seized him and planned to return him to London, but Scott escaped to the protection of an old friend from his days of diplomatic sway, Don Alonso de Cardenas, the former Spanish ambassador to London.

Scott was in a perilous position: he was a figure of particular hatred, not only for the evident pride he had in his part in the killing of the King, but also for having caused the Royalists such anguish during his days as a highly effective intelligence chief. Added to that, he had been a destructive figure in Commonwealth London, being amongst those who took over Lambeth Palace. There he had the bones of Archbishop Parker, a sixteenth-century champion of Anglicanism, dug up and thrown into a rubbish tip. Although Scott had fallen out with Oliver Cromwell and had no respect for the succeeding Lord Protector, Richard ('I have cut off one tyrant's head,' he had threatened, 'and I hope to cut off another'[30]), Scott was a marked man.

The Spanish could not guarantee his long-term safety, now his true identity was known, and so Scott decided to take his chance back home. He applied for royal clemency during the advertised fortnight time limit, and surrendered to Sir Henry de Vic, Charles's ambassador to Brussels. On 12 July, as soon as he arrived back in England, he was committed to the Tower. It was made clear to Scott that his only hope of salvation lay in giving up the names of all the agents he had employed against the Stuarts, when spymaster. His efforts in this regard were half-hearted at best, and the apologies he offered for his incendiary words in Parliament also fell short. Scott awaited his trial, which would be alongside a growing band of those who had been denied a pardon, or who had been successfully hunted down.

In Colonel John Jones's case, it was not so much a hunt as a gentle gathering. The Welshman, married to Cromwell's sister Catherine, had been released on parole in January 1660, following his arrest in Ireland. Jones was now picked up while walking the newly laid gravel paths of Finsbury Fields, outside the City of London. The colonel had been a prominent enemy, helping to subdue the Royalist strong-hold of Anglesey, and he had been a scourge of the Crown and Catholicism in Ireland. He was a long-time correspondent with

Harrison, whose Fifth Monarchist beliefs he shared. Jones must have known the dangerous attention that all the regicides were receiving. Perhaps his declining to flee can be put down to the same refusal to apologise for a cause he believed in, and the same cussed fatalism, as Harrison had demonstrated? Or maybe he miscalculated, placing too much importance on his earlier parole? Either way, he now joined the number of imprisoned regicides awaiting punishment.

Colonel Hutchinson was not one of the publicly condemned ten. His relieved friends told him to take advantage of the offer of royal clemency, and turn himself in as soon as he could. Hutchinson agreed that this was sensible, but his wife thought otherwise. She refused to trust the new regime, even when the colonel and his friends thought her misgivings ridiculous. In the end, the couple compromised: Hutchinson consented to test the sincerity of the offered pardon through a ploy that would keep him out of Parliament's hands, while not alienating the resurgent Royalists.

On his wife's advice, Hutchinson wrote politely to the Speaker, saying that he was inconvenienced, and therefore unable to surrender himself into a general custody. That said, he would of course stand ready to make himself available if and when his presence was required. In the meantime, he would give his word not to abscond. While his letter was being digested, Lucy Hutchinson built up a bloc of goodwill towards her husband. It was constructed upon the social ambitions of a man at court to whom her brother, Sir Allen Apsley, had promised an introduction to the new King. Excited by the promise of this favour, the pushy courtier took it upon himself to act as Colonel Hutchinson's unofficial advocate, spreading the false rumour that Charles very much wished the colonel excused of his crimes. Those eager to ingratiate themselves to royalty heard this with great interest.

When Hutchinson's letter was discussed in Parliament, such sycophants presented it as proof of Hutchinson's moderation, humility and repentance. First to speak on the colonel's behalf was Roger Palmer – whose new wife, Barbara Villiers, was Charles's

primary mistress at the time – and Heneage Finch, MP for Canterbury. Their testimonies opened a floodgate of support in
Hutchinson's favour, 'and,' recalled his wife, 'there was not at that
day any man that received a more general testimony of love and
good esteem of all parties than he did.'[31] He was 'cleared by vote'.

Hutchinson was informed that he was safe from the threats of
capital punishment or imprisonment. His penalty was merely to be
dismissed from public office for ever, including his seat in Parliament. A levy would also need to be paid. Hutchinson wrote such an
emotive letter (the Commons recorded that it was one of 'signal
repentance'[32]), in gratitude for this generosity, that he was then
informed that there would be no fines or confiscations against his
property either. It was an outcome beyond anything that he could
reasonably have hoped for. Aware that names were still being added
to and removed from the Act of Indemnity, Hutchinson lay low,
staying out of sight from those who were making these life or death
decisions. Eager for tangible proof of his sympathetic treatment, he
sent a letter to the Commons requesting they write to 'confirm that
favour and mercy'[33] granted him.

It was as well that he did. As more and more documents were
unearthed by Parliament's clerks, so the number of men held
responsible for the killing of the King increased. Records appeared
detailing the members of the various committees that were involved
in the intricacies of the King's trial: the sourcing of chairs, the selection of cushions, the formalities of the procedure. Hutchinson had
been pardoned as a reluctant, obscure, bit player in it all: that was
how he had presented himself. 'But as soon as they had passed their
votes for his absolute discharge,' Lucy Hutchinson wrote, 'he was
found not to have been one day away from the trial.'[34] The question
was, what could be done to bring this willing and attentive regicide
to justice, now that he had been pardoned? There was a precedent
for overturning such decisions, after all.

Adrian Scroope was one of nineteen regicides to surrender to the
royal proclamation of 4 June 1660, confident that by doing so he

would be assured of his life. The cavalry colonel was allowed to present his defence, after which he had quickly been released on parole, having been fined a year's income from his estate.

However, the House of Lords refused to agree to his pardon. On 20 July the Upper House sent a message to the Commons: 'They desire,' it was announced in the chamber, 'that this House will be pleased to send the instrument under the Hands and Seals of those Persons who gave Judgment against the King; and what other Evidences you have, to inform their Lordships touching that Matter.'[35]

The Lords had decided to arrest all regicides. With regard to Scroope, they wanted him named specifically as excepted from pardon, as they had learnt of a conversation between him and Major General Browne. This had taken place earlier in the summer, outside the Chamber of the Speaker of the House of Commons. Scroope had introduced himself to Browne. Realising that he was talking to a regicide, Browne said, 'What a sad case have we brought this Kingdom unto?' Scroope asked him why he said that. 'You see,' continued Browne, 'how it is ruined now the King is murdered.'

Scroope replied, 'Some are of one opinion, and some of another.'

Browne then asked, 'Sir, do you think it was well done to murder the King?'

To which Scroope replied, 'I will not make you my confessor, Sir.'[36]

Despite the Commons's wish to spare Scroope, the Lords refused to grant him leniency. Report of his exchange with Browne was enough to have Scroope's merciful treatment overturned. On 28 August he was added to the list of those to be tried for their life; this would be the very last day on which that list was being composed. He was committed to the Tower, where he was kept a close prisoner, awaiting trial.

The Tower of London had been the grimmest of gaols since 1100, when Ranulf Flambard (who had overseen the building of Westminster Hall, where the King was tried) became its first escapee, thanks to a rope smuggled in to him in a cask of wine. It certainly proved to be a miserable prison for the regicides. Its garrison in the early 1660s included Colonel William Legge's regiment. Legge had suffered several times as a prisoner of Parliament, enduring a spell in the Tower in 1659 for high treason. Many of his men were Irish Catholics, who held raw memories of the New Model Army's massacres in their homeland. These were not men who were likely to be gentle on their charges.

The newly installed Lieutenant of the Tower was Sir John Robinson, who also had personal reasons for hating his regicide inmates: he was a nephew of Archbishop Laud, Charles I's premier churchman who had been tried and executed by Parliament in 1645. Indeed one of the prisoners now in Robinson's charge was Isaac Penington, who had been Lieutenant at the time of Laud's execution, and had overseen the Archbishop's beheading on Tower Hill.

Described by Pepys as a 'talking bragging bufflehead', Robinson helped himself to funds that were earmarked for the prisoners' supplies, and treated them with casual cruelty. When one of the imprisoned colonels and his retainer were suffering from violent dysentery, Robinson denied them access to their latrine, despite there being two further doors beyond it, blocking any hope of escape. Many of the regicides had been stripped of all their property on arrest. They were unable to pay the high charges Robinson set for basic provisions, and so 'he gave them none', recalled the wife of one who suffered under him, 'but converted what the King allowed to his own use, and threatened some of the prisoners with death if they offered to demand it; and suffered others, at twelve of the clock at night, to make such a miserable outcry for bread that it was heard in some parts of the city, and one was absolutely starved to death for want of relief, although the King at that time told a prisoner that he took more care for the prisoners than for his own table.'

Inmates who could usually afford Robinson's outrageous charges, but from time to time were late with payments, found their prison conditions made suddenly even harsher. Meanwhile Robinson insisted on keeping the wealthiest regicides in his lodgings, so he could charge them directly for any services received. The rest had to rely on the charity of friends, who sent them food. A lot of this was pilfered before reaching those it was intended for.

The warders found common cause with the prisoners, through their mutual loathing of Robinson. He had a reputation for being a nasty drunk, who harangued them and who frequently withheld their wages – this, while charging them extortionate rents for their modest accommodation. The warders 'pitied the poor gentlemen that were so barbarously used', recalled the same regicide's wife, 'and whether out of humanity or necessity or villainy ... they would offer the prisoners many courtesies, and convey letters between them'.[37] The brutality of the place could take its toll. John Downes was so despondent after three years in the Tower that he asked Robinson if he could be 'thrust into some hole where he might silently be slain'.[38]

There had originally been approximately eighty regicides, when the fifty-nine who had signed the death warrant were added to the legal team that had tried the case, as well as to those on the scaffold who oversaw and administered the execution. Of these, more than a quarter were dead by the time Charles II returned in glory to England: Cromwell, Bradshaw, Pride, Deane and Dorislaus; also the quartet who had perished during active service in Ireland: Ireton, Ewer, Horton and Moore; as well as Danvers and Lord Grey of Groby. Others who escaped royal vengeance by dying before the Restoration were a trio of Yorkshire army officers: John Alured, Sir William Constable and Sir Thomas Mauleverer, and seven politicians: John Blakiston, Humphrey Edwards, Sir Gregory Norton, Peregrine Pelham, William Purefoy, Anthony Stapley and John Venn.

Retribution could still be exacted from the dead, however. The Commons heard with satisfaction, on 31 May 1660, of the seizure of some of Blakiston's property by the Sheriff of County Durham. Blakiston, one of the most powerful Parliamentarians in the north of England and a great radical, had been an eager member of the High Court of Justice. However, he only outlived the monarch he helped to condemn by four months. The Commons had granted his widow and children £3,000 on his death, and now the Convention Parliament wanted to reclaim that sum, as well as whatever else it could confiscate from his estate. Many of the other dead regicides had their family wealth seized – though Pelham had died so poor, ruined by the withholding of debts owed to him and by the Civil War, that he had been unable even to pay the doctor that had tended him at the end.

Now it was time for the Royalists to have a closer look at the remaining sixty regicides, and see which of them could be put on trial not just for their possessions, but for their lives.

Chapter 6

A Bloody Sacrifice

We deal not with men, but monsters, guilty of blood, precious blood, royal blood, never to be remembered without tears.
Sir Harbottle Grimston, Speaker of the House of Commons

At first the captured regicides' only visitors in the Tower were officials involved in their prosecution, as well as a committee of three – Secretary Morris, Sir Anthony Ashley Cooper and Arthur Annesley – charged with finding the true identity of 'the person in the frock' who had cut off the head of the King. This trio paid particular attention to Colonel Hercules Huncks, John Cook and Captain William Hewlet, but several others were interrogated roughly in an attempt to resolve the mystery.

Huncks gave up Colonels Hacker and Axtell at this point, preserving his life by offering damning evidence against his former colleagues – an irony, Axtell would note, given that 'Colonel Huncks . . . was the uncivillest of all about the late King, and yet he comes in as a witness against us'.[1]

Francis Hacker received no warning of his arrest. He had remained in charge of his regiment of horse guards in the City of London for several weeks after Charles's return, reassured by General Monck that he would be excused any past wrongs. Hacker was at home on his Leicestershire estate when he was summoned to London. On arrival, on 4 July, he went to see Monck, 'who could not be ignorant of the design that was against him', Edmund

Ludlow believed, 'yet received him with as much show of affection as ever, enquiring of him with much kindness where he lodged. But the next day after he was thus caressed, he was seized, examined, [and] sent to the Tower of London.'[2] Hacker was taken into a small room in the Tower where, he later recalled, 'the Gentlemen were very strict with me'.[3]

Colonel Hacker's problems stemmed from the original death warrant of the King: he had kept it safe throughout the Commonwealth years. Hacker's wife, Isabell, mistakenly believed she could now spare her husband by presenting the document, trusting its words demonstrated that the colonel had only been obeying orders. However, Mrs Hacker had in fact produced incontrovertible proof not only of her husband's direct involvement in the killing of the King, but also that of all of the warrant's signatories. On 1 August the Lords added Hacker's name to the list of those to be treated without mercy.

Hacker and his fellow prisoners in the Tower had much time to contemplate what might happen to them. They tried to make sense of what they assumed to be imminent execution. John Cook found comfort in a rational breakdown of his condition. He calculated that, being aged fifty-two, 'I can expect to do little more for God. I am three parts dead (seventy being divided into four), the shades of evening are upon me and aches and pains are inseparable companions.'[4] Meanwhile, Colonel John Jones reminded his distressed well-wishers that he had had no right to survive a particularly savage storm at sea during a crossing to Ireland, years earlier; so every day of his life since then should be counted as a bonus and a blessing. But these were brave words for outward consumption; Cook, for one, admitted that his spirit was frequently cast into the depths by the horror and hopelessness of his situation.

Colonel Henry Marten, regicide, republican and roué, handed himself in on 20 June 1660, on the proclamation of Charles II, sure that such a surrender would guarantee his life. As bitterness towards the regicides mounted, and the thirst for reprisals grew, Marten found himself one of nineteen men excepted from pardon: they would be tried, their only hope being the mercy of Parliament. The colonel remarked with grim humour that this was the first royal proclamation that he had ever obeyed, and he very much hoped he would not be hanged for having trusted the word of the King.

In a letter that he intended for publication, to gain his jury's sympathy, Marten addressed the charges he faced, mixing self-serving justification with remarkable broadmindedness. He acknowledged where the desire to try him and his companions stemmed from: 'Upon serious consideration (it seems to me) the Royal party could contrive no one sacrifice so proper to appease the ghost of their often soiled cause, both in point of revenge & interest, as the persons who had the boldness to make an example of their Ring-leader.' He was quick to recognise how difficult a task he and his fellow commissioners of the High Court of Justice now faced in escaping condemnation, given the skill of the legal minds arrayed against them: he and his co-defendants would, he wrote, have to 'fence for their lives with Masters in the Art'.[5]

Marten shared his sorrow at having been instrumental in helping to start the Civil War: 'Could I have foreseen how dearly public freedom must be bought, and how hardly it can be kept, I would have used only my passive valour against all the late King's oppressions, rather than voted, as I did, any War at all, though a defensive one.' He was insistent that the fighting, and the King's trial and execution, could not be seen as separate events, 'for you must understand that this act,' he stated, 'whether its name be Treason and Murder, or Reason and Justice, its Parent was a Civil War.'

As for regrets, he was happy to admit that he had some, but he was adamant that they centred around Cromwell, not the cause he had fought for: 'Had I suspected that the Axe which took off the late King's head, should have been made a stirrup for our first false General, I should sooner have consented to my own death than his.' Further, he felt obliged to concede, 'I am satisfied in my conscience that the said King thought in his conscience he died unjustly.'[6] This was a great sadness to the colonel.

When it came to the King's trial, the lawyer in Marten made him agree that Parliament was not the place for a person to be tried, since its responsibilities were legislative, never judicial. 'My opinion is,' he continued, 'that the . . . trial by Commissioners without a Jury was yet more irregular, for he ought not to have been put into a worse condition than the meanest Englishman, who may claim to be tried in a known Judicatory before sworn Judges, and by a Jury of twelve men, all agreeing; if it be for his life, by two Inquests upon oath one after another.'[7]

Despite the shortcomings of the legal process, Marten was adamant that, 'In all this I take no murder to myself, nor Treason, as being sure I had no murderous nor treasonable intent about me in what I did.' He saw an absolute distinction between the deed of judgment itself, and the interpretations that could be placed on that deed. 'My plea therefore is, that I judged the late King.'[8]

Henry Marten had, according to a contemporary, 'lived from his wife a long time. If I am not mistaken, she was sometime distempered by his unkindness to her.'[9] This was his second wife, the first, Elizabeth, having died in childbirth in 1634, when young. At the time of the King's execution he had taken a permanent mistress – 'Mary Marten', as she styled herself – and had three daughters with her: Peggy, Sarah and Henrietta (the last two he nicknamed 'Poppet' and 'Bacon-hog'), in addition to the six children from his two marriages. Through his private letters to Mary we can see the ups and downs of Marten's hopes and fears, as well as his reliance on their love to keep him focused on happier thoughts than imminent trial for high treason. Before his detention in the Tower he wrote to her: 'As for news, it cannot be worth the gaping after (any more than the weather) the worst will come soon enough; the best is like to be welcome whensoever it comes.' But, he admitted, 'I confess what I hear is not very good.' What kept him consoled in such perilous times is the intimacy they share, when he and Mary are 'snug like a snail within our own selves, that is, our minds, which nobody but we can touch'.[10]

In another letter Marten was distressed to hear that Mary had been unwell. 'I am afraid I can guess too right at the greatest part of thy disease,' he wrote, 'or at least, the ground of it, which is melancholy and thoughtfulness for things which I can apply no remedy to.' Marten reminded his lover not to underestimate his ability to bounce back from disaster: 'I have been on bare board a thousand times in my life, and yet still found a twig or something to hold me up,'[11] he boasted.

His main hope at this time of terrible uncertainty remained Charles's word that those who handed themselves in would have their lives spared. 'Tomorrow morning,' he reported, 'we are all to appear at the House of Commons, to show cause why the sentence given against us should not be executed. I think we can show a very good one, wherein the King's honour and the Parliament is concerned,' before adding, less optimistically, 'if they think otherwise, who can help it?'[12]

Marten sustained Mary and their children with all the provisions he could afford: 'a leg of mutton, two loaves, a peck of flour . . . and four bottles of William Parker's Lemon Ale', one day; 'a piece of cake, and some Bergamot pears from Hollingbury, a piece of sturgeon, and a bottle of liquor',[13] as well as venison and cheese, on another. He asked frequently about their daughters (his 'pesky rogues'): 'Now I care for nothing but knowing how my three biddies do,' he declared. Elsewhere, he took a father's pride in the attributes the girls had inherited from him: 'Look upon my little brats, and see if thy dear be not among them; has not one of 'em his face, another his brains, another his mirth?'[14]

When the news came that he was, after all, going to be tried, Marten wrote to let Mary know with startling honesty, while reassuring her that all would work out well in the end:

My sweet Dear, brave gallant Soul,

Now stand thy ground; I was told on Tuesday night, that the House of Commons had given us all up on Monday, and had appointed a Committee to bring in a bill for that purpose, which cannot require much time, and if I wish any thing in the world, it is, that thou hadst been with me, when the tidings came, and ever since, to see if thou couldst find any alteration in me, sleeping or waking . . .

Perhaps the bill will not pass when it comes in, perhaps the Lords will not pass it, when it comes there; perhaps the King has given way to his friends to set this on foot, on purpose to have the whole honour of pardoning to himself; perhaps some names may be excepted in one House, or in the other; and thy Dear may be one of them. He that has time, has life; a thousand things happen betwixt the cup and the lip; and it is some comfort that we can still send to each other . . .

I was not so hasty to send thee this news yesterday; I believe I had not now neither, but that I was afraid thou wouldst hear it from another hand, that would make it worse . . .

Pluck up thy strength, my good Heart, conquer this brunt, and thou art a man for ever.

Marten was sent to the Tower with the others who would be on trial for their lives. There, gossip was rife. He wrote to Mary that he had heard that two of his fellow accused would be pardoned, while he and the rest would be sent into exile. All he could hope for, he said, was time to prepare himself for this journey overseas.

While waiting to see where he would be sent, Marten fed his lover snippets about life in the Tower. He had heard that various of Charles II's courtiers wanted 'to set up a trade of granting leave to visit prisoners' – something that Lambert and Heveningham's wives had suggested. Meanwhile his critical, womanising eye led him to fault the drab appearance of one of his fellow inmates' daughters. At the same time Marten explained how each prisoner's wellbeing in the Tower was dependent on the attitude of his individual guard: 'This Keeper of mine,' he wrote, 'is a very civil person to me when he is with me, and swears he will visit thee, and bring thee to me whatever it cost; but he is just the worst Keeper in the Tower for keeping his times, when he is from me, that he makes me so uncertain in sending [letters] to thee, whereas all other prisoners are unlocked before 7 in the morning; he makes me stay till 8, 9, 10, and past; it is almost 9 now, yet I am fast.'[15]

The one piece of news that neither Marten nor any of his fellow regicides could communicate was the date of their trial, for none of them knew when that would be. That choice was down to their accusers.

The trial was committed to senior Royalist lawmen, who were aware of what was expected of them after five months of escalating antagonism towards the regicides. Alongside them were fifteen men who had actively been for Parliament against the late King. Many of their former comrades were aghast at the shameless way in which they had become not just turncoats, but also leaders of the retribution being meted out against their own kind. 'Colonel George Monck being commissionated to be of this number,' Ludlow wrote, 'was not ashamed to sit among them, any more than Mr Denzil Holles and the Earl of Manchester.' Holles and Manchester had been two of the six men that Charles I had sought to arrest, in person, just before the Civil War broke out. Ludlow remembered how they were 'therefore personally concerned in the quarrel, had contributed the utmost of their endeavours to engage divers of the gentlemen (upon whom they were now to sit as judges) on that side, [and] were not contented to abandon them in this change, but assisted in condemning them to die for their fidelity to that cause, which [they] themselves had betrayed'.[16]

The senior judge in the case against the regicides was Sir Orlando Bridgeman, a man of sharp eyes and hollow cheeks, who had recently been created Lord Chief Baron of His Majesty's High Court of Exchequer. Bridgeman's father had been chaplain to King James, and one of his brothers would become a bishop. Bridgeman had long shone as a lawyer. By the time he was thirty-one he had served as solicitor general to Charles when Prince of Wales. He entered Parliament, where he was a forthright Royalist. However, when Charles I's controversial favourite, the Earl of Strafford, was impeached, Bridgeman voted in favour of the charge. When it became clear that a majority in the Commons were after Strafford's life, wanting him charged with treason, Bridgeman argued vigorously that it was inappropriate to attach a capital penalty to the charges against the earl. Although unsuccessful – Strafford was executed – Bridgeman had at an early age become adept at discerning precisely what treason was, and what it was not. This would be crucial in the trial of the regicides.

Bridgeman had served the King faithfully during the Civil Wars, at first in and around the important city of Chester, before joining the King's parliament in Oxford. Charles relied on him during failed peace negotiations with Parliament in 1645, and he was again one of the King's legal advisers during the final attempt at a treaty, during Charles's imprisonment on the Isle of Wight. It seems likely that he was one of those to counsel the King not to recognise the court, if and when he was brought to trial.

Now the tables were turned. The accused would be confronted by a bevy of the King's appointed judges, performing their professional duties against the backdrop of calls for vengeance. Some sincerely wanted the killers of the late, venerated, King held to account. Others, who had supported Parliament against Charles, but now welcomed his son as their King, were happy for a few dozen men to be scapegoats for half the kingdom. As Lucy Hutchinson noted, 'Many who had preached and led the people into [fighting the King], and of that Parliament who had declared it to be treason not to advance and promote that cause, were all now apostasised, and as much preached against it, and called it *rebellion* and *murder*, and sat on the tribunal to judge it.'[17]

The attorney general was Sir Geoffrey Palmer, at sixty-two, eleven years older than Bridgeman, but his contemporary when entering the Commons in 1640, and his equal in outspokenness. A bon viveur, famed for his hospitality on his Midlands estates and at his Hampstead home, Palmer's legal speciality was not treason, but conveyancing: he had an eye for detail. Ludlow tracked his methods during the trials of the regicides and called Palmer one of 'the tyrant's bloodhounds at the bar'.[18]

Sir Heneage Finch, the solicitor general, was one of those who had spoken on Colonel Hutchinson's behalf in the Commons, in the mistaken belief that Hutchinson's pardon was the King's secret wish. Finch had lived quietly during the Commonwealth because of his widely known Royalist sympathies. He resided with his wife and fourteen children in Kensington House, which would become the principal royal palace in London from 1689 until 1760. Before the trials, Finch had chaired the committee that decided who would be covered by the Act of Indemnity. He had therefore already examined the individual cases of each of the prisoners in great detail. To legal historians, Finch is known as 'the father of equity',[19] the legal principles whereby strict rules of law are subject to modification, where appropriate. The unyielding laws of treason allowed no such latitude.

Sir Edmund Turnor had helped to ease the Restoration, after professional disappointment. Passed over as Speaker of the Commons in favour of Harbottle Grimston, he used his consolation position as Chairman of the Elections Committee to ensure that, in the many disputed elections for the Convention Parliament, the Royalist candidate was returned at the expense of his Presbyterian rival, wherever possible. Turnor was known for his cloying servility to the Crown, and for his vindictiveness. His was not a welcome face to those on trial.

The proceedings against the accused opened on 9 October in Hicks Hall, the sessions house in Clerkenwell that was the judicial and administrative centre of Middlesex. On the first day, Sir Orlando Bridgeman addressed the twenty members of the grand jury without the defendants present. He gave a full and clear statement of the case, which included a ringing definition of high treason: 'By the Statute of the twenty fifth of Edward the Third (a Statute or Declaration of Treason) it is made High Treason to compass, and imagine, the Death of the King.'[20] Bridgeman confirmed that this was the only crime in English Law where just imagining or 'compassing', without actually committing an offence, could result in punishment. He explained: 'Then what is an imagination, or compassing the King's death? Truly, it is any thing which shows what the imagination is. Words in many cases, they are evidences of his imagination: they are evidences of the heart.'[21] The judge also made clear the guilt attached to all involved in any stage of the crime of high treason: 'If two, or more, do Compass, or Imagine the King's Death, if some of them go on so far, as to consultation; if others of them go further, they sentence, and execute, put to death: in this case they are all guilty; the first consultation was treason.'[22]

Bridgeman made clear why the death of a King was such a uniquely heinous crime: 'The reason of it is this, in the case of the death of the King, [it is] the head of the Commonwealth that's cut off: and what a trunk, an inanimate lump, the body is, when the head is gone, you all know.' Sir Orlando then harked back to the ancient laws that Charles I had in mind when justifying his dogged belief in the Divine Right of Kings. Bridgeman touched on statutes from the late eleventh century, through to Tudor times:

> How do they style the King? They call Him, 'The Lieutenant of God', and many other expressions, in the Book of *Primo Henrici Septimi* states that book there: 'The King is immediate from God, and hath no superior.' The Statutes say: 'The Crown of England is immediately Subject to God, and to no other Power.' 'The King' (says our books) 'He is not only *Caput Populi*, the Head of the people; but *Caput Reipublicae*, the Head of the Commonwealth, the three Estates.'[23]

Bridgeman anticipated the likely defence of those on trial: that they had acted under the authority of Parliament. 'Gentlemen,' he advised, 'if any person shall now come, and shroud himself under this pretended authority, or such a pretended authority, you must know, that this is so far from an excuse, that it is an height of aggravation.'[24]

The judge pointed first to the pledges that those in authority had taken. In particular, he reminded the grand jury that anyone sitting in the Commons or the Lords was obliged to take the Oath of Supremacy before taking their seats: 'They that take the Oaths of Allegiance, and Supremacy, they swear, that they will, to their power, assist, and defend all Jurisdictions, Privileges, Preeminences, and Authorities, granted, or belonging to the Kings, His Heirs, and Successors, or annexed to the Imperial Crown of this Realm.' He next quickly dispensed with the idea that a king could be placed on trial: 'I must deliver to you for plain, and true, Law; that no authority, no single person, no community of persons, nor the people collectively, or representatively have any coercive power over the King of England.'[25]

Bridgeman deviated from the specifics of the case with emotional passages, designed to remind the grand jury of the uniqueness of the case they were to hear: 'No story, that ever was, I do not think any Romance, any Fabulous Tragedy, can produce the like.'[26] He also pointed to the individual qualities of the late King, as compounding the tragedy of his loss, especially when, Bridgeman recalled, he had agreed to concede so much in the treaty agreed on, the month before his execution, while prisoner on the Isle of Wight. The calamity was compounded by the place of the King's beheading, 'before his own door, even before that place, where he used in Royal Majesty to hear ambassadors, to have his honourable entertainments'.[27]

'To conclude, you are now to enquire of Blood, of Royal Blood, of Sacred Blood; Blood like that of the Saints under the Altar, crying . . . "How long, O Lord," etc. This Blood cries for Vengeance, and it will not be appeased without a Bloody Sacrifice.'[28]

The jurors can have been left in no doubt as to what was expected of them.

The twenty-nine prisoners were told at nine o'clock that night that the following day would see them in court, facing charges that they had yet to learn.

They were woken by their guards early on 10 October, before being handed over at six o'clock in the morning by Sir John Robinson to the sheriff. He transported them – Harrison, Marten, Scroope, Scott, Jones, Clements, Cook, Peters, Axtell and twenty others – in a convoy of carriages, with a strong, mixed guard of cavalry and infantry, to Newgate, the notoriously grim prison on

the edge of the City of London. At nine o'clock, after making brief
and shocking acquaintance with the squalor of Newgate, they
found themselves ushered across to the sessions house of the Old
Bailey – a shuffling column of elderly men in chains, hobbling
towards their destiny.

The accused were divided into five groups, the first of which, the
smallest, comprised just Sir Hardress Waller, William Heveningham
and Thomas Harrison. On being told to approach the bar, they
were instructed to raise their right hands. Harrison interjected, 'My
Lord, if you please, I will speak a word . . .' The court was quick to
establish its authority: 'Hold up your hand, and you shall be heard
in due time. Mr Harrison, the course is, that you must hold up your
hand first.'[29]

The defendants listened to the indictment that imperilled their
lives, delivered by the clerk of the Crown, Edward Sheldon. It
accused them, among other wrongs, of 'not having the fear of God
before [their] eyes, and being instigated by the Devil'; of acting
'contrary to . . . due allegiance, and bounden duty'; and of 'signing
and sealing the warrant for the late sovereign's execution'. The indictment read, the three prisoners were asked in turn to plead guilty, or
not guilty. Sir Hardress Waller was shaken by the starkness of the
choice, which resulted in much dithering. 'My Lord, I do desire some
time to consider of it, for it is a great surprisal.' He was told he had to
plead one way or the other, and that he must not drift off into irrelevant asides. 'Shall I be heard, my Lord?' implored Waller.

'Yes, upon your trial. There is but two ways. Plead "Not Guilty",
or confess it. Sir Hardress Waller, we would not have you be
deceived. If you confess, and say, you are guilty: there is nothing
then, but Judgment. If you say "Not Guilty": then you shall be
heard with your evidence.'

Waller's claim that his case differed to that of all the other defendants, because he had been in Ireland for so many years, was rejected
by the court. The clearly bewildered Waller then pleaded, 'In as
much as I have said, I dare not say "Not Guilty". I must say
"Guilty".'[30]

The prisoners seem to have assumed that they would be given the chance to speak freely, before pleading. Harrison and Robert Lilburne protested that being held close prisoner had deprived them of any legal advice. The majority pleaded not guilty, most likely because they now understood the finality of opting for 'guilty', which left the mercy of Parliament as their only hope. Pleading not guilty seemed to offer a prospect of salvation, a chance to be heard.

At the end of the long day, the court was told to reconvene at seven the next morning. Any jurors or witnesses who were late or absent would be fined £100. Samuel Pepys committed his view of these early proceedings to his diary: 'At night comes Mr Moore, and tells me how Sir Hardress Waller (who only pleads guilty), Scott, Cook, Peters, Harrison, &c., were this day arraigned at the bar of the Sessions House, there being upon the bench the mayor, General Monck, my Lord of Sandwich, &c., such a bunch of noblemen as had not been seen in England. They all seem to be dismayed, and will all be condemned without question ... Tomorrow they are to plead what they have to say.'[31]

Now the trial proper started, with Harrison, Scroope, Carew, Jones, Clements and Scott brought forward. It proved impossible for these six men to agree on who should be selected for their jury, out of the pool of eighty-six candidates, so Sir Orlando Bridgeman ordered that they should be tried individually. He selected Harrison as the first to be brought to the bar.

Finch, the solicitor general, gave the opening address. This must have been galling for the defendants: Finch had himself been accused of treason, twenty years earlier, and had only saved himself by fleeing his accusers, several of whom were now on trial for their lives.

In his account of the trials, the regicide Edmund Ludlow referred to Finch with loathing – a common reaction among Puritans, scandalised by his immoral ways. Ludlow variously described him as 'that grey-haired traitor and inveterate enemy to the good of the

public', 'the old fornicator', and as a man 'old in wickedness as well
as years'. Finch began by leading the court through the enormity of
the crime of which he had once been accused, but which he now lay
at the feet of others. 'These things were not done in a corner', he
claimed, for 'every true English Heart still keeps within itself a
bleeding register of this story.'[32]

Now, Finch asserted, those who had overseen these infamous
deeds must be punished: 'My Lords, the actors in this tragedy
were many, very many, so many, that sure their name is legion, or
rather many legion.' He then calculated who, and how many,
comprised the body that could be termed as 'regicides': 'The
judges, officers, and other immediate actors in this pretended
court, were in number about fourscore. Of these some four, or
five, and twenty are dead, and gone to their own place.' He calculated that another eighteen or nineteen had fled abroad, in a state
of constant fear that they would be hunted down and brought to
justice. Therefore, Finch concluded, 'Twenty-nine persons do
now expect your Justice.'[33]

Sir Edmund Turnor followed Finch, opening with a biblical
reference to how Amaziah, King of Judah in the 8th century BC, had
avenged his father King Joash's death by slaying ten thousand
victims. Turnor claimed that it was a sign of Charles II's great mercy
that he wanted only this select group of miscreants to stand trial for
their lives. Turnor made it clear that the conviction of the accused
was both vital and inevitable. He then turned his attention from the
pack, to the singular figure of Harrison: 'and so we shall call our
witnesses, and doubt not, but to prove, that this man at the bar was
the first, and not the least of these offenders'.[34]

Edmund Ludlow heard with disgust that Harrison had not only
to contend with an apparently predetermined guilt, but also faced
the basest form of intimidation from his accusers. 'I must not omit,'
he wrote, 'that the executioner in an ugly dress, with an halter
[noose] in his hand, was placed near the major general, and continued
there during the whole time of his trial, which action I doubt
whether it was ever equalled by the most barbarous nations.'[35]

Harrison was now presented, one after the other, with the names of those who might sit in the jury to hear his case. He refused the first seven, which provoked laughter in the public gallery. The major general was unflustered. It was not until the twelfth candidate that he found a juror he would accept. Not long afterwards, he had used up his entire quota of thirty-five objections.

Five witnesses for the prosecution were sworn. The first four told how they had seen Harrison sitting as a judge in the High Court of Justice – some of them had taken note of those commissioners attending on each of the days. Each agreed that Harrison had been there on the final day of the King's trial. They recalled seeing him rise to his feet with the others, in approval of the sentence of death.

The fourth witness, James Nutley, added colour to the picture. He remembered Harrison as a leading participant in the trying, then killing, of the King. Nutley was the junior colleague of John Cook, who had tearfully begged Cook not to take part in the prosecution of the King. Nutley had been a frequent presence in Westminster before and during the trial. He remembered seeing Harrison sitting in a committee in the Exchequer Chamber, a few days before the trial, as the charge was being crafted. 'I do remember well, it was in the evening, they were lighting of candles, they were somewhat private,' Nutley said, before gesturing towards Harrison. 'This gentleman was there, I saw him.'

Nutley recalled Harrison regaling everyone present with an account of his conversation with Charles, after the King asked if the intention was to murder him. Harrison told his audience that he had informed the King that this was not their plan – it was, rather, to have Charles be 'a public example of Justice'.

This evidence was enough in itself to confirm Harrison's damnation in the court's eyes. Nutley recollected that some on the committee felt that the wording of the royal impeachment was overlong. 'They were offering some reasons to contract it, and I heard this Prisoner at the Bar vent this expression: "Gentlemen, it will be good for us to blacken him, what we can – Pray, let us blacken him", or words to that purpose. I am sure "blacken" was his word.'[36]

A sixth witness was now produced, and sworn. Lord Newburgh, who had been the King's host at Bagshot Park during his brief, distressing, visit, spoke of the tight guard Harrison had placed around the monarch: 'When the King had dined, he [Harrison] carried him to Windsor, and appointed several of his officers to ride close to the King, as he was riding, lest he should make his escape from them.'[37] The prosecution reminded the jury that such an imprisonment of the monarch would, on its own, be enough to constitute high treason.

Wadham Wyndham had been appointed a sergeant-at-law earlier in the month. He now brought forth the papers that would seal the fate of many: the first related to the convening and summoning of the High Court of Justice; the second was the warrant for execution. With the bar set so low for guilt for treason that even imagining the deed could lead to conviction and execution, signed and sealed documents that confirmed the accused's intentions in tangible, legible, form constituted unshakable evidence. Isabell Hacker had produced the warrant in the misguided hope that it would excuse her husband. Instead, it established his guilt, and that of all of its signatories, beyond any doubt.

Meanwhile a man called Jessop, a junior bureaucrat at the House of Commons, produced the forms relating to the convening of the High Court of Justice. He explained that, on the instructions of Henry Scobell, the recently deceased clerk of Parliament, he had carefully filed away all records relating to Charles I's trial. Jessop was a meticulous and obedient man: all the paperwork was there, relating to the preparation, conduct and conclusion of the proceedings. The bulk of this was passed to one side, to be sifted through in time.

The production of the two key documents – Hacker's warrant, and the summoning of the High Court of Justice – caused immediate consternation: their implication was clear. Yet Harrison was matter of fact. 'I desire to see the Instrument,' he said. Looking at his signature on the form, he confirmed, 'I believe it is my own hand.' He was then shown the execution warrant, and said, 'I do think this is my hand, too.' Realising he now had his man for sure, Wyndham added, 'If you think it, the jury will not doubt it. That's the bloody Warrant for Execution. And we desire they may both be read.'

Questions were raised as to whether the documents should be read out as evidence, but Harrison overruled such objections on the basis that he had nothing to hide: 'I do not come to be denying any thing, that in my own judgment, and conscience, I have done, or committed; but rather to be bringing it forth to the Light.'[38]

Wyndham summed up his evidence to the jury, stressing Harrison's leading role in the King's death: 'You see this prisoner was no ordinary actor in it: his hand is in at all games, taking of him, imprisoning of him, bringing him to London, and setting guards on him. You see also his malice, "Let us blacken him", for they knew his innocence would shine forth, unless it was blackened by their imputations.' In a crescendo of outrage, Wyndham concluded, 'He sat many times, as you hear, and sentenced him, and assented to that sentence by standing up, and likewise by concluding the catastrophe of that sad beginning of our sufferings, his making a warrant for his execution, and accordingly you know what did follow. I think a clearer evidence of a fact can never be given, than is for these things.'

The irresistible confidence of the prosecutor's close made the public gallery buzz in excited anticipation. Bridgeman was appalled: 'Gentlemen, this humming is not at all becoming the gravity of this court. Let there be free-speaking by the Prisoner and Counsel. It is more fitting for a stage-play, than for a Court of Justice.'[39] It was now time for Harrison to speak. The arguments he had formed during his six months in prison blended with his profound religious beliefs to form a defence that he believed to be robust. He began by reiterating that the King's fate 'was not a thing done in a corner', but was rather of international renown. Harrison claimed that he had examined his conscience, in tears and through prayer, many times. His all-powerful, all-knowing God had consistently assured him he had done no wrong, and Harrison warned the court that God would soon appear to the world, to explain that which might seem inexplicable to the human mind.

In the meantime, Harrison would justify his actions through the revisiting of events that all were familiar with. 'You know,' he told the court, 'what a contest hath been in these nations for many years. Diverse of those, that sit upon the bench, were formerly as active.'

Harrison was daring to speak the truth: that many of the jurors and legal officers present had actively sided against the King in the previous two decades. What they had done was also treason, by the court's own definition: the breaking of the Oath of Supremacy, the armed opposition to God's anointed. Yet it was a subject not to be touched upon, a crime not to be prosecuted: rather, it was to be quietly forgotten, a veil pulled over it, while the regicides alone were pushed forward for sacrifice.

'Pray, Mr Harrison,' the judge cut in; 'do not thus reflect on the court. This is not to the business.'[40]

Realising he was to be denied use of this, his most compelling claim, the major general redirected his defensive fire. He claimed he had acted out of conscience, and in the belief that he had been doing God's bidding, rather than out of any personal conviction. Harrison also pointed to the status quo in England eleven years earlier: 'I say what was done was done by the authority of the Parliament, which was then the Supreme Authority, and that those, that have acted under them are not to be questioned by any power less than them ... And whereas it hath been said, we did assume, and usurp an authority, I say, this was done rather in the Fear of the Lord.'

This provoked an explosion from Bridgeman: 'Away with him! Know where you are, sir! You are in the Assembly of Christians. Will you make God the author of your treasons and murders?'[41]

Harrison had nowhere to go, now the court had demolished the two main struts of his defence: that all that had been done had been at the bidding of a Parliament of England, and that no other organisation could question that supreme body's authority. The solicitor general dismissed these interlocking points with equal contempt, insisting that the defendant's reference to them comprised a fresh act of treason, which on its own demanded the death sentence.

Now the various other legal figures joined in the destruction of Harrison's attempted justifications. Sir Arthur Hazlerig asked mockingly, why, if he held Parliament in such very high esteem, had he pulled the Speaker from his chair during Cromwell's termination of the Rump Parliament seven years earlier? Harrison made his final, forlorn, counterattack. 'I would not willingly speak to offend any man,' he began, ominously, 'but I know God is no respecter of persons. [The King's] setting up his standard against the people—

'Truly, Mr Harrison,' interjected Bridgeman, 'this must not be suffered! This doth not at all belong to you!'

Harrison persevered. 'Under favour, this doth belong to me. I would have abhorred to have brought him to account; had not the blood of English men, that had been shed—'

Wyndham cut in. 'Me thinks he should be sent to Bedlam, till he comes to the Gallows to render account of this!'

Turnor added his disgust. 'My Lords, this man hath the plague all over him! It is pity any should stand near him; for he will infect them.'[42]

Harrison now returned to less inflammatory talk, settling on the evidence against him. He denied that he had sought to 'blacken' the King, during his trial. He maintained that he had brought Charles from the Isle of Wight out of obedience to the orders of his commander-in-chief, Fairfax. He persisted in saying he had acted under the umbrella of Parliamentary authority. He expressed his grave disappointment that his lines of justification had been closed to him by the deliberate obstruction of the Court.

When Harrison had finished, the judge addressed the jury. He noted of the accused: 'He hath been so far from denying, that he hath justified these actions. The evidence is so clear, and pregnant, as nothing more. I think you need not go out.'[43] The jurors huddled together, very briefly, at the bar.

Their foreman was Sir Thomas Allen, part of the Restoration establishment. Five months earlier, as lord mayor of London, he had greeted the King on his return to the capital. Allen now stood to deliver the inevitable, unanimous, verdict: 'Guilty.'

The court was eager to deal with its first victim. The solicitor general asked for the sentence against Harrison to be carried out as quickly as possible. 'His demeanour hath been such,' he claimed, 'that he doth not deserve a reprieve for so many days, that you are like to spend in this session.'[44]

Harrison was given one final chance to speak. He had nothing further to say, since the Court refused to consider his defence. The judge then pronounced the sentence that would loom over all the accused:

You, that are the Prisoner at the Bar, you are to pass the Sentence of Death, which sentence is this. The Judgment of this Court is, and the Court doth award, that you be led back to the place, from whence you came, and from thence to be drawn upon an hurdle to the place of execution, and there you shall be hanged by the neck, and being alive shall be cut down, and your privy members to be cut off, your entrails to be taken out of your body, and (you living) the same to be burnt before your eyes, and your head to be cut off, your body to be divided into four quarters, and your head, and quarters, to be disposed of at the pleasure of the King's Majesty: and the Lord have mercy upon your soul.[45]

Chapter 7

Men of God

The doctors did prescribe at last
To give 'em this potation,
A vomit or a single cast,
Well deserved, in purgation;
After that to lay them down,
And bleed a vein in every one,
As traitors of the nation.

Anonymous Restoration ballad, 1660

Hanging, drawing and quartering had been the prescribed form of execution for high treason since the thirteenth century. Previously the sentence had tended to be just hanging, without macabre additions. There had been a time when throttling the life out of an offender had been considered enough, but Henry III wanted the guilty sent on their way with more of a flourish, and an unimaginable amount of pain, so as to deter others from attempting this king of crimes. A would-be assassin of Henry's, and later the man behind the plot, both suffered hanging, drawing and quartering, in 1238 and 1240 – but they were disembowelled *after* death.

Early forms of the sentence involved the condemned being dragged through the street on the end of a rope. But the resulting repetitive impact of the head on the ground could result in near death before the gallows – the fulcrum of suffering – had been reached. It therefore became normal practice for the victim to be transported to his place of death on a low hurdle, or sledge, on which he would receive the projectiles of the crowds, but arrive intact.

On reaching the gallows, the condemned man (women guilty of high treason were burnt at the stake) was allowed to address the people. He was urged by the presiding sheriff to confess his crime and to incriminate accomplices. A priest encouraged a final search for forgiveness which, it was promised, would give the condemned a chance of seeing Heaven, rather than the otherwise inevitable descent into Hell. There was then time for praying aloud. The only clothes worn by the prisoner were his shirt, and a cap that would be drawn down over the eyes just before the drop.

The executioner would ask for forgiveness from his charge. It was wise to concede on this difficult point, and also to offer a financial gift, for the way in which the killing was performed was largely at the discretion of this master of suffering. He could favour you by allowing you to hang until dead; or he could cut you down after the 'short drop' (which garrotted the throat, but left neck and spine intact), then continue to the sharp end of proceedings – the chopping off of genitals, then the disembowelling with a red-hot metal gouge – while keeping the screaming victim alive, leaving his vital organs till last.

The crime was defined by the Treason Act of 1351, passed during the reign of Edward III. This was the law that Sir Orlando Bridgeman had selectively highlighted to the grand jury before the regicides were brought before it. He had quoted the part of the Act relating to, 'When a Man doth compass or imagine the Death of our Lord the King', as the basis for this capital trial. The savagery of the sentence was meant to deter subjects from killing leading male members of the royal family, or from defiling their queens, 'companions' and princesses.

Celebrated victims of this vicious and protracted style of execution included Guy Fawkes, who in 1605 had prepared to blow up King James and the House of Lords during the State Opening of Parliament. Caught near his bank of gunpowder, Fawkes endured relentless torture as the King's agents sought to extract the names of co-conspirators from him. Broken and bloody, Fawkes was condemned to a traitor's death. But on the allotted day he cheated the executioner by throwing himself from the scaffold, and dying instantly from a broken neck.

Behind each phase of the execution lay more than just sadism: this was a symbolic process that led the criminal to oblivion. The drawing through the streets provided a final, degrading journey from the living world. Hanging was the normal mode of dispatch for condemned criminals – the swift cleanness of beheading was generally reserved as a privilege for nobility and royalty.

The implement for castration was a sharp blade which not only cropped a man's masculinity, but also symbolically terminated his power. The removal of sexual organs also underlined that the children of the dying man were disinherited: all possessions of those executed for treason were confiscated. The disembowelling related to medically ignorant and religiously superstitious medieval beliefs about the composition of the body and the spirit. Corrupt people were thought to harbour their malice in their hearts and in their innards. In tearing into the bowel with red-hot implements, to excavate these infected parts, the executioner was aiming to negate their evil through incineration in a purifying fire.

The head was cut off, not only as a mark of the conclusion of the sentence's course, but also because it was believed to be the repository of the evil designs that had formed and flourished there. Along with the heart, the head was customarily raised high by the executioner, to mark the subject's eventual death.

The head would be stuck on a pike, and placed with its dead eyes cast in the direction of the site of the crime. It was often encased by a metal brace, to hold it together for a little longer during putrefaction. Ravens were famed for picking the flesh, and feasting on the eyeballs, of those executed at the Tower of London.

The regicides seem initially to have been expecting to be hanged, or beheaded, as relatively orderly exits from the world: Scott had famously claimed in the Commons that an ending of the Long

Parliament would see his and other heads on the block, and Cook had spent much time trying to make logical sense of his fate. This had included dwelling on the likely method of his dispatch, and the ordeal that they represented: he calculated that, 'The axe or the halter [noose] will be less pain than the pangs of childbirth.'[1]

There had been examples of people being similarly condemned, within the previous decade and a half. After a failed plan to capture Dublin Castle, Connor Maguire, Baron of Enniskillen, had been captured and found guilty by the Parliamentarians in London of being 'the chief contriver of the late Irish Rebellion and Massacre of the Protestant English'. After sentencing, the twenty-nine-year-old nobleman wrote a humble letter to the Commons that 'showeth that your petitioner stands condemned for his life, and adjudged to be drawn, hanged, and quartered: the performance whereof (he humbly conceives) in some more favourable manner, will be satisfactory to justice'.[2] Maguire pointed out that, given his rank, he should be afforded a quicker, more dignified, end. The Commons denied him, and he was hanged, drawn and quartered in February 1645, bullying officials and Protestant priests repeatedly interrupting his final prayers because they despised his Catholic words of comfort and supplication.

Thirteen years later, Cromwell insisted that a new High Court of Justice be set up to try the fourteen principal conspirators in a freshly unearthed Royalist plot. They were condemned to death for treason. Three of them – the brother of an earl, a knight and a priest – were granted the swift end offered by beheading. Another three, who were colonels, 'were treated with more severity', Clarendon reported, 'and were hanged, drawn, and quartered, with the utmost rigour, in several great streets in the city, to make the deeper impression upon the people'. But the ghastliness of the procedure was too much, and 'all men appeared so nauseated with blood, and so tired with those abominable spectacles, that Cromwell thought it best to pardon the rest who were condemned; or rather to reprieve them'.[3]

While the Royalists had loudly complained at the barbarity of hanging, drawing and quartering when it had been used against their own, they now insisted on it as the correct form of punishment for the killers of their late King. They were delighted Harrison would be the first to sample the agony and the humiliation of it all. 'No man in the kingdom was regarded with so much detestation as this, by all parties,' remarked the Reverend Mark Noble, an eighteenth-century biographer of the regicides, 'except the few remaining fanatics, who looked upon him as a saint and martyr, and firmly believed to see him arise – to see, rather his mangled scattered remains re-unite in glory amongst them.'[4]

From the moment he had been sentenced, Thomas Harrison had shown an astonishing bravery nurtured by his religious intensity. Led from the court, he was immediately surrounded by a crowd howling with delight at what lay in store for him. In reply to the gloating taunts, he shouted, 'Good is the Lord for all this! I have no cause to be ashamed of the cause that I have been engaged in!'[5]

Harrison remained upbeat during the two days between his being sentenced and his execution. He stayed unshakeable in his conviction that the ordeal he and his fellow regicides were facing was part of God's plan, before the imminent Second Coming. He greeted the confiscation of his entire £17,000 estate by bequeathing to his wife the one object that remained to him – his Bible. This, he maintained, was an object with a value far beyond human understanding.

On 13 October he emerged from his cell, was tied to a sledge and was then pulled from Newgate prison, along Fleet Street, towards his place of execution. Charing Cross had been the site of one of the twelve Christian crosses erected in the late thirteenth century by Edward I, in memory of his dead and much-mourned wife Queen Eleanor. Parliament had destroyed this memorial to romance and royalism in 1647. Now some of its cause's most ardent supporters would be slain on this same spot, within sight of Whitehall, where the King had been beheaded.

The crowd was seething and hostile. 'Where is your good old cause now?' one man taunted, as the major general rattled past on his hurdle. 'With a cheerful smile,' Ludlow recorded, Harrison 'clapped his hands on his breast and said, "Here it is, and I go to seal it with my blood." '6

Far from being cowed by terror, Harrison presented a brave and defiant farewell to those who had come to celebrate his end. When he stood on the scaffold, about to give his final speech, it was noticeable that his legs were shaking. This provoked coarse heckling from those convinced he was quaking with fear. But the major general would have none of it, shouting out that his many wounds in battle had left him with a legacy of quivering limbs. He delivered his words within sight of the rope that would hang him, and of the instruments that would tear him apart.

There was to be no last-minute repentance of his part in the death of the King. Instead, Harrison chose his final moments to justify his actions: 'The finger of God hath been amongst us of late years in the deliverance of his people from their oppressors, and in bringing to judgment that who were guilty of the precious blood of the dear servants of the Lord.' To any sympathisers in the crowd, he gave this rallying cry: 'Be not discouraged by reason of the cloud that now is upon you, for the Sun will shine and God will give a testimony unto what he hath been doing in a short time.'7 There must have been many former Parliamentarians present who felt a tingle of satisfaction at their soldier's heartfelt defiance.

When the moment came for him to be put to death, Harrison recalled achievements from the past, while entrusting his future to God: 'I have served a good Lord and Creator; he has covered my head many times in the day of battle: by God I have leapt over a wall, by God I have run through a troop, and by God I will go through this death and He will make it easy for me. Now into thy hands, O Lord Jesus, I commit my spirit.'8

He was hanged with the short drop, to ensure no easy departure from this world, and only when the frantic thrashing had stopped was he cut down. As Harrison regained consciousness his shirt was pulled away. The executioner used his knife to cut off Harrison's genitals, which were presented to him before being tossed into a bucket. He was then held down while red-hot metal bored into his belly.

It was while his innards were being burnt in front of him that Harrison summoned up his remaining strength, and swung a punch that caught the executioner off-guard. This brought an abrupt end to the major general, as he was immediately dispatched by the irate and embarrassed hangman. Harrison's head was severed, his heart cut out, and then his body was cut up into four.

One who witnessed this blood-drenched ordeal was Samuel Pepys. The diarist was a Parliamentary sympathiser who was adapting to life under the Restoration. 'I went out to Charing Cross, to see Major General Harrison hanged, drawn, and quartered; which was done there, he looking as cheerful as any man could do in that condition. He was presently cut down, and his head and heart shown to the people, at which there was great shouts of joy. Thus it was my chance to see . . . the first blood shed in revenge for the blood of the King at Charing Cross.'[9]

There was plenty more to come.

The trials had continued during Harrison's final days. At the end of 12 October, with Scroope, Scott, Carew, Jones and Clements found guilty, Judge Bridgeman encouraged them to face up to 'the foulness of this horrid offence', in advance of appearing before 'God's tribunal'. He said he was sad to see the fatal fall of such men, several of whose qualities he knew personally. He painted Charles I's reign before the Civil Wars as a period of unmatched peace and prosperity, and attacked the five men for being among those who had condemned a monarch who he believed to possess extraordinary personal virtues: 'I urge this unto you, only that you would lay it to your hearts, that you would consider what it is to kill a King, and to kill such a King.'[10]

Bridgeman was at great pains to distinguish between the King's Parliamentary adversaries, and those directly involved in his conviction and execution: 'They were not guilty, but some few ambitious, bloody, guilty persons, who contrived the same, and others misled by them.'[11] Sir Orlando refused to allow fanciful religious beliefs to forgive earthly conduct, declaring, 'There is a spiritual pride, men may overrun themselves by their own holiness, and they may go by pretended revelations ... You must not think that every fancy and imagination is conscience; the Devil doth many times appear like an Angel of Light.'[12]

When thirty-eight-year-old John Carew learnt the tone of Bridgeman's comments, he said that he would be the first to follow Harrison, for he shared the same Fifth Monarchy beliefs that the Court and the Crown were identifying as a particular menace.

Carew was regarded as second only to Harrison in the sect, and had suffered similarly under the Protectorate, after (like Harrison) some prominence in the years immediately after Charles's execution: he had represented Devon during the experiment of Barebone's Parliament. However, he came to believe that Cromwell's personal ambitions flouted God's will, prompting him to write a tract that included the accusation: 'There are those who suspect you'll King it, and procure your Heir to succeed it.'[13] For this, and other acts that Cromwell viewed as sedition, Carew had been imprisoned in Pendennis Castle in Cornwall.

The Restoration would provide no respite for Carew. He had become one of Charles I's judges by accident, his name not featuring in the original list of commissioners, but being added later – seemingly as an afterthought. Carew had asked to be excused the responsibility, but eventually agreed to sit when satisfied as to the authority of the High Court of Justice. Aside from his status as a regicide, Carew was a figure of special contempt in Royalist circles for not having attempted to plead for mercy for his half-brother, Sir Alexander Carew. Sir Alexander had been condemned to death for trying to betray the port of Plymouth to the King during the Civil War: he was beheaded in December 1644. One of Charles II's supporters asserted, 'It is no wonder that he was one of the Judges of the King, who was consenting to the death of his own brother.'[14] The Commons voted for John Carew to be excluded from the Act of Indemnity by a majority of eighty votes to seventy.

Carew had been the focus of public displays of intense hatred on his journey from Cornwall to the Tower of London. Contrary to the reports that had troubled the Commons earlier in the year he had not tried to flee abroad, even though he had had the opportunity to do so. He shared Harrison's belief that running away would denote the abandonment of an honourable and blessed cause. He also swore by the apocalyptic Scriptures, and held dear a verse in the Book of Revelation that resonated with his beliefs: 'And I saw the souls of them that were beheaded for the witness of Jesus, and for the Word of God, and which had not worshipped the Beast. And they lived and reigned with Christ a thousand years.'[15] He believed he could be certain of a place among the Elect.

In several towns that he passed through on his way to London there had been calls to hang or shoot Carew there and then, rather than let him live a day longer. 'He had a gracious presence of the Lord with him,' recalled a Puritan witness to his journey; 'Otherwise the many reproaches and hard usage in the way had been sufficient to have troubled his spirit.'[16]

Carew remained calm but forthright during his trial. He readily admitted his presence at the King's prosecution, and confessed his signature on both of the key documents. He justified his actions as being in tune with God's will. 'As for that I can say in the presence of the Lord, who is the searcher of all hearts,' he offered, 'that what I did was in his fear; and I did it in obedience to his holy and righteous laws.' This provoked high excitement in the public gallery, but Bridgeman allowed Carew to continue, reminding the court and the accused, 'Go on, he stands for his life, let him have liberty . . . Go on, you shall not be interrupted.'[17]

There was less tolerance of Carew's secondary defence: that he had acted under the authority of Parliament, when sitting in judgment of the King. Mr Justice Foster reminded Carew that there was no precedent for the House of Commons to act in such a way, to which Carew calmly countered, 'Neither was there such a war, or such a precedent.'[18] It was a brilliantly telling point, and he refused to retract it: 'Gentlemen of the Jury, I say I shall leave it with you. This authority I speak of is right, which was the supreme power, it is well known what they were.'[19] This was an argument that the Royalist court repeatedly disparaged, but never convincingly rebutted. Fellow regicide Edmund Ludlow referred to the Court's counter-arguments on this point as being so flimsy that they were no more than mere 'cobweb-coverings'.[20]

At the end of the day, when Bridgeman asked the five who had been found guilty if they had anything further to say before he proceed to sentence, the other four cast themselves on the King's mercy, while Carew bypassed earthly authority altogether. 'I commit my cause unto the Lord,'[21] he said. His family begged him to reconsider and seek clemency: then, even though his life may remain forfeited, they might have a chance of retaining his property. But he refused to compromise his most closely held beliefs for their material benefit.

When the time came for his execution, everyone noticed how happy Carew looked. 'Coming down Newgate stairs to go into the sledge,' wrote an eyewitness, 'in a very smiling and cheerful manner, his countenance shining with great glory, he uttered words to this effect: "My Lord Jesus endured the Cross, whose steps I desire to follow." '[22] Royalist reporters, deeply troubled by another demonstration of pious bravery so soon after Harrison's, wrote that Carew's demeanour should be put down to drunkenness rather than courage: they claimed he had downed three pints of sack – fortified wine – before setting off for his execution. This, the Royalist scribes maintained, explained Carew's excessive sweating that day, which even his handkerchief could not assuage.

The day had started with threatening autumnal clouds hanging low, and they released their drops as Carew mounted the scaffold. He gave a fiery speech in the rain, warming the hearts of the Fifth Monarchists watching. He then met his death with a serene defiance and acceptance that drew reluctant admiration from many who had come to watch a wretched fanatic suffer.

Part of the thinking behind the regicides' trials had been the hope of drawing attention to what contemptible beings the defendants were. But the courage and piety of Harrison and Carew had drawn admiration from the watching crowds, and news of their stoicism spread quickly. The remaining doomed men aspired to match the example of the Fifth Monarchy duo for grit and dignity, when their time came.

But another Man of God was finding the imminent prospect of excruciating death too much to bear. Hugh Peters was sixty-two, and in poor health. Eleven years earlier he had led Charles in triumph from Windsor to London for his trial, and had since combined his religious calling with command of a regiment during Cromwell's Irish campaigns. Peters came from a well-to-do background: his father was an émigré from Antwerp who settled with Peters's maternal family in Fowey, on the Cornish coast. A Cambridge graduate, Peters was filled with religious fervour as a young man, inspired by an electrifying sermon during a visit to London. It was a potent enough dose to last a lifetime.

Peters's certainty in his beliefs made him an outspoken opponent of royal policy and religion. He had been imprisoned in 1627 after openly condemning Charles's French queen, Henrietta Maria, for the 'idolatry and superstition'[23] of her Roman Catholicism. His licence to preach was suspended, prompting him to move to the greater tolerance of the Netherlands. There he served as a military chaplain, before briefly becoming a prominent pastor in Rotterdam. Even there, the long arm of the Anglican Church caught up with him, pricked by his outspokenness. Peters decided to join the Puritan trek towards the far-flung, colonial communities of America's eastern seaboard. An ocean away from Europe, they offered the chance of political and religious liberty.

Peters had been intrigued by possibilities across the Atlantic for some time. He was an early investor in the New England Company, which bought a grant of land between the Charles and Merrimack Rivers (which makes up much of the central part of present-day New England). The settlers forcibly colonised land that had been home to the Massachusett, Nauset and Wampanoag tribes, who lost much of their population to disease as a consequence.

In 1629 the trading body changed its identity to the Massachusetts Bay Company, acquiring a royal charter from Charles I that
recognised it as being 'one body corporate and politic', able to pass
its own laws provided they were 'not contrary' to those of England.[24]
Now it carried the quiet hopes of many who were eager to create a
refuge from religious intolerance in England. This was the one
English colonial body in America that did not require its board
members to meet in the motherland, meaning that control of
company stock provided a unique measure of independence.

Hugh Peters took up his new life in New England in 1635,
bringing energy and ideas to the colony. He used knowledge
gleaned from his youth in Cornwall to advise the settlers on how to
develop both their fishing trade and their shipbuilding. He helped
spread the gospel among the Native Americans, later claiming that
as a result of their newfound godliness, 'in seven years among thousands there dwelling, I never saw any drunk, nor heard an Oath,
nor any begging, nor Sabbath broken'.[25]

Peters was one of 17,000 Puritans who had migrated to New
England by the mid-1630s. The preacher was among those anxious
that this growing community of godliness should be led by suitably
trained clergy. He became a prime mover in the establishment of
Harvard College, by vote of the Great and General Court of the
Massachusetts Bay Colony, in 1636. Harvard was established to
provide an annual harvest of spiritual leaders. At the end of the
same year Peters became pastor of the first church in Salem, which
was, along with Boston, one of the two main settlements in the
colony. He asserted his authority over the community, combining
strong leadership with a compelling example of simple living. In the
process he earned considerable respect and popularity.

There was consternation in his congregation when it was learnt
that Peters would be part of a three-man delegation from the colony
to England, in 1641, 'to negotiate for us ... both in furthering the
work of reformation of the churches there which was now like to
be attempted, and to satisfy our countrymen of the true cause our
engagements there have not been satisfied this year'.[26] It was an

important mission, and demanded the vivid oratory of the passionate preacher. Peters promised to return to New England, which he would from now on frequently refer to as 'home'. However, to his bitter regret, this was not to be. Years later, when facing death, Peters would write: 'It hath much lain to my heart above any thing almost, that I left the people I was engaged to in New England, it cuts deeply, I look upon it as a Root-evil.'[27]

Peters arrived to find England 'embroiled in troubles and War', and was pressured to join the other leading ministers on campaign. The preacher quickly found himself in Ireland, before being assigned to ministry in the fleet. He was in demand from the great men of the cause: his particular patron was the Earl of Warwick, commander of the Parliamentary navy, and a colonial pioneer in North and Central America. Peters was also a valued presence in the retinues of successive lords general – the Earl of Essex, Lord Fairfax and Oliver Cromwell. These immensely powerful figures valued Peters's extraordinarily infectious words, which could rouse men to fight with a courage reserved for those utterly confident in God's blessing.

Peters whipped up New Model Army troops before battle, or in the prelude to attack on a besieged position. He was then repeatedly chosen to report their resulting victories to Parliament: he could be relied on to fire his audience, raise morale and stiffen resolve. 'In all which affairs I did labour to persuade the Army to do their duty,'[28] was how he coyly recorded the impact of his remarkable eloquence. Often, and intentionally, his triumphant reports resulted in increased money being allocated by Parliament to their troops in the field.

During the build-up to the King's trial, Peters was busy. He addressed congregations in London that included a high proportion of soldiers, and persuaded them that a king was eligible for trial and condemnation, if his actions demanded punishment. A Mr Beaver would recall how, in December 1648 (he could remember the date exactly, because it was while Parliament was observing a fast), he had listened to Hugh Peters preaching in the church of St

Margaret's, Westminster. Peters's New Testament text that day was the story of the freeing of the criminal Barabbas in place of Jesus – an error by the misled mob that had led to that greatest of historical wrongs – Christ's crucifixion.

From the pulpit Peters chided those who might repeat the travesty, and allow the wrong man to escape justice now. He reserved particular condemnation for London's merchants, accusing them of being prepared to reach a shameful compromise with the defeated King in order to line their pockets. Beaver remembered Peters's words: ' "I have been in the City," he said, "which may very well be compared to Jerusalem in this conjuncture of time, and I profess these foolish citizens, for a little trading and profit they will have Christ" (pointing to the redcoats on the pulpit stairs) "crucified, and that great Barabbas at Windsor released ... O Jesus, what should we do now?" with such like strange expressions, and shrugging of his shoulders in the pulpit.'[29] Beaver heard Peters continue in this melodramatic vein for two or three hours, justifying and encouraging the King's execution, while warning the military that if they failed to see the appropriate sentence passed they would invite destruction on themselves.

Peters also worked on the King's judges. The diarist John Evelyn recorded on 17 January 1649: 'I heard the rebel Peters incite the Rebel powers met in the Painted Chamber, to destroy his Majesty and saw that arch traitor Bradshaw, who not long after condemned [the King].'[30] Four days later Peters preached to a congregation of the commissioners of the High Court of Justice, taking as his text Psalm 149, verse 8, which exhorted, 'Bind your Kings with chains, and your Nobles in fetters of iron.' Warming to his theme, Peters said, 'What, will ye cut off the King's head, the head of a Protestant Prince and King? Turn to your Bibles and you shall find it there, "Whosoever sheds man's blood, by man shall his blood be shed" ... and I see neither King Charles, nor Prince Charles, nor Prince Rupert, nor Prince Maurice [Rupert and Maurice were nephews and leading generals of the King], nor any of that rabble excepted out of it ... This is the day that I and many saints of God besides have been praying for these many years.'[31]

A man named Chase recalled Oliver Cromwell laughing while Peters preached that day, apparently in appreciation of Peters's eccentric style of delivery: it was theatrical to the point of absurdity. To worldly observers it was all a bit much: Samuel Pepys would later record listening to a learned but overblown sermon by Dr Creeton, a chaplain to Charles II, pronouncing him 'the most comical man that ever I heard in my life. Just such a man as Hugh Peter[s].'[32]

But the extravagant delivery enchanted the less sophisticated. A historian of Salem noted of Peters that, 'his language was peculiar to himself. He had a power of associating his thoughts in such a manner, as to be sure to leave them upon the memory. If his images were coarse they were familiar, and never failed to answer his purpose.'[33] His purpose in early 1649 was to push on to condemnation of the King. Thomas Richardson would say of Peters, after the first day of the royal trial, 'I heard him commend Bradshaw, the carriage of him in the trial of the King, and another, Cook's carriage: to be short, Mr Peters holding up his hands said, "This is a most glorious beginning of the work." '[34] Sir Jeremy Whitcot remembered Peters's rapturous delight as the High Court of Justice gathered steam towards its goal of convicting the King. 'I cannot but look upon this Court with a great reverence,' he heard Peters say, 'for it doth resemble in some measure the trial that shall be at the end of the world by the Saints.'[35]

On three occasions, Peters recalled, he had spoken with Charles I, advising him on how to achieve salvation, and offering to preach to him the true word of God. 'The poor wretch would not hear me,'[36] Peters said, with pity.

In the early years of the Commonwealth, Peters seems to have enjoyed being a prominent figure at the execution of leading Royalists. He had arranged the surrender of the Duke of Hamilton to Parliament at Uttoxeter in 1648, and was with him on the scaffold the following year, when the duke was seen to embrace Peters warmly, before he was beheaded. He also delighted in saving others from execution, including the Earl of Norwich.

Peters's years in the Netherlands, the American colonies and Ireland gave him a very broad perspective. He had deep knowledge of Ireland, and was sympathetic to the plight of its Protestants. He also assisted the oppressed Protestant minority in Catholic Piedmont. Peters's strong attachment to the Netherlands led to his disagreeing fiercely with Cromwell about the Anglo-Dutch War – Peters feeling strongly that the two Protestant powers should work together, not blow one another apart on the seas.

At the death of his master, the Lord Protector, Peters had given the sermon, taking as his text, 'My servant Moses is dead.' His steps in Cromwell's funeral procession were the prelude to his retire-ment: his health was poor. Peters was heard from intermittently after that, most vocally when recording his dismay at Richard Cromwell's fall. He rose again from his sickbed in January 1660, when Parliament instructed him to intercept Monck with words of guidance during the general's advance towards London. He caught up with Monck at St Albans, delivering a poorly received address in the daytime, which he followed with an equally ill-judged prayer that evening. These blunders would remain fresh in the minds of the new regime, after the Restoration.

Peters seems to have remained strangely oblivious of the approaching danger. Confident that he would live out his days in peace, he wrote to Monck reminding him that he was chronically ill, while pointing to his having abstained from public life in the year since the collapse of Richard Cromwell's Protectorate. Peters hoped his total submission would guarantee his future safety.

But the Restoration provided the perfect opportunity for reprisal against those whose unpopularity matched their former power. Peters was a symbol of the republican, Puritan, decade that now demanded total rejection. In January 1660 the infirm preacher was banished from his set of rooms at Whitehall. Four months later he was relieved of the library that had been entrusted to him in 1644: it had belonged to William Laud, Charles I's Archbishop of Canter-

King Charles I of England out Hunting, Sir Anthony van Dyck, *c.*1635

Charles's refusal to engage with Parliament, as well as his High Church sympathies, resulted in tensions that erupted into the English Civil War in 1642.

A great and bloudy

FIGHT

AT

COLCHESTER,

AND

The ftorming of the Town by the Lord Generals Forces, with the manner how they were repulfed and beaten off, and forced to retreat from the Walls, and a great and terrible blow given at the faid ftorm, by Granadoes and Gunpowder. Likewife their hanging out the Flag of Defiance, and their fallying out upon Tuefday laft, all the chief Officers ingaging in the faid Fight, and Sir *Charles Lucas* giving the firft onfet in the Van, with the number killed and taken, and Sir *Charles Lucas* his Declaration.

uly London Printed for *G. Beal,* and are to be fold in the Old. Bayley, and neer Temple Bar, 1648.

Battle of Marston Moor, John Barker, 1644

The New Model Army, in alliance with the Scots, destroyed the King's army at the battle of Marston Moor, Yorkshire in 1644. Charles lost control of northern England in a day.

Through secret dealings with his allies, Charles I brought about the Second Civil War in 1648. It was put down with ruthless efficiency by the Parliamentarians; after the Siege of Colchester, senior Royalist officers were executed by firing squad.

John Bradshaw was known by his colleagues for scrupulous honesty. He was made Lord President of the High Court of Justice, formed to try the King.

Charles I before his judges. He is seated in the centre, with his back towards us, facing the dozens of men trying him for his life. The King consistently refused to recognise the right of this assembly to sit in judgement of him.

An Eyewitness Representation of the Execution of King Charles I in 1649, John Weesop, *c*.1653

Charles faced his execution with poise and courage, leaving his followers with the myth that he had suffered with Christ-like dignity.

Charles II, John Michael Wright, *c.*1661–66

Charles II, soon after his Coronation. His life as an impoverished exile ended
when the British people returned to kingship as their chosen form of rule.
The hunt for his father's killers continued throughout his 25-year reign.

The first harvest of the regicides, in 1660, resulted in the hanging, drawing and quartering of ten men. The ghastliness of this form of execution was a spur to the others to run for their lives. Not all of them got away.

Going to Execution.

Dun vpon the Devill

He that set them at worke hath payde them their wages.

Traytors Rewarded.

The bodies of three prominent regicides – Oliver Cromwell, his son-in-law Henry Ireton, and John Bradshaw – were exhumed so their bodies could suffer the punishment that they had escaped through death.

Major General Thomas Harrison was Charles I's guard from prison at Hurst Castle to his trial in London. A much-hated religious zealot, Harrison was the first to be sentenced at the trial of the regicides.

Lieutenant General Edmund Ludlow was greatly feared by Charles II, being a gifted soldier and effective politician. Ludlow fled to Switzerland, and was the target of Royalist kidnappers and assassins.

Colonel John Hutchinson timed his appeal for clemency perfectly, but the Royalists discovered incriminating documents that made them hell-bent on vengeance.

Hugh Peters, pastor of Salem, Massachusetts, returned to England to breathe fire into the Parliamentary cause. His passionate sermons convinced many that a king could be put to death if guilty of tyranny.

Colonel Adrian Scroope was fined just one year's income for his part in the King's death until a conversation was recalled in which Scroope showed no remorse for his actions. This sealed his fate.

Colonel John Okey had commanded the New Model Army's only regiment of dragoons. After the Restoration, Okey's former chaplain Downing set about hunting Okey and his colleagues. Okey was captured in the Netherlands.

Colonel Daniel Axtell roused Parliamentary troops to shout for 'Justice!' in the trial against the king. His later presence on the scaffold was, he said, just a case of a soldier obeying orders.

William Goffe fled to America with his father-in-law, Edward Whalley, once the Restoration was inevitable. At first the major-generals were greeted in Massachusetts with respect, but were soon hunted for their lives.

William Goffe has entered mythology as 'the Angel of Hadley' – the deliverer of the colonial outpost Hadley from an attack by Native Americans in 1675. He is depicted directing the defence that saved the women and children from massacre.

Judges Cave, West Rock, New Haven, George Henry Durrie, 1856

Judges Cave in New Haven, Connecticut, is one of the supposed hiding places of Goffe and Whalley. The two fugitives believed this to be a safe refuge until it was discovered by a Native American hunting party, forcing them to flee.

bury, who had been executed for his role as the King's religious henchman. Also in May, a spate of cartoons and ballads greeted the order for Peters to be apprehended: the masses were baying for his blood. Effigies of Peters were burnt in public, along with Cromwell's. He was suspected of being one of the King's brace of executioners. On 19 June a pamphlet appeared detailing an alleged confession by Peters to his doctor, in which he was presented as a more than willing hand in the King's trial and execution.

On 18 July, Peters learnt that his application for the royal mercy offered in the Act of Indemnity had been rejected. This unexpected news sent him into hiding, from where he composed a robust defence of his actions, and submitted it to the House of Lords. His self-justification was later published as *The Case of Mr Hugh Peters, Impartially Communicated to the View and Censure of the Whole World*, and opened with a complaint at the overwhelming prejudice he faced without even being heard. 'Before his holy Majesty, Angels and Men,' Peters swore he had nothing whatsoever – whether in thought, or by action – to do with Charles I's death. He reminded his readers that he had helped Royalists during the Commonwealth, while admitting, 'It is true, I was of a Party, when I acted zealously, but without malice or mischief.'[37] It is clear that he thought this lack of forgiveness from the new King was a mistake, 'unless my evil be only for acting with such a Party'.[38] Surely this was not possible, he said, for it would lead to half the nation remaining unpardoned, and vulnerable to reprisal.

Peters panicked, in the face of terrible and unforeseen danger. He seems to have chosen to forget the public nature of his attacks on the King – the whipping up of congregations and assemblies, so they would contemplate putting Charles I on trial for his life; the riding at the head of the crowd-drawing procession that hurried the King from Windsor to St James's – and tried to pretend that things had not been as they had appeared.

This involved some nimble reinventions. He maintained that he had not been party to Pride's Purge when, in truth, he had been one of the few preachers to support it; that he had never profited from the war, despite receiving not just Laud's library, but also an annuity from Parliament, as well as confiscated Royalist property; and he vigorously dismissed the many reports that he had been unfaithful ('unclean', in the language of the time) to his mentally ill wife – a particularly serious accusation, since in the Puritan colony where he was alleged to have strayed, adultery was a capital offence. He pointed to his Christian creed, and his status as a gentleman, to lend weight to his version of events, before swearing to be loyal to Charles II, and 'to be passive under Authority, rather than impatient'.[39]

This failed to satisfy his enemies, and the hunt for the preacher continued. It ended in success on 2 September when Peters was found hiding under the bed of some Quaker friends in their Southwark home. The man who had urged the New Model Army to perform brave deeds discovered quickly that he was not, himself, a man of courage. There was a tangible desperation about his addled remarks in Court that betrayed his disbelieving terror at the very real prospect of a traitor's death.

At his arraignment, on 10 October, when asked to plead, he replied in consternation, 'I would not for ten thousand worlds say, I am guilty. I am not guilty.' When asked how he would be tried, the controversial preacher offered, 'By the Word of God.' Those in the public gallery recognised this as an erroneous reply, put forward by a defendant desperate to wrap himself in protective religious clothing, and erupted in derisive laughter. The question was put to him again, and Peters was obliged to reply, this time, correctly, 'By God, and the Country.'[40]

During his trial, on 13 October – the day Harrison was castrated, gutted and chopped into five parcels of flesh – Sir Edward Turnor told the court not to be misled by Peter's priestly status, for, 'He did make use of his profession, wherein he should have been the minister of peace, to make himself a trumpeter of war, of treason and sedition in the kingdom.'[41]

A devastating witness was produced, who illuminated the deep hatred for the King and the royal family that lurked within Peters.

Dr William Young had looked after the preacher when he had been desperately ill with dysentery in Ireland. It took Peters a week to get over the worst of his sickness, and he then convalesced for nine further weeks in the physician's home. During those two months in 1648, the priest had been open with his thoughts, often staying up till the early hours to dissect the minutiae of recent wars. 'Many times I should hear him rail most insufferably against the Blood Royal,' Young told the court, 'not only against our Martyred King, but against his Royal offspring.' Peters had also shared with Young his true and secret purpose for returning home from New England: 'He told me that for the driving on of this interest of this Reformation, he was employed out of New England for the stirring up of this war, and driving it on.'[42]

Dr Young next recounted that Peters told him that it was the King's being taken by the army from Holdenby, when he moved from Parliament's control to that of the military, which had led to thoughts of executing the monarch. Oliver Cromwell had learnt that Parliament was plotting to have him arrested. He and Peters had escaped from London to Ware. The two men concluded there that the only way to restore peace was through the trial and death of the King. Young believed that it was Peters who originally proposed this plan, and it was Cromwell who agreed to it.

This theory was given further substance through the testimony of Sir Jeremy Whitcot, who recalled hearing Peters 'speak very scurrilously of the King. Among the rest, he was making some kind of narration of Cromwell making an escape, and that he [Cromwell] was intended to be surprised, "that if he had not presently gone away, he had been clapped up in the Tower and declared a traitor". He said there was a meeting of the officers of the Army, where he used this expression, "And there we did resolve to set aside the King." '[43]

Other witnesses were called, who spoke of Peters's presence at meetings where the agenda was hostility to the King. Wilbert Gunter, who drew ale at The Star pub in Coleman Street, recalled seeing Peters sitting with Cromwell and others for many hours after the King's arrest, and heard Peters referring to the monarch repeatedly and dismissively as 'Charles Stuart'.

It was shown that Peters had long been an outspoken critic of the King. George Starkey came from Windsor, the birthplace of the New Model Army. Starkey's family lived near the castle, and their home had been requisitioned as lodgings by Henry Ireton. It contained a large room that the Council of War used for meetings. It was in this that Starkey frequently saw Cromwell, Ireton and Peters, together with two others whose names he did not know, sitting up till two or three in the morning, talking with intensity and passion.

Starkey had a clear memory of Peters's relentlessly poor opinion of Charles I: 'I remember some of his expressions were these, that he was a tyrant, that he was a fool, that he was not fit to be King or bear that office; I have heard him say, that for the office itself (in those very words which shortly after came into print) that it was a dangerous, changeable, and useless office.'[44] Starkey told the court how his elderly, Royalist father had quietly seethed with resentment at the presence of his compulsory houseguests. But when news came of the King's imprisonment on the Isle of Wight, it was too much for the old man: he vowed to make his true feelings known. His first act of defiance was to hide the key to his wine cellar. Then, while saying grace at dinner that night, he dared to throw in an impudent barb: 'God save the King's most excellent Majesty,' he said, 'and preserve him out of the hands of all his enemies.' At this, Peters turned deliberately towards his elderly, reluctant host, and coldly declared: 'Old gentleman, your idol will not stand long.'[45]

Peters's guilt as to 'contriving' the death of the King was established under this great weight of evidence. What remained unproven was the suspicion that he was one of the two royal executioners – either the man who swung the axe, or the one who then held high the King's dripping head. Richard Nunneley swore that he had seen Peters prior to the beheading, busy round the scaffold. Nunneley specifically remembered Peters summoning a carpenter from

Houndsditch named Tench, whom he instructed to beat four iron staples into the floor of the scaffold. These were to be used for securing the King, if he refused to submit to death.

Nunneley maintained that Peters disappeared from view an hour before the King walked on to the scaffold. It was not until after Charles's head had been severed that he spotted Peters again – wearing a black cloak and wide-brimmed hat, in conversation with the hangman. Nunneley swore that he later saw the two men drinking water together.

Peters excitedly rebutted this evidence, claiming that he had been confined to bed at home during the execution, too ill to move. He produced a servant to back up this version of events; but this witness was, the judge would conclude, deeply unsatisfactory.

Although the identity of the two men on the scaffold has never been proven, there were eyewitness accounts – including that of a waterman, whose job it was to taxi people along the River Thames – that the man who swung the axe so expertly that day was the regular hangman, Richard Brandon. According to the waterman, Brandon was in his boat later that day, in a terrible state, his conscience in turmoil at the thought of having beheaded the Lord's anointed.

It seems unlikely that Peters, who was accustomed to chronic ill health, had absented himself from a moment of such unique magnitude as the death of the King. This was by some distance the most sensational event that this busy, fervent, involved preacher would ever witness – the thrilling collision of his devout religious theories with his radical political aims.

On a practical level Parliament needed the execution to be performed clinically, so that it did not descend into bloody chaos. The man most likely to deliver death in one clean stroke was Brandon, the seasoned axeman. But, even with added financial inducements, Brandon was conscience-stricken by the task in hand. What better comfort for a God-fearing executioner than to give him a preacher as a scaffold companion? Might not Peters have been the man to hold aloft Charles I's severed head?

Despite his role in the execution remaining unproven, there was no escape for Peters at trial. In his summing-up, the solicitor general said: 'What man could more contrive the death of the King than this miserable priest hath done? . . . For many come here, and say they did it "in the fear of the Lord" – and now you see who taught them.' After sentencing, Peters admitted that the testimony he had presented had not been as truthful as he would have liked: 'I will submit myself to God, and if I have spoken anything against the Gospel of Christ, I am heartily sorry.'[46] Regret was soon replaced by terror, as Peters plunged into a gloom of despair.

Peters had been tried alongside the lawyer John Cook, who had mounted a brilliant legal defence that led to awkward questions as to the validity, the procedure and the content of the charges against him.

Cook claimed he had only accepted the case against the late King because he needed the fee: he assured the court that he had no malice in helping the prosecution; rather his involvement was down to avarice. This raised the vital question as to whether a lawyer paid to represent a cause could be condemned for doing so, since he was performing his professional duties. With similar ingenuity Cook stated that he could not be guilty of contriving or plotting the death of the King, since he was only engaged as solicitor to the court the day after the charges against Charles I were proclaimed.

On a more mundane level he also pointed out that the charge against him had been drawn up in the name of 'I. Cooke', not 'J. Cooke'. This sort of administrative error could, Cook knew from experience, lead to cases being dismissed.

But none of Cook's clever points could penetrate the all-enveloping hostility of this Royalist court. They had come to condemn the prime movers in the death of the King, and the case's lead prosecutor could not be allowed to elude them. Additionally, Cook had been a legal pioneer who had tried to straighten out some of the abuses of his profession, and who had recommended that lawyers should donate one-tenth of their fees to the poor. Accordingly, as Ludlow noted, 'The malice towards this gentleman was very great from those of his own robe.'[47] He was not going to receive any favours from disgruntled colleagues.

Cook and Peters received their death sentence at the same time. They were manacled together and escorted back to prison.

Chapter 8

A Time to Die

How long, Lord, holy and true, will it be ere thou avenge our blood on those who dwell on the earth?
Lieutenant General Edmund Ludlow, regicide

The prisoners had been kept in solitary confinement when in the Tower of London, but in Newgate prison they were held together. Cook generously offered legal advice to those comrades whose trials were still to come, giving detailed guidance to Colonel Axtell in particular, who took numerous notes for his defence.

Cook also became the compassionate advocate for Peters in his vulnerable and miserable state, repeatedly seeking a stay of execution for the preacher so he could prepare himself for death while in better mental health. These requests failed, the Anglican priests who heard them seeing them as further evidence of Cook's wickedness: why else would he seek to help someone as evil as Hugh Peters?

Cook's wife, Mary, was staying with relatives of fellow regicide Edmund Ludlow. She had been so persistent in her attempts to visit her husband in the Tower that the gaolers there threatened to move him to Newgate before the transfer was due. Cook offered that he would not mind the move, since Newgate provided an equally direct gateway to heaven.

Now that Cook was committed to Newgate, as a man condemned, Mary was openly distraught at what was about to befall her husband: her worst fears had come true. He tried to lighten her load, telling her not to waste money on buying mourning clothes after he had gone, since he would by then be in the glory of heaven, resplendent in white – a reason for joy, not grief.

The evening that Cook and Peters were formally served with their death warrants, which stated that their executions would be performed the following day, they were removed from the other prisoners to spend their last night in Newgate's dungeon. There, Cook wrote a restrained but loving letter to his baby daughter, Freelove, addressing her tenderly as 'My Dear Sweet Child', and advising her of the virtues that must guide her life: humbleness, meekness, courtesy; and above all, the twin obediences – to God, and to her conscience. The doomed father presented himself to his daughter's memory as one that God had chosen to suffer in his cause, and who would therefore be assured of a place in heaven. There, he told her, he would be joyfully reunited with the son – Freelove's brother – who had predeceased him.

Cook slept briefly, before waking to the continuing burden of Hugh Peters, who remained trapped in profound despair, and who was now rambling incoherently after heavy, all-night, drinking.

That morning Cook was visited by his wife, who was weeping uncontrollably at the horror that awaited her husband, and at the imminence of their separation. 'My dear lamb,' he chided, lovingly, 'let us not part in a shower. Here, our comforts have been mixed with a chequer-work of troubles, but in heaven all tears shall be wiped from our eyes.'[1]

Cook and Peters were led to their separate sledges. There was a sharp pole on Cook's on which was fixed the severed head of Thomas Harrison, the soldier's lifeless face placed opposite that of the lawyer. It was a base form of intimidation, this macabre accompaniment on the men's journey from Newgate to Charing Cross, through animated, abusive crowds. When they arrived, the executioner beckoned for Peters but Cook, pointing to the wretched condition of his comrade, volunteered to die first. Peters was secured by the rails to Charing Cross, where he was evidently crazed with fear, swigging back alcohol, his eyes casting about wildly for a source of deliverance.

Peters was forced to watch his companion's final agonies, which were preceded by a very long speech from the lawyer. In this, Cook found time to make one last plea for the postponement of Peters's execution. 'Here is a poor brother coming,' said Cook, gesturing towards the tethered priest. 'I am afraid that he is not fit to die at this time. I could wish that his Majesty might show some mercy.'[2] Cook also asked that the King might spare the remainder of the condemned men, accepting his life in their place.

After praying, Cook was hanged to the point of unconsciousness, cut down, and castrated. Death was denied him at this point because many in the crowd insisted on some sport: seeing the pathetic, blathering state that Peters was in, a Colonel Turner shouted for him to be released from the railings, and be brought forward to get a close-up view of what was about to happen to him. 'Come, Mr Peters,' the hangman leered, rubbing his bloodied hands together, before wiping them on his apron, 'how do you like this work?'[3] Peters was held close as Cook was torn open, the crude, scorching instruments burrowing into his stomach to extract the meat of his bowels. These were then slowly roasted in front of his eyes.

It was a protracted and agonising end, the stench of cooked flesh hanging in the air. The executioner eventually confirmed that Cook was dead by holding his knife aloft, a dripping organ impaled on its point. His triumphant cry was, 'Behold, the heart of a traitor!' Cook's head was presented next.

It was now Peters's turn. As he approached the ladder, he saw a friend in the crowd and gave him a gold piece, asking him to take it to his daughter with a message that – by the time she received the coin – he would be with God. Peters was most likely in no state to give a speech. Royalist reports stated that he died 'sullenly and desperately'. Others recalled him mumbling a short prayer, before taking the drop from the ladder, apparently with a smile on his face. Ludlow – more charitable, and naturally eager to afford his friend a martyr's exit – wrote that Peters found his courage at the very end, and told the sheriff that his attempt to terrify him through Cook's appalling suffering had, rather, given him strength. 'Sir, you have slain here one of the servants of the Lord before mine eyes,' Ludlow recorded him as saying, 'and have made me behold it on purpose to terrify and discourage me, but God hath made it an ordinance to me for my strengthening and encouragement.'[4]

Whatever the truth about his demeanour, Peters was hanged, drawn and quartered that morning. His and Cook's heads were placed on poles overlooking the north end of Westminster Hall, where the trial of Charles I had taken place more than a decade earlier with the approval and collusion of both men.

The next day, 17 October, was the turn of Thomas Scott, Gregory Clements, Colonel Adrian Scroope and Colonel John Jones. Scott and Clements were sent ahead, to die together.

The four men had been allowed visits by their family and close friends the previous Sunday – an intolerably sad time, alleviated slightly by the condemned men's determination to raise the spirits of those they were leaving behind. Jones took one of Scroope's distraught daughters by the hand, and said, 'You are weeping for your father, but suppose your father were tomorrow to be King of France, and you to tarry a while behind, would you weep? Why, he is going to reign with the King of Kings in eternal glory.'[5]

Meanwhile Scott was bitterly regretting having returned from the Continent in the mistaken belief that he would receive the King's mercy. His provocative words in the Commons, about his pride at being one of those responsible for the King's death, were retold to the court by a succession of prominent witnesses. Scott countered repeatedly that what was said in Parliament was protected by privilege, so his words there could not be used against him. But the court ruled that treason was a crime of such enormity that it could have no hiding place, not even in the precious forum of the House of Commons.

Scott's fate had finally been sealed by the testimony of William

Lenthall, Charles I's Speaker of the House of Commons, who had clung on to office long after his master's execution. At the Restoration, Lenthall had been selected by the Commons as one of twenty men who were not to benefit from the Act of Indemnity: they would be punished, but their lives would not be at risk. It was only the pleading of General Monck (now the Duke of Albermarle) in the Lords that downgraded Lenthall's punishment to one of lifetime exclusion from public office.

Desperate to regain royal favour, Lenthall had sent £3,000 as a gift to the new King. The money was banked, but resulted in no encouraging signs from the Crown. Lenthall now offered himself as a witness against Scott, claiming to have heard his treasonous words, even though he had been forced to concede that from the Speaker's chair he had not been able to see who spoke them. As a reward for his useful testimony Lenthall was granted an audience with Charles II. But, to the delight of the many who held the former Speaker in contempt, on being presented to the King, Lenthall misjudged his courtly bow, lost his balance, and toppled over on to his back.

Lenthall retired from public life after this, retreating to his two Oxfordshire estates: Besselsleigh Manor and Burford Priory. There, with plenty of time to look back on his life, he became racked with guilt at his shortcomings, especially his words that had damned Scott. Lenthall died in November 1662, insisting that he was such a miserable, flawed human being that there should be no great memorial to him, such as might have been expected of one who had achieved great political office. Instead he ordered that a simple slab would serve, and he had two Latin words carved on it: *Vermis sum* – 'I am a worm'.

Lenthall would have learnt that Scott had gone to his death in an altogether more honourable manner, his absolute belief in his cause helping him to face his horrifying end with defiance. Sir Orlando Bridgeman had asked to come to visit him in Newgate prison – a request that held out the possibility of last-minute forgiveness. But Scott refused to give into this temptation: he knew that any mercy offered would be in return for his public condemnation of all he had stood for. 'Truly,' he said, 'I bless God I am at a point, I cannot, no, I cannot desert the cause.'[6]

Scott faltered, the night before his death, when the full reality of the ordeal struck home. However, he steeled himself through a night-time of prayer. When his wife, Alice, came in the morning with their daughter and two sons for the agonising farewells, they found him reconfirmed in defiant contempt for those who were ending his life. He made his family promise not to beg for his body to be spared the customary mutilations and indignities after death: his pitiless enemies could do what they wanted with his mortal remains, for his spirit would by then be in a far better place.

On reaching the place of execution, Scott mounted the ladder from which he would soon step away and be hanged. He began to address the crowd gathered to witness his end, with a prepared speech:

> Gentlemen, I stand here a spectacle to God, angels, and men: to God and angels, to whom I hope I shall speedily go, and now to you. I owe it to God, the nation, and myself, to say something concerning each. For myself, I think it may become me to tell you how and why I came hither, and something in general concerning my capacity. In the beginning of these troubles I was, as many others were, unsatisfied. I saw liberties and religion in the nation in great danger. To my best apprehension, I saw the approaching of popery in a great measure coming in upon us. I saw—

The sheriff interrupted at this point, refusing to continue justify his actions, or those of the men who had taken up arms against the Crown eighteen years earlier. If Scott wanted to turn to his prayers, the sheriff explained, that would be in order – but this dangerous talk must stop.

Scott promised not to reproach anyone, if allowed to carry on with his intended speech. But the sheriff was adamant: 'Sir,' he said, 'you have but a little time, therefore spend that little time in prayer.'

Scott, a man who was used to having his say, had put together words that were of the utmost importance to him, so he persisted: 'I shall speak—'

The sheriff cut in again, saying he would only allow the condemned man to pray.

'It may become me to give an account of myself,' continued Scott, 'because—'

But the sheriff, clearly under orders to put a stop to such inflammatory speeches, that were received with sympathy and fascination by the many onlookers, was adamant: 'It doth not become you to speak any such thing here,' he directed, 'therefore I beseech you betake yourself to prayer.' Then he repeated his earlier advice: 'It's but a little time you have to live, you know that is the most needful thing.'

The exchanges between the two men became shorter and sharper. Scott insisted he wanted to explain why and how he had come to this place of execution. Another voice shouted out from the crowd: 'Everybody knows that!'

Scott, still astonished that he was being denied what he viewed as his native right, said with indignation, 'It's hard [that] an Englishman may not have liberty to speak.'

But there was no shaming the determined official. 'I cannot,' he explained, with finality, 'suffer you to speak any such thing.'

Scott reacted with scorn: 'I shall say no more but this, that it is a very mean and bad cause that cannot bear the words of a dying man; nor hath it been ordinarily denied to persons in my condition.'

When Scott had outwardly accepted that he was to be denied his final words, he lay down in the dust and prayed to God, exalting him while acknowledging his own sins. He managed to weave in a political subtext to these prayers, stating that he felt strong because God had promised him a place among the saints and angels, for the Lord approved of his stance. Scott emphasised to the watching crowd that his was 'A cause not to be repented of, I say not to be repented of.'[7]

At this, the sheriff stepped in, saying that this was not a prayer but a speech, and it must stop. Scott's words continued, in a subtler vein, but he still managed to insinuate his real thoughts: he said he hoped that all kingdoms would unite under the Lord, that the blood shed in the cause of civil and religious liberty should not be forgotten, and that his enemies would be shown the error of their ways. Then, he was put to death.

Gregory Clements climbed the ladder now. Originally, in court, he had declared himself not guilty. But his relatives had urged him to change his plea to guilty, in an attempt to preserve his £40,000 fortune for their benefit once he was gone; if he had persisted in claiming his innocence, but had then been found guilty, he would have surely forfeited his estate, as well as his life. So he had accepted his fate, the final transaction of this most successful of merchants being his life, as payment for his family's continued worldly comfort. Perhaps out of disillusionment at his relatives' greed, he remained quiet in the days before his death, and offered few words in the moments before his execution.

The hurdle that had carried Scott and Clements to Charing Cross now returned to collect the condemned colonels, Scroope and Jones, whom Ludlow described affectionately as 'two comely ancient gentlemen'.[8] When Scroope had been sentenced, one of his children reportedly clung to him, sobbing loudly. 'Peace child,' he soothed, 'Peace – be still – not a word . . . Who would be troubled thus to die, for can anyone have greater honour than to have his soul carried to Heaven upon the wings of the prayers of so many Saints?'[9] Scroope's spirit was so at peace that he spent the time between the sledge conveying Scott and Clements to their deaths, and its return for him and Jones, fast asleep. He snored loudly. A friend woke him to say it was time to go, then hugged him tight, and asked him how he felt. 'Very well,' he replied, 'I thank God never better in all my life. And now,' he continued, 'I will wash my hands in innocency, and so will I compass thine altar, O Lord.'[10]

His final speech was a rousing glorification of God, and a public forgiveness of all his enemies – although he did refer to one in particular, 'through whose means I was brought hither to suffer'.

Some in the crowd knew this to be Major General Richard Browne, one of Parliament's busier and more successful generals of the First Civil War, who had been loathed by Royalists: they looked down on him as 'the faggot man' because his wealth came from trading timber and coal. However, in the tug-of-war over the late King in the late 1640s, Browne had sided with the Presbyterians in Parliament against the army and the Puritans. After Pride's Purge, Browne's reward for this stance had been five years' harsh imprisonment. The Restoration had brought about Browne's resurgence. He was elected lord mayor of London in the month of the regicides' trials, and had appeared as a witness against some of them. Browne had betrayed to the court Scroope's private but fatal views on Charles I's execution: the colonel had justified it, and declined to see it as murder. This had seen Scroope transferred from the list of those covered by the Act of Indemnity, to that of the condemned.

During his final moments, Scroope clearly had his nemesis very much in mind, but preferred to leave him anonymous. 'I say once more,' Scroope continued, 'the Lord forgive him; I shall not name him, for I came not here to reflect on any man's person.'[11]

In reference to the cruel reversal that had seen his initial penalty – the payment of a fine equivalent to one year's rent from his estate – replaced by the imminent agony of a barbaric death, Scroope spoke passionately about the purity of God's justice, contrasting it wistfully with the sad fallibility of the judgment of Man. Scroope had shown the same concern during his trial, which he had faced unprepared, after six weeks' close imprisonment. He had attempted to justify his conduct then, reminding the court that he had not been a Member of Parliament, but rather part of a commission summoned by Parliament, a body that he had not felt able to disobey since it was at that point 'accounted the supreme authority of the nation'. This was a point absolutely rejected by the court.

Scroope had been provoked to utter the great unspoken truth, under which the regicides' trial was conducted. Looking round at the many former Parliamentarians sitting in judgment, he offered, 'I could say, but I think it doth not become me to say so, that I see a great many faces at this time that were misled as well as myself; but that I will not insist upon.'[12]

It was a point that he had expanded upon, after a witness called Kirke confirmed to the court that he had been surprised to see Scroope sitting as one of the commissioners in the High Court of Justice on the day of sentencing. Addressing the Lord Chief Baron, Scroope had said, 'In all humbleness I do speak it to your Lordships, that your Lordships will please to consider that if he [Kirke] had any employment in that business himself, how fit a witness he is against me?' The judge replied, 'Much fitter.'

Accepting how the cards were stacked against him, Scroope replied with a shrug, 'If it be so, I have done.'[13] He maintained that, if he was guilty of anything, it was an error of judgment, not malice.

At the conclusion of his case, the Lord Chief Baron turned to the jury and conceded: 'Mr Scroope, to give him his right, was not a person as some of the rest; but he was unhappily engaged in that bloody business, I hope mistakenly, but when it comes to so high a crime as this, men must not excuse themselves by ignorance, or misguided conscience.'[14] The jury agreed, and declared Scroope's guilt.

In his final speech, from the executioner's ladder, Adrian Scroope claimed no great compliment should be paid to him, other than he hoped that he would be remembered as 'a tender-hearted father'. His was another valiant death that added lustre to the Good Old Cause of Parliament, and brought further quiet consternation to the avenging Royalists. Lucy Hutchinson noted that the colonel 'had the honour to die a noble martyr'.[15]

The same description applied to Jones, who had remained remarkably accepting of his fate ever since his gentle arrest in Finsbury. He greeted the sight of the sledge that was to pull him to his death with a joke: 'It is like Elijah's fiery chariot – only it goes through Fleet Street!'[16] He told those who loved him not to mourn, but to take this opportunity to 'take off your mind from me, and fix it immovably upon your eternal relation with the Lord Jesus Christ, in whose glorious and blessed presence we shall meet ere long, to our eternal rejoicing'.[17] By the time that Jones was put to death, the executioner was, according to eyewitnesses, so sated with blood that he stood down, allowing his apprentice to castrate, gut, behead and quarter the old colonel.

Jones met his death with such courage and faith that minor miracles were believed to have occurred that day in his honour: among them, despite it being autumn, a crab apple tree was said to have come into bloom on his family's estate in Merioneth. (These lands were now confiscated by the King and his brother, the Duke of York.)

It was a bloody week. Friday 19 October saw the end of two army officers intricately involved in Charles I's trial and execution. Colonel Daniel Axtell and Colonel Francis Hacker had been found guilty of 'imagining and compassing' the death of the late King. Axtell had been tricked into arrest in July, when a Royalist posing as a potential purchaser of some of the colonel's property requested a meeting with him. There, he revealed his true purpose, taking Axtell prisoner, 'who being thus betrayed into the hands of this bloody enemy, who had creatures enough in both houses to gratify his lust', according to a contemporary, 'he procured them to except [Axtell] out of the Act of indemnity; by which means . . . he came to be thus inhumanely and cruelly treated'.[18]

Axtell offered the legal defence proposed to him in Newgate prison by John Cook. 'May it please your Lordships,' he said, 'my case differs from the rest of the Gentlemen.'[19] Axtell stated that, whereas the others were being tried for their actions, he was only accused of using words against the late King. In any case, he claimed to have acted under the authority of Parliament, insisting that, 'if the House of Commons who are the representatives of the whole nation, may be guilty of treason, it will follow that all the people of England, who chose them, are guilty also, and then where will a jury be found to try this cause?'[20] The colonel presented himself as a simple soldier, who had merely obeyed the orders of his superiors: his presence in Westminster Hall had not been voluntary, he pointed out, but by command. If that obedience to Parliament made him guilty of anything, he maintained, then similarly culpable was the Earl of Manchester, and several of the other Parliamentary military leaders now sitting in judgment of this case.

This was an embarrassing line for many to hear. The court rejected such a defence out of hand. Axtell was hated by the Royalists, in particular for his cold-blooded murder of prisoners of war during Cromwell's Irish campaigns, and they wanted him dead.

Axtell was condemned for whipping up the soldiers in Westminster Hall, so that they influenced proceedings by calling for 'Justice!' and then 'Execution!'. He was also convicted for being in charge of the soldiers who oversaw the King's beheading. Testimony given by Colonel Hercules Huncks, who had rejected Cromwell's command to sign the order for executing Charles, proved to be devastating. (Huncks, who had been well known as a passionate supporter of Parliament's cause, would be pardoned three months later for having given his evidence.) There was the added problem for Axtell that Huncks had suffered no harm for refusing to comply with his orders, which undermined Axtell's claim that disobedience would have inevitably resulted in his being shot.

Colonel Hacker must have felt the least fortunate of all those sentenced to death. As Lucy Hutchinson wrote, 'Poor Mrs Hacker, thinking to save her husband, had brought up the warrant for execution, with all their hands and seals.'[21] It was damning enough evidence to allow the court's Serjeant Keeling to claim, in a vivid image of guilt, that Hacker 'had the axe in his hands'.[22]

Hacker had admitted his role in keeping Charles guarded prior to his execution. Under questioning he was obliged to go further, conceding that he had also marched the King to the scaffold, and signed the order to the executioner to carry out his duties. Sir Orlando Bridgeman thought Hacker an especially blameworthy defendant. 'Either he is guilty of compassing the death of the King, or no man can be said to be guilty,'[23] he directed. The jury had no need to retire, instead forming a whispering huddle in court, before the foreman swiftly returned the guilty verdict.

Axtell was in his cell when he heard Scott, Clements, Scroope and Jones being led to their execution sledges. He was barred from saying farewell in person to the quartet, so shouted out their names, with blessings: 'The Lord go with you! The angel of his presence stand by you!'[24] Axtell was pleased to hear later that the four had died 'cheerfully'. He asked how the executions had been performed. When told from a ladder, he seemed content, choosing to see this as a manifestation of the Old Testament tale of Jacob's ladder.

Axtell's daughter came to visit her father, bringing questions from friends who remained troubled by his bloody record in Ireland. 'I can say with all humility that God did use me as an instrument in my place for the suppressing [of] the bloody enemy,' he said, in justification; 'And when I considered their cruelty in murdering so many thousand Protestants and innocent souls, that word was much upon my heart, "Give her blood to drink for she is worthy." And sometimes we neither gave nor took quarter, though preservation might have said, "Give that which ye might expect to have."'[25]

Axtell and Hacker prayed together, attended by preachers, on the morning of their deaths. They were taken on a single sledge three miles west of the City, to Tyburn: the inhabitants of Charing Cross had complained about the foul stench of burning bowels during the earlier executions, prompting this return to the traditional site of London's executions. At Tyburn, the condemned mounted the executioner's cart. It was noted how quiet and respectful the crowd was: Ludlow learnt that when two present shouted out, 'Hang them, hang them, rogues, traitors, murderers! Hangman, draw away the cart!', one who was more in tune with the general mood that day countered, 'Gentlemen, this is not civil. The Sheriff knows what he hath to do.'[26]

Axtell spoke to a muted audience. During his speech, which lasted several minutes, he earned a sharp reprimand from the sheriff after saying, 'I was fully convinced in my conscience of the justness of the war, and thereupon engaged in the Parliament's service, which as I did and do believe was the cause of the Lord. And I adventured my life for it, and now die for it.'[27]

Hacker, a man of few words, read out a carefully written statement in which he also expressed his pride at having served the cause
of Parliament. 'And as for that for which I am condemned, I do
freely forgive both judges, jury and witnesses, yea all others,' he
continued. 'And I thank the Lord to whom I am now going, at
whose tribunal I must render an account, I have nothing [that] lies
upon my conscience as guilt, as to that for which I am condemned,
and do not doubt but to have the sentence reversed.' He urged his
friends to pray, 'that I may have a sweet passage from this mortal
life to that which is immortal'.[28] Hacker then asked that Axtell pray
aloud for both of them, since he had no pretences as an orator.

When he had finished, Axtell thanked the sheriff for allowing
him to speak. He then turned to his fellow sufferer, and the two
colonels embraced. Their caps were pulled over their eyes and
Axtell, expecting the cart to be pulled away from beneath them,
shouted, 'Lord Jesus, receive my spirit!' But the cart failed to budge.
Axtell then implored, 'Into thy hands, O Father, I commend my
spirit!' Again, the cart did not move. The carman, whose duty it
was to draw the cart away, was refusing any part in the death of the
two men. The hangman then jumped down, and led the horse
forward. Axtell gave a third cry to God, before the drop.

While Axtell was hanged, drawn and quartered, Hacker was, 'by
his Majesty's great favour', simply hanged, then, as John Evelyn
noted, 'given entire to his friends, and buried'.[29] This may have been
thanks to Monck's unease at having promised Hacker his safety,
before having him seized and sent to the Tower.

John Evelyn had been travelling frequently to and from London
during the week of these executions, the electrifying buzz
surrounding such public sufferings matched by the mundaneness of
the reason for being in town: he was there to be sworn in as
Commissioner of Sewers. On 17 October he recorded in his diary:

This day were executed those murderous Traitors at Charing Cross,
in sight of the place where they put to death their natural Prince, &
in the presence of the King his son, whom they also sought to kill:

taken in the trap they laid for others. The Traitors executed were
Scott, Scroope, Cook, Jones. I saw not their execution, but met their
quarters mangled and cut and reeking as they were brought from the
Gallows in baskets on the hurdle: O miraculous providence of God;
Three days before suffered Axtel, Carew, Clements, Hacker, Hewson
and Peters for reward for their iniquity.[30]

Evelyn's dates were wrong. Less surprisingly, so was his identification of some of the chopped-up limbs and torsos in the baskets:
indeed, Colonel Hewson had not been killed, having escaped to the
Continent. But the pungent odour of the freshly butchered corpses
was real, and the Royalist delight at this rich harvest of revenge was
truer still. There had been around sixty regicides alive at the Restoration. In just a few days, ten of these had been dispatched. The
remaining fifty were acutely aware that the fierce appetite for retribution was roaring still, and that their lives were in the gravest of
danger.

Chapter 9

Surrender or Else . . .

Upon His Majesty's gracious declaration from Breda, and the
votes of Parliament, and His Majesty's proclamation, published
by the advice of the Lords and Commons then assembled in
Parliament, they did render themselves, being advised that they
should thereby secure their lives; and humbly craved the benefit
thereof, and the mercy of the Houses, and their mediation to His
Majesty in their behalves.

'Contention of the Regicides who came in upon the
Proclamation of Charles II'

Edmund Ludlow had been anxious about what the return of the
Stuarts might entail, long before the Restoration transpired.
He realised that vengeance would be an integral part of the process,
when and if the cause fell, and he assumed that he would be among
the most vulnerable to such a sea change. Ludlow was an extremely
important figure in the cause of Parliament: politically, he was a
radical republican who had been a prime mover behind Charles I's
trial; militarily, he was a heavyweight in the New Model Army,
serving lately as a lieutenant general of cavalry. Of all the surviving
regicides he was the most capable of successfully leading armed
resistance against the new order.

When it had become clear that the dead King's son would be
gifted the vacant crown, Ludlow had hoped that the extent of royal
retribution might be limited to token action against the fallen

figureheads of republicanism. In the spring of 1660 this had seemed possible, when the talk was of Cromwell and Bradshaw being the posthumous recipients of revenge. Soon afterwards there had been rumours of a plan for one or two of the surviving judges to be made examples of: the new King was concerned that to do nothing against those who had, so outrageously, put his father to death would mark him from the outset as a weak ruler.

Ludlow was wily and well connected. He had friends in the Royalist camp. He also had, in his loyal Welsh wife, a willing inter-mediary, eager to protect her husband. Elizabeth Ludlow was happy to talk to whoever might act as political barometers in the aftermath of the Restoration – this unexpected storm that had hurled republicanism onto the rocks. Meanwhile Ludlow quickly assumed a low profile; unseen, he watched his triumphant enemies intently, the better to fathom their purpose. In May, out of the windows of his home in Holborn he had viewed, with disgust, the new King's triumphant return to London. From his lonely vantage point he had become a disbelieving eyewitness to the wave of Royalist sycophancy that seemed to have engulfed all, including many who had, he knew, until recently spoken of 'Charles Stuart' with dismissive contempt.

It sickened the lieutenant general to see the men of his once committed and proud cavalry squadrons riding in joyful, servile escort to the resurrected Stuarts. He recalled how these units had been raised to fight for the civil rights and religious beliefs that the new King's father was seen to imperil. Ludlow wrote with sad acceptance that these troops had 'been corrupted under the tyranny of Cromwell, and kept up as a standing force against the people', so 'they had forgotten their first engagements, and were become as mercenary as other troops are accustomed to be'.[1]

Ludlow resolved never to join in this betrayal of the cause to which he remained proudly devoted. Earlier that month he had made a dangerous and deliberate stand, refusing to have anything to do with the appointment of the commissioners sent by Parliament to acknowledge the exiled Prince of Wales as the new monarch. His election as an MP was annulled soon afterwards: none of the late King's judges were to be allowed to continue in public office. Feeling the net closing in on him, Ludlow felt a responsibility to avoid punishment, not just out of self-preservation, but also in the hope that he could be useful to the cause, when it rose again.

Ludlow's excellent contacts warned him that he was being considered for one of the quartet of vacant names in the Bill of Indemnity that had demanded the death of seven regicides. He knew he had enemies, and that they would be happy to see him suffer. He learnt that one of these had written to General Monck, falsely claiming that Ludlow had led two or three hundred men into hiding, planning to rise up against the new order when the time was right. It seemed most likely that, on the back of this misinformation, Ludlow would become one of the fated seven. But, out of the blue, Parliament was suddenly adjourned: this was the first of several lucky breaks that came his way.

A Royalist acquaintance indebted to Ludlow used this interlude to coordinate a group of sympathisers in the Commons, who would do all they could to block Ludlow's condemnation. This ally sent Ludlow a message through his sister-in-law: if this plan was to have a chance of success, Ludlow must immediately confirm that he was no longer in armed resistance to the Crown. The sister-in-law took it upon herself to offer that reassurance there and then, without the delay of referring back to Ludlow.

Three more names – Jones, Holland and Scott – were added by the Commons to the list of the doomed. Thomas Skipwith, the MP for Grantham, proposed that the seventh should be Ludlow; however nobody seconded him. It was at this point that the reviled Colonel John Barkstead was suggested and promptly included. Oliver Cromwell had once complimented Barkstead with the words that: 'There never was any design on foot but we could hear of it out of the Tower.'[2] For the new regime it was time for vengeance against one of the Lord Protector's trusty henchmen. Ludlow's relief at his exclusion from the list of seven was short-lived as calls for more wide-ranging vengeance grew in the heady days of resurrected Royalism. Soon Parliament was insisting that every one of the late King's judges hand themselves in within fourteen days, or lose their lives and possessions. Ludlow learnt of this deeply troubling development first hand: he heard the news being proclaimed to the listening crowds in the street outside his quarters. He carefully monitored the effect of this decree, weighing up whether to follow the surrender of twenty-two of his colleagues in mid- to late June, or to join the dash for seeming safety overseas that required separation from loved ones and property.

Ludlow hung back from making the decision. He asked his friends and relations what they thought he should do. Several thought surrender the safer course; others refused to give any opinion on a question that involved his life or death, but they suggested caution. There was one contact, unnamed but well informed, who firmly advised that surrender should not be contemplated: it was too dangerous an option, he insisted, given the growing desire in Charles II's court for extensive retribution.

Ludlow realised that he would need to tidy up his business affairs, whether he chose to flee or not: if he was to run, he would need funds; if he was to surrender, he would have to account for his estate as a prelude to the inevitable financial penalty. A straightening out of his finances would not be possible if he was in hiding. He therefore decided to promise to hand himself in.

At the same time Ludlow prepared a written defence of his past deeds. He sent its completed draft to Arthur Annesley, a leading MP, for his comments. Having read it, Annesley advised Elizabeth Ludlow that it did not go far enough: it did not admit guilt. 'My wife told him,' recorded the lieutenant general, 'that what was contained in that paper was as much as my conscience would give me leave to say.'[3] In that case, Annesley cautioned, it would be better to say nothing: not to admit guilt would be seen as seeking to justify the unjustifiable. This, in turn, would inflame the vengeful.

Ludlow looked to others for advice. His military service had brought him into conflict with James Butler, then the Marquess of Ormonde, the Royalist leader in Ireland whose inadequate defences had been no match for Cromwell a decade earlier. Over time, Ormonde and Ludlow had developed a mutual respect, which the Parliamentarian hoped to exploit now. Ormonde had endured years of hard exile with the Prince of Wales on the Continent prior to the Restoration. His rewards, now Charles was King, included a dukedom and the office of Lord High Steward of England.

Ludlow sent his wife to ask Ormonde what his best course of action would be. 'He received her with great civilities,' Ludlow recorded, 'and made her large promises, pressing her with great importunity to acquaint him, if I were in England.'[4] Elizabeth Ludlow, sensing her host was looking to secure her husband rather than save him, refused to answer. She concluded that Ormonde was not to be trusted.

At this stage Ludlow felt more inclined to surrender than not. But the knowledgeable friend who had insisted that real peril awaited those who handed themselves in now reiterated his advice. He warned that the mood in the Lords was more severe than in the Commons: there was an appetite in the Upper House for many more men to suffer. This flew in the face of advice that Ludlow's wife was receiving elsewhere: Sir Harbottle Grimston, Speaker of the House of Commons, told Elizabeth he felt certain that none would be held to account beyond those already named. If Parliament went back on its word on such a point, he said, 'it would be the most horrid thing in the world'.[5] Grimston promised to sound out other important members, and soon reported back that these men shared his optimism. The Speaker repeated his recommendation to Elizabeth that Ludlow hand himself in during what remained of the window of opportunity offered by the proclamation. He passed her a letter that guaranteed Ludlow's safety, as he made his way to surrender.

After bringing the majority of his affairs up to date, Ludlow proceeded to the Speaker's Chamber to hand himself in. Finding Grimston absent, Ludlow went with James Herbert, an MP in the new Parliament who was a friend, to turn himself over to the serjeant-at-arms. There, Herbert pledged a bond of £3,000 to guarantee Ludlow's appearance in front of the authorities, when required. Eager to free Herbert from this potentially ruinous commitment, Ludlow arranged for his bond to be substituted with one made by four others. These were men who he knew could never be successfully pursued for debt: a penniless Royalist uncle; a colonel – recently knighted by the new King – whose apparent fortune was in reality owned by his wife; another acquaintance, who was thought rich, but who had secretly fallen on hard times; and his tailor. Ludlow rewarded the first two of the four with a little, welcome, cash. To all appearances the lieutenant general had obeyed the royal proclamation, but in truth he had pulled off a sleight of hand: his finances were in good order, while his options remained open.

Ludlow was unable to rest. He heard persistent rumours that Monck and his wife, the Duchess of Albermarle (to whom Ludlow referred as 'the dirty duchess', and whom he viewed as the epitome of self-serving greed), were adamant that he be added to the register of the doomed. Monck was said to have warned Charles II that Edmund Ludlow was the most dangerous man in the land: as such, he must not be allowed to remain at large.

Of even greater concern to Ludlow was word secretly sent to him by Secretary of State Sir William Morice, an academic cousin of Monck's, whose promotion to a position of great power after the Restoration had surprised many. Morice had been one of the members excluded from the Commons by Pride's Purge. He and Ludlow had since found common ground in their resistance to Oliver Cromwell's rule. Believing the lieutenant general to be still in hiding, he told a mutual friend to advise Ludlow to keep up his guard, and at all costs to remain at large – for, if captured, he would be a dead man.

It was while finalising his financial affairs that Ludlow received a fresh alarm. Sir Charles Coote, who had tricked Chief Justice John Cook into capture in Ireland, now refused to comply with requests from Ludlow's brother to deliver up stock that belonged to the lieutenant general. Eager to be rid of his tiresome creditor, Coote wrote a letter to the King, blackening Ludlow's name. Coote claimed that, at a dinner at Ludlow's home, his host had claimed to be the man who had forced Cromwell to proceed to Charles I's execution. Coote told the King that, if he needed confirmation that this conversation had taken place, he should check with another present, Lord Broghill. But Broghill refused to corroborate Coote's story, saying it was ungentlemanly 'to remember any thing to the prejudice of a gentleman who had spoken freely at his own table'.[6]

Ludlow now warned the four men who had stood bail for him that if he felt his life in any greater danger than it already was, he would be forced to flee. While Parliament was sitting, when any changes to the Bill of Indemnity could be sudden and fatal, Ludlow placed armed guards on each of the gates to his home – though he rarely stayed there, preferring to lie up at a secret address. Meanwhile he took daily soundings from his friends in the Commons as to which way the chill wind of revenge was blowing.

The Bill of Indemnity picked up renewed energy when it reached the Lords. Their lordships were keen to hear from Royalists whose relatives had been executed under the Commonwealth. They were particularly moved by the words of two widows: one had been married to Charles I's chaplain, Dr Hewett, who had been beheaded for treason in 1658; the other was Arundel Penruddock, whose husband had lost his head following a failed uprising in 1655. There were so many other Royalists seeking satisfaction for the loss of loved ones that a committee had to be appointed to sift through their applications. The Lords also wanted to avenge those of their number who had been tried and executed during the previous decade and a half – especially those dispatched after the Second Civil War, in the wake of the King's death. They allowed the next of kin of each of those slain lords to select one judge from their relatives' trial: that man would atone for his actions with his life.

Ludlow's friends became increasingly shrill in their advice to him. Sir John Winter, private secretary to Charles I's widow, Henrietta Maria, warned him that there was now a move to exclude *all* the King's judges from the benefit of the Bill of Indemnity. Indeed, Winter cautioned, Ludlow had become a particular figure of hatred in royal circles, since Monck had shared with the King his belief that Ludlow's military power in Ireland had threatened the viability of the Restoration.

It was while digesting this latest warning that Ludlow learnt with bemused disbelief that two of his fellow regicides were to be excused their part in Charles I's trial and execution. He accepted with sadness that it was Colonel Ingoldsby's treacherous capture of Major General Lambert (in the stand that Ludlow had been too slow, through caution, to join) that had secured his pardon. Ludlow was more bewildered by Colonel Hutchinson's forgiveness, since Ludlow clearly remembered that Hutchinson 'had been as zealous against the late King, at the time of his trial, as any other of his judges'.[7] Ludlow suspected that, in addition to his timely apologies and justifications in the Commons, Hutchinson must have come to some secret agreement with Monck; otherwise, his being spared was impossible to comprehend.

During the summer of 1660, while factions in the Lords and the Commons traded favours, adding and subtracting names from the list of the condemned, Ludlow wrote a robust, anonymous, paper confirming the rights to be enjoyed by those – such as himself – who had surrendered under the terms of the proclamation. Among the points he made was a rejection of the Commons's ability to increase the number of those to suffer beyond the agreed and advertised seven. Ludlow asked Henry Marten to read through his points and comment on them as a lawyer. Marten advised that the paper, as constructed, would be deemed libellous: rather than being presented as factual, he suggested that it would be preferable if Ludlow submitted his case in the form of a personal petition. This was too dangerous a course for Ludlow to contemplate.

As the summer passed, the eagerness of the regicides to know their fate was matched by the king's growing impatience at the lack of progress in holding his father's killers to account. When senior courtiers failed to force the Lords to a conclusion, Charles II appeared in the House to address its members in person. He reminded his audience that those who had judged his father 'were guilty of such a crime, that they could not pardon themselves, much less expect it from others'.[8] To Ludlow such regal interference was an outrageous violation of parliamentary privilege. It also under-lined the King's determination to see all the regicides brought to punishment. 'Finding my friends to grow every day more appre-hensive of the dangers that threatened me,' Ludlow wrote, 'I removed from my house; and on this occasion received a signal testimony of the friendship of Chief Justice Coke [John Cook], who being little solicitous for himself, solemnly protested in a message he sent me, that if he were in no hazard on this occasion, he would willingly lay down his life to secure mine, who he was pleased to say, might be more useful to the public, than he could hope to be.'[9]

The seizure and imprisonment in the Tower of various Scottish and Irish noblemen who had come to London to pay homage to the new King added to Ludlow's fears. The diplomatic prince, who had soothed his subjects with overtures of harmony from Breda, was revealing himself to be a man of vengeance. He was now safely installed on the throne, with members of the House of Lords baying for regicide blood. The terms and spirit of the original proclama-tion, that offered two weeks in which to surrender without fear of a loss of life, continued to be undermined. The Earl of South-ampton, appalled at this injustice, proposed that it was only fair to give those who had, in good faith, handed themselves in, a fresh two weeks in which they could flee. This suggestion was overruled by Sir Heneage Finch.

Sir John Bourchier, a Puritan who had attended all four days of Charles I's trial and then signed the death warrant, was one of those who had submitted to the proclamation in the permitted timeframe. The sixty-five-year-old was suffering from plummeting health, and so was allowed to be looked after at the home of one of his daugh-ters. His family realised that death was imminent. They were fearful that if he died while still accused of high treason, all of his property would be liable to confiscation. They encouraged him to repent publicly for his actions, in the hope that forgiveness might secure his estate for them.

For several days Bourchier sat in a chair, his life ebbing away. Suddenly, he forced himself to his feet and gave a clear and determined justification of the moment that would define his life: 'I tell you it was a just act! God and all good men will own it.'[10] Then he slumped back, wearied by his defiant last words: soon afterwards he died.

Meanwhile Ludlow decided to absent himself from Westminster. He moved down the Thames to Richmond, where he enjoyed the summer days walking in the deer park – grounds created a quarter of a century earlier by Charles I, the man he had helped send to his death. While in Richmond he heard of the frantic horse-trading in Westminster, as the Bill of Indemnity at last neared its completion. Charles II's advisers were increasing pressure on the Commons to commit to punishing all the late King's judges. Ludlow heard that the chancellor, Lord Clarendon, had offered that those named by the Lords would only be punished if a later Act of Parliament deemed it necessary. The chancellor meanwhile insisted that any of Charles I's judges who had surrendered, then went back on their word would not be considered for clemency – 'which last clause,' Ludlow wrote, 'I took to be particularly levell'd at me, having been informed that the serjeant's deputy, attended with soldiers, had very lately searched my house.'[11]

The Commons buckled, agreeing to hand over to the Lieutenant of the Tower of London all who had yielded in good faith to the House's serjeant-at-arms. From being men on bail, sure of their lives, the surrendered men now found themselves confined to the nation's most dreaded prison, from where traitors rarely emerged alive.

Ludlow's failure to appear at this point meant he could now be added to the list of those who would answer for their crimes with their life. However, the authorities had no idea where he was. They decided to lure him in rather than frighten him off, and claimed they would carefully examine the terms of his bail before acting against him. In the meantime, they said he would be best served by handing himself in.

Elizabeth Ludlow revisited Grimston to gauge afresh what, now, was the best way ahead for her husband. The Speaker repeated his earlier advice that Ludlow must surrender. Mrs Ludlow countered that she thought this a very dangerous course, given the extent to which the Commons had already yielded to royal pressure. Surely yet more concessions were likely to follow? And, she went on, what was to stop the current House of Commons from being replaced by another, whose members might vote through even stricter retribution against the Stuarts' historic foes? 'The Speaker seemed much offended with this discourse,' Ludlow wrote, 'and going down the stairs with her, told her he would wash his hands of my blood, by assuring her, that if I would surrender myself, my life would be as safe as his own; but if I refused to harken to his advice, and should happen to be seized, I was likely to be the first man they would execute, and she to be left the poorest widow in England.'[12]

But the advice Ludlow was receiving from other more trusted parts of the enemy camp was consistent: his life was in peril. After weeks of uncertainty, he now knew it was time to escape.

Ludlow sent a letter explaining his decision to Speaker Grimston, and 'told him that he had withdrawn himself, not out of distaste to the House of Commons upon whose words he had rendered himself', reported Sir Thomas Gower, a Royalist who had raised a regiment for Charles I during the Civil War, 'but that he saw blood was thirsted for by those, who hardly ever had attempted to draw any in either sort, and that [they] attempted to invade the liberties of the Commons of England, of which he hoped they would be careful; that whenever the House of Commons signified their pleasure, and that they would maintain what they had promised, upon notice left at a place he named, he would readily return to the place from whence he left.'[13]

Ludlow let his family and closest friends know his decision. He told them he would be using his mother's maiden name as an alias; when they heard from him next it would be as 'Edmund Phillips'. Wearing a new beard as a disguise, he said his goodbyes, unaware of when or if he would see them again. With evening descending, he was taken by coach through James's Fields (which would soon be built on, and become St James's Square), and into the City, passing over London Bridge. At St George's Church, Southwark, he was met by a guide leading a spare horse. The two men then headed south, towards the coast, travelling by lesser roads, avoiding towns, and steering clear of places where soldiers might be: the military would be looking out for fleeing regicides, and many of them would know the distinguished lieutenant general by sight.

The fugitive and his guide rode through the night, safely reaching the Sussex town of Lewes by daybreak. There Ludlow boarded a shallop, a small covered boat, but sea swell forced a switch to another craft until conditions improved. (This second vessel had a recent history that must have encouraged Ludlow, for he learnt that it had already successfully spirited away another leading Parliamentarian, Oliver Cromwell's heir, Richard.) The squall was so strong that it made this new vessel run aground on the sand. It was now that a Royalist search party appeared. They inspected the covered boat, but decided against approaching the one beached on the sandbank, feeling sure that a boat in such a condition must be empty.

After a day and a night waiting for the storm to pass, Ludlow was able to slip out of English waters towards the French port of Dieppe. The crew was evidently unaware of the identity of its fine-looking passenger: Ludlow described in his memoirs a conversation he had with the ship's master, who had worked out of Irish ports during the years of Ludlow's military command there. The master asked the bearded traveller of news from London: did he happen to know if General Ludlow was one of the judges taken prisoner recently? Ludlow coolly replied that he had not heard of any such thing.[14]

At Dieppe, Ludlow went to the home of Madame de Caux, a sympathiser who welcomed him with a choice of staying with her in town, or moving to her house in the country. Worried that one of the many Irishmen he had seen in the port might recognise him, Ludlow opted to move inland. He was keen to get some country air, and even keener to avoid the fate of Isaac Dorislaus.

After a few days in this new hideout, Madame de Caux forwarded to Ludlow letters received from England. One of these contained a written proclamation from Whitehall, dated 1 September 1660, which recalled the regicides' obligation to surrender during the two-week window in June earlier that year, 'and whereas Edmund Ludlow, Esq., being one of the persons therein named, did there-upon render himself', it announced, 'nevertheless hath since escaped from out the custody of the serjeant-at-arms attending on the House of Commons, and is fled, or doth obscure himself to evade the justice of a legal trial'.[15] The decree warned that nobody must assist Ludlow in any way; rather, they were to apprehend him. The reward for success in this was a temptingly generous £300, the equivalent of almost twenty years' wages for the average farm labourer.

Ludlow made plans to head for Geneva, a city with a long history of tolerance and where many British religious exiles had led un-troubled lives for well over a century. Ludlow hoped to find himself among like-minded compatriots, for he knew several of the other regicides had talked of fleeing to Switzerland.

He set off to the southeast, passing through Rouen, before arriving three days later in Paris, where he stayed with a Protestant, Huguenot, family. This was a place of repugnant fascination to Ludlow, both for its rampant Catholicism, and because it was the fulcrum of Louis XIV's absolute hold over France. The Englishman levelled his contempt at the monarch and his religion with equal ferocity: 'I saw the King's stable of horses,' the old cavalryman wrote, 'which though not extraordinarily furnished, gave me more pleasure than I should have received by seeing their master, who thinks fit to treat them better than his miserable people. But I loathed to see such numbers of idle drones, who in ridiculous habits, wherein they place a great part of their religion, are to be seen in every part, eating the bread of the credulous multitude, and leaving them to be distinguished from the inhabitants of other countries by thin cheeks, canvas clothing and wooden shoes.'[16]

From Paris, Ludlow aimed for Lyons, joining a group of international travellers which included a friendly German aristocrat. On arrival, he was troubled to see how closely newcomers to the city were scrutinised: all were obliged to disclose their details to government officials. Ludlow, somehow, was spared such questioning; his luck was continuing to hold. Relieved, he settled into an inn with his travelling companions. It was not a happy experience. He recorded with disgust how they were forced to share the premises with friars from various orders, one of whom Ludlow took to task for making lewd suggestions to a Parisian youth in their party. Many of his prejudices seem to have been confirmed during his journey through 'profane France' towards the promised land of republican, Protestant, Geneva.

The last stop before reaching Switzerland was Fort l'Ecluse, a border garrison between the Vuache hills and the Jura mountains, which controlled the Rhône valley. Ludlow had been advised that the examination he had avoided in Lyons would be inevitable here, but the warnings came from those unacquainted with the slack discipline at Fort l'Ecluse. Some well-placed bribes, which paid for soldiers' drinks, saw this last obstacle evaporate. The next day he crossed the River Rhône, and soon afterwards entered Geneva.

Here, there were few reminders of home. During his journey Ludlow had heard that his fellow regicide William Cawley was heading for Geneva, but he discovered that neither he nor any of the other fugitives were there. Geneva itself was a disappointment. 'Neither in doctrine nor discipline, principle nor practice,' he wrote, 'have they made such progress since the time of the first Reformation as might have been hoped for, but have rather gone backward and brought forth sour grapes.'[17]

Eleven days after arriving in the Swiss capital, Ludlow was shocked to read of the executions of Harrison, Carew, Cook and Peters. The following week's gazette gave detailed accounts of the ends of Scott, Scroope, Clements, Jones, Axtell and Hacker. If he had not run away when he did, Ludlow knew he would have been among the same batch of hanged, drawn and quartered Parliamentarians.

Further news reached Ludlow from England, including concocted accounts of his fate. The Royalist publication *Mercurius Politicus* declared in early September, 'We have omitted the proclamation for £300 to any that should apprehend Col. Edmund Ludlow, in regard we hear from very good hands he is already in custody.'[18] The following week the paper was less bullish. 'Ludlow was nearly taken,' it reported, 'they took his hat and the coats and cloaks of two or three that were with him.'[19] Elsewhere there were rumours that the lieutenant general had been captured while trying to flee the country in disguise.

Although the bulletins were wildly inaccurate, they reconfirmed the energy that Charles II's men were putting into apprehending Ludlow. It seemed impossible to his enemies that a man of such high profile could really have got away. The Royalists convinced themselves that such an easily identifiable figure must still be in England, and they redoubled their efforts to hunt him down.

December brought further false reports, alleging his capture in England: 'On Saturday night at midnight was Major Gen. Ludlow taken at one Michael Oldsworth his house, secretary to the late Earl of Pembroke; Ludlow married this Oldsworth his sister; he got out of the house, but was taken endeavouring to make his escape.'[20]

That same month he learnt that the House of Commons had voted to have the bodies of Cromwell, Ireton and Bradshaw dug up from their burial places and hung from the gallows. This desecration followed the precedent established after the Gunpowder Plot in 1605, when the bodies of Catesby and Percy – two of the conspirators who had died before facing trial and execution – were exhumed and decapitated. Their heads were placed on spikes outside the House of Lords.

As part of the posthumous retribution against Cromwell, Ireton and Bradshaw, a mason named John Lewis was given fifteen shillings to break open the leading regicides' lavish tombs so their corpses could be retrieved. He found Cromwell's remains wrapped in a green wax cloth. The Lord Protector's torso was clad in a copper gilt breastplate emblazoned with the arms of the Commonwealth, while the reverse recorded the span of his life, and his full title, in Latin. Two days later, on 28 January, Cromwell's and Ireton's bodies were taken on carts from Westminster to the Red Lion Inn in Holborn, where they spent the night, side by side. They were joined by Bradshaw's corpse the following day.

The thirtieth of January 1661 was the twelfth anniversary of the execution of Charles I. Parliament decreed this day should become, as John Evelyn recalled, 'the first solemn fast and day of humiliation to deplore the sins which so long had provoked God against this afflicted church and people: ordered by Parliament to be annually celebrated, to expiate the guilt of execrable murder of the late King'.[21] A symbolic centrepiece was needed as a focus for the first festival of atonement. That morning the three regicides' coffins were dragged on sledges to the gallows at Tyburn. There, the caskets were broken open, and the bodies pulled from them. The remains were hanged together, from nine in the morning until six in the evening, dangling on a gibbet in front of a crowd of thousands. Three men of exceptional distinction and power in their lifetimes, under the restored monarchy they were just a trio of traitors swivelling in varying states of decay. That evening their remains were beheaded, the bodies slung into the deep common pit. The three heads were stuck on spikes in Westminster, their unseeing eyes directed towards the spot where the King's scaffold had stood.

Now the hunt restarted for the remaining men who had shared in the killing of the King, but who had yet to face justice. Charles II instructed his agents to track them down, even if they had managed to flee overseas.

Chapter 10

Strangers in a Strange Land

The first sight of your handwriting filled my eyes with such floods of tears, that for some hours I could not recover my sight to read it; yet at last to reading I went, but then every line, yea every word called back my tears, and so overwhelmed my affections, that I could not get through it till between one and two of the clock that night.

Colonel John Barkstead, writing to a friend in London,
while in hiding in the Netherlands

On 11 October 1660, during the trial of the twenty-nine regicides, Sir Heneage Finch had addressed the court with words of warning for those men who had so far evaded the reach of Charles II: 'Some eighteen or nineteen have fled from Justice, and wander to and fro; about the world with the Mark of Cain upon them, a perpetual trembling, lest every eye that sees them, and every hand that meets them, should fall on them.'[1]

Just before his execution, Colonel John Jones had written to a friend: 'O dear hearts, in what a sad condition are all our dear friends beyond sea, where they may be hunted from place to place, and never be in safety, nor hear the voice of the turtle dove. How much have we got the start of them, for we are at a point, and are now going to heaven.'[2] Jones preferred the certainty of imminent death, followed by eternal paradise, to a life on the run.

From his Swiss sanctuary, Ludlow kept track of the whereabouts and fates of his fellow commissioners from the High Court of Justice of January 1649. He learnt that four of the court's other military men – Colonels Valentine Walton, John Dixwell, John Barkstead and John Okey – had managed to get to apparent safety in Germany.

Walton had served as a captain in his brother-in-law Oliver Cromwell's regiment: in 1617, aged twenty-four, he had married the sixteen-year-old Margaret Cromwell. The Waltons lost their eldest surviving son at the battle of Marston Moor in 1644, when a Royalist cannonball shattered his leg and desperate surgery could not save him. Around this same time Margaret died, after which Walton married again. In 1646 he co-authored the letter to Parliament from Norfolk, recording sightings of the fugitive Charles I and his chaplain, Michael Hudson, as they attempted to reach the Scots.

A committed republican, Walton had been keen for Charles I to stand trial in 1649. He attended many of the sittings, and signed the death warrant without hesitation. After the royal beheading, Walton became a prominent figure, sitting on all five councils of state during the Commonwealth. He was one of the numerous committed Parliamentarians who fell out with Cromwell when he ruled as Lord Protector. Further disillusioned by what he had seen of the army's role, in the late 1650s, Walton sided with the House of Commons against the military. He secretly communicated with Monck, but as soon as Monck was made commander-in-chief he took away the Puritan Walton's command of a cavalry regiment, and gave it, tellingly, to a Catholic Royalist officer instead.

When Walton realised that Monck was working to restore the monarchy, he was quick to flee. According to Ludlow, though, he only 'narrowly escaped'[3] overseas. Walton travelled to Hanau, a walled metropolis on a river near Frankfurt am Main that contained two separate entities. One of these, 'new Hanau', established a couple of generations earlier, included a large population of Calvinist émigrés from France and the Spanish Netherlands (modern-day Belgium). Many of these were successful merchants.

They demanded and gained religious tolerance and other privileges from the reigning count, Frederick Casimir, on whose land their new settlement stood. The count was a Lutheran, impoverished by the ravages of the Thirty Years War (during which Hanau's impressive defensive walls withstood its one attempted siege with ease), as well as by his own personal extravagance. Frederick Casimir had travelled to Britain as part of his Grand Tour during the English Civil War, and so understood something of the conflict whose aftershocks had brought this trickle of refugees to his city.

Walton became a burgess of Hanau, which entitled him to the city's protection; but he remained deeply concerned for his safety. He was troubled by reports that the Royalists were sending forces after the escaped regicides, to assassinate them or take them back to England: he knew that accused men, such as himself, who had fled, were seen to have acknowledged their guilt. They were no longer eligible for trial. If caught, they would simply be formally identified, and then brutally dispatched.

Walton decided that the safest course was no longer to remain as a respected but recognisable guest of this independent German city, but rather to disappear quietly into obscurity. This he succeeded in doing: he became a humble gardener in the Lowlands and is believed to have died soon afterwards, possibly in 1661.

John Dixwell had wrong-footed his enemies in England, pretending that he was on the point of surrendering, while in fact sorting out his finances before fleeing. He was, for now, content to reside in Hanau. Another 'friend' in the city was Colonel John Barkstead, the unpopular but effective Lieutenant of the Tower, who was also steward to Oliver Cromwell's household. The manner in which he profiteered from prisoners in the Tower during his seven years in charge there had scandalised even his own side, and he had been fortunate to escape punishment during Richard Cromwell's brief Protectorate. After being named as the seventh regicide to be executed, he escaped, but he found exile an unbearable separation from those he loved, replying to a letter from London:

My dear friend,

    I am very sensible of my great neglect of that duty which is incumbent upon me . . . that I had not long before this given you an account how it has been with me, and what the Lord hath done for me his poor unworthy servant since I last saw you; that I have been a stranger in a strange land I need not tell you, I am persuaded you will judge favourably of me till you understand how it hath pleased the Lord to deal with me. The truth is, my condition in some respect may resemble the dove that Noah sent out of the Ark that could find no place to set the sole of her foot on, thus hath it been for some months with me, so that I could not with any consistency (because of those that bear an evil will to Zion) write to you; but my dear friend though I have been absent from you in the body, yet I can say truly I have not been so in my spirit; the Lord knows how my soul hath both night and day longed after you and all the rest of my Christian friends in Christ Jesus . . .[4]

Barkstead eventually settled in Hanau: the free city was an important centre for jewellery manufacture and the working of gold – an attraction for Barkstead, who before the Civil Wars had been, along with his father and brother, a prosperous London goldsmith. Barkstead also had some German roots, his grandfather having emigrated from there to Staffordshire. He felt he could make a home in Hanau, but looked forward to his wife coming to join him there.

John Okey also encouraged his wife to quit England for a new life with him in Hanau. During the Civil War he had risen from being a quartermaster to command of the New Model Army's sole regiment of dragoons. He and his men had performed with gallantry throughout the Civil Wars, their flanking fire troubling the sweeping charge of Prince Rupert's Royalist cavalry at Naseby. In the Second Civil War they were among the victorious Parliamentarians at St Fagans, and at the taking of Pembroke Castle. A ready judge at Charles I's trial, he also signed the death warrant, before helping to oversee the military arrangements surrounding the execution.

Okey was opposed to Oliver Cromwell's Protectorate. In the autumn of 1654 he was one of those to draw up *The Humble Petition of Several Colonels of the Army*, which was designed to rein in Cromwell's ambitions and return a parliament free from his meddling. This resulted in Okey's trial for sedition, and he was sentenced to death. Cromwell commuted this to the loss of his commission, and enforced retirement. During this he lived off the income from the property he had acquired during his years in power. Okey reappeared in public life in 1657, joining those opposed to the calls for Cromwell's coronation.

There was a brief resurrection of his military career after the fall of Richard Cromwell. At the end of 1659 he was among the soldiers who tried forcibly to stop the secluded members from gaining access to Parliament. Monck lost no time in taking his new regiment from him. Okey's last stand as a soldier was an ignominious one, fleeing from Major General Lambert's side when surprised by Ingoldsby near Daventry.

Mrs Barkstead and Mrs Okey had agreed to travel through the Netherlands to Hanau. They knew that theirs was a one-way journey into a lifetime of exile: they would not be able to return to England, once they had settled with their condemned husbands overseas. The two colonels wanted to meet their wives in the Netherlands, in order to reunite with them as quickly as they could, and so as to help them on their way to Germany. They received 'encouragement to undertake the voyage from a friend whom they had employed to solicit some of the States-General', a friend wrote, 'that they might abide for a short time within their jurisdiction unmolested'.[5]

Okey and Barkstead knew Charles II's envoy to the Netherlands: he was a former colleague of theirs. A devout Parliamentarian who had aided the soldiers of the New Model Army, George Downing was a figure whose background extended to both sides of the Atlantic. His maternal uncle was John Winthrop, the first governor of the Massachusetts Bay Colony. The Downings were encouraged by their relatives to move to Massachusetts, and settled in Salem, where their preacher was Hugh Peters.

In 1640, Downing entered the first year of undergraduates at Harvard College. Two years later he passed out in the inaugural class, taking second place academically. At the end of 1643 he was taken on to Harvard's teaching staff, receiving £4 per year 'to read to the Junior pupils as the President shall see fit'.[6] But Downing was restless. His thirst for travel led him to become a ship's chaplain in the Caribbean. From there he crossed to England, arriving in 1646 in poverty – Ludlow recalled that Downing at this time 'was not worth a groat'[7] – to find a nation torn apart by civil war. John Okey had taken the destitute Downing in as chaplain and preacher to his regiment. Reacquainted with Hugh Peters, the men worked alongside one another, urging Parliament's troops on towards final victory.

Oliver Cromwell recognised Downing's qualities: in 1649, the year of Charles I's execution, he made him his scoutmaster-general in Scotland. There he directed Parliamentary spies, gathering intelligence and transmitting it to London. He also used his powerful position to start the building of that personal wealth which was to become one of his most remarkable achievements. This quest was assisted by his marriage to Lady Frances Howard, an aristocratic beauty.

In January 1657, the first public proposal was made to have Cromwell take the Crown. It was George Downing who seconded the motion with enthusiasm. Later that year, perhaps in gratitude, Cromwell gave him the important diplomatic role of Agent in the Netherlands. In August 1658, Downing was writing to London, with terror, of rumours that Walter Whitford, the Royalist who had murdered Dr Dorislaus, had returned to The Hague to kill him.

Downing's self-preservation and canniness made him a speedy defector to the Prince of Wales in the run-up to the Restoration. He wanted Charles to know that he 'wished the promoting of your Majesty's service, which he confessed he had endeavoured to obstruct . . . alleging to be engaged in a contrary party by his father who was banished to New England, where he . . . had sucked in principles that since his reason had made him see were erroneous'.[8]

As proof of his newly Royalist loyalties, Downing forwarded a letter he had that day received in code from Thurloe, Cromwell's intelligence chief, which contained fresh and secret military information. He was happy to turn his back on a failing cause.

Whatever Charles II thought of this old enemy, who had revealed himself to be a shameless and opportunistic turncoat, he was too useful to punish, too cunning to leave unemployed. The new King kept Downing in the Netherlands as his own man, hoping to profit from the diplomat's underhand effectiveness. Downing had shared some of his successes with his secretary, the diarist Samuel Pepys, who recorded of his master: 'He had so good spies, that he hath had the keys taken out of [the Dutch leader] De Witt's pocket when he was a-bed, and his closet opened and the papers brought to him and left in his hands for an [hour], and carried back and laid in the place again and the keys put in his pocket again.'[9] Downing was a man who would stop at nothing to achieve his goals.

Fleeing regicides were passing into and through the Netherlands. Thomas Chaloner, Marten's fellow bon viveur among the ranks of prim Puritans who had signed away Charles I's life, had fled England on learning that he was to be denied the mercy of the Act of Indemnity. Dutch sympathisers wrote of him at this stage as being 'an old man, full of grey hairs; a thick, square man'.[10] His age and poor health meant he enjoyed only the briefest of freedoms that summer, dying in mid-August 1660. Chaloner's body was committed to the graveyard of the Old Church at Middelburg, the assumed name of 'George Sanders' carved on his gravestone in order to protect his remains from desecration.

Meanwhile, Sir Michael Livesay, who had been an MP and a regimental commander before sitting every day on the High Court and signing Charles's death warrant, was known to be in the Netherlands in the autumn of 1660: reports that he had then been pulled apart by a murderous mob of vengeful Royalists proved to be incorrect, but there was no doubt that he was somewhere on Dutch territory, in hiding.

Downing lay ready to pounce on any of Chaloner and Livesay's comrades, should they stray within his reach. He was nervous of revealing his plans to the Dutch because he felt sure they would block the abduction of foreign refugees on their soil. 'I am very much afraid lest that if I should go to De Witt, or any other, for an order to seize them,' he wrote home in early July 1661, 'it should somehow or other be discovered; for I know the humour of these people; and therefore if I might have my own way, I would in such a case employ three or four resolved English officers, and seize them, and then immediately give notice to the burgomasters of the place, and States General. Or, if the King would adventure, without more ado, if possible, to get them aboard some ship. Let me know the King's pleasure herein.'[11]

A week later his network of spies had sent reports of the scurrying regicide activity along and around the corridors he controlled. It became clear they were heading for Germany: 'Dendy is yet at Rotterdam and I am put in hopes of finding Corbet. I hear that Okey and some others of them are at Strasbourg, and have purchased their freedom there publicly; and that Hewson is sick, but intends thither also with one or two more by the first occasion.'[12]

Edward Dendy had followed his father as serjeant-at-arms to the Commons. On 8 January 1649 he had proclaimed the establishment of Charles I's trial. Miles Corbet was a constitutional lawyer who had served as Lord Chief Baron of Ireland. He had meanwhile been one of Norfolk's MPs for thirty-seven years. It was in that capacity that Corbet had written to Parliament, in 1646, relating sightings of Charles I in disguise with his chaplain, after the King had slipped away from beleaguered Oxford. A busy bureaucrat, Corbet had been an effective chairman of the Committee of Examinations, helping to suppress Royalist propaganda news-sheets. That, and his chairing of the committee that drew up the capital prosecution against Archbishop Laud, had marked out Corbet as one of a handful of fellow Parliamentarians (the others were Cromwell, Ireton, Scott, Marten and Peters) subjected to those publications' coarsest broadsides. Corbet's sallow complexion prompted his attackers to virulent anti-Semitism, calling him a 'bull-headed, splay-footed member of the circumcision', and a 'bacon-faced Jew'.[13] The fact that Corbet was the most devout of Christians was irrelevant: in the minds of bigots, his physical appearance fitted that of the stereotype of the Jew.

Although appointed to the High Court of Justice, Corbet had refused to sit in judgment of the King during its preliminary phases, arguing against the trial's validity in law. But a verse from the Book of Revelation kept coming to him, pricking his conscience: 'The fearful and unbelieving shall have their part in the lake that burns with fire and brimstone.'[14] Corbet felt compelled to answer his summons to sit as a commissioner, and on the day of sentencing he went to assure himself as to the legality of the proceedings. Satisfied that all was in order, he added his signature to the death warrant.

Colonel John Hewson, a former shoemaker, was a fellow signatory. He had served in Ireland with uncompromising vigour, losing an eye during the siege of Kilkenny in 1650, before being made governor of Dublin later that year. In 1659 he had become deeply unpopular for attacking demonstrators in London when they called for a free Parliament: some had died during his troops' heavy-handed suppression of the protest, and Hewson was blamed.

That August, after some delay, Downing secured a blank arrest warrant from the representatives of the Dutch States-General. By the time he was ready to use it, his quarry had scattered. Dendy had slipped away, alerted, as Downing had predicted, by powerful Dutch friends that his capture was imminent. Dendy would join the growing band of regicides settling in Switzerland. Corbet temporarily disappeared. Hewson melted away for ever, the place and time of his eventual death unrecorded.

Clarendon wrote consolingly to Downing: 'I do not know that you could do more than you did in the case of Dendy; yet it is plain that upon the granting of any such warrant notice will be given them [the regicides]; but I like your design well,' the chancellor urged, 'of causing any of them to be arrested, and afterwards they will not so easily get from you.'[15]

Confident that its time would come, Downing filed away the blank arrest warrant for future use.

John Okey, 'little thinking,' as a friend wrote, 'that his New England tottered chaplain whom he clothed, and fed at his table, and who dipped with him in his own dish should prove like the Devil among the twelve to his Lord and Master',[16] assumed that he and Barkstead would be left alone during their travels through the Netherlands. He quickly checked through an intermediary that this would be the case, and received assurances of their wellbeing from Downing, who claimed that he had no orders to look out for them.

The travellers were also confident in the Dutch as guarantors of safe passage. Theirs was a country that had come into being after ridding itself of the oppressive rule of the Spanish – its prize for enduring, then winning, the bruising Eighty Years' War. They prided themselves on their tolerance, and they enriched themselves through trade. The Dutch were famed for putting commerce before all else – and that included not bothering themselves overmuch with the religious, political or criminal concerns of their neighbours. Okey and Barkstead were unaware, however, that at the time of their expedition, the Dutch were interested in forming a trade alliance with Charles II's England. To secure this, they might be prepared to sacrifice something of their famed reputation for tolerance.

Ignorant of the danger they were in, Okey and Barkstead started out for Delft, the southern Dutch city that was still being rebuilt after an enormous, accidental gunpowder explosion in 1654: more than a hundred citizens had been killed, and thousands injured. The two men set off expecting a speedy reunion with their wives.

On reaching Delft the pair settled into their lodgings. There they were visited by Miles Corbet, happy to see friendly faces after spending much of his time in exile in prayer, meditation and reading the scriptures. During those times of quiet he had examined his conscience about his role in Charles I's execution – an event he referred to as 'that necessary and public Act of Justice'. A chronicler later recorded of Corbet that 'he did never repent at all that he had a hand in it, nor, after all the searchings of heart about it, did see cause to do so, when at any time he had the most serious and calm reflections upon it'.[17]

Corbet would also recall the lack of food that he endured during his time in hiding in the Netherlands, 'and yet,' he claimed, 'I found God all sufficient to me, even in my short commons.'[18] More challenging was the fear of being discovered, which meant that he 'did the best to secure myself, and was careful not wilfully to run into any danger'.[19] As part of his strategy of self-preservation he had not dared to send a letter to his wife for eight months. He went to see Bradshaw and Okey to learn how he could safely communicate with her in future, without compromising his liberty.

Corbet was so happy to be reunited with these English friends that he delayed his planned journey home that evening, and stayed with them late into the night. The three men were at last saying their farewells when Downing and his henchmen pounced: cornered, the fugitives were quickly rounded up, placed in chains and assaulted by their captors, before being escorted to prison. There they were again treated roughly, their wrists and ankles manacled, before they were committed to a dungeon, where the only place to sleep was on the wet floor.

Early the next afternoon a delegation of Dutch politicians came to visit them. Their leader conducted the examination, asking them to explain why they had been taken, and what their roles had been in England before their self-imposed exile. Barkstead answered most of these questions. He spoke clearly, convincingly and well, appealing to his audience's liberal, republican, sympathies. The three regicides were relieved to hear the Dutchmen confirm that they would be granted a public hearing in Delft, before there was even a possibility of their being handed over to their Royalist compatriots for extradition.

Downing, though, had other ideas – he would later be called by the French first minister 'the greatest quarreller of all the diplomats in Europe'[20] – and now he displayed his combative streak. Having finally caged three of his prey, he was not prepared to contemplate their release. He bullied the Dutch officials, insisting on his jurisdiction over men who had killed his royal master's father, and insinuating dark consequences if he did not get his way. He pointed to his blank arrest warrant, and insisted it had been granted him precisely for this sort of eventuality. The Dutch capitulated, a disbelieving friend of the regicides writing, 'By order from the States-General at two o'clock in the morning [the three men were] taken out of prison, and thrust into a vessel lying at Delft, and from thence conveyed into one of the King of England's frigates provided for the purpose, and so in a few days were brought for England, where they arrived at the Tower of London upon the Lord's Day in the evening.'[21] There, they were led to separate cells.

Barkstead was treated vindictively. The Royalists enjoyed the delicious vengeance of placing the hated former Lieutenant of the Tower, who had been such a cruel gaoler to their comrades, in despicable accommodation. He managed to smuggle out a letter to a friend, detailing the conditions in which he was kept:

> I being now a close prisoner in the Tower, in one of the (as they conceive) meanest and securest Prison lodgings, in which when it rains I have no place to sit dry but in a high window, being attended with a life guard of two warders and two soldiers day and night, and denied the use of pen, ink, and paper; so that what I write is so by stealth, and that so by bits, that I am forced sometimes before I have writ two lines to tear what I have written, and with much trouble to secure my paper, ink and pen; but yet I have adventured on a line or two to you, to let you know that I received your welcome letter.[22]

Barkstead's health soon faltered because of the rain and cold, but he told his friend that his resolve was such, that 'the dungeon, chains, bolts and manacles have not had the least hardness in them; no, I must say again, through free Grace, the Lord hath not only made them easy, but pleasant, yea kickings and buffetings, when in irons, by some of Downing's men, yet the Lord strengthened me'.[23]

On 16 April 1662, the prisoners were transported up the Thames to the bar of the King's Bench in Westminster for judgment. This area had formed part of the courtroom for Charles I's trial. The three were asked in turn to confirm their identities, which was the only formality required before sentencing. Yet, when it was put to them that they were the Barkstead, Corbet and Okey who did 'maliciously, wickedly, and traitorously imagine, contrive or endeavour to murder the late King', the lawyer Corbet said he could not admit to being one who had acted maliciously to Charles I, therefore he must not be the man mentioned in the charge. He offered that there must be many others who also shared those names, and maybe one of those had possessed the malice referred to?

The court, keen to be done with its work, summoned a jury. The three accused were not allowed to challenge any of its members, since this was not a trial for treason, but rather a process to prove their identities. The jury promptly ascertained that the three well-known men before them were indeed the signatories of Charles I's death warrant named in the charge. Judgment was given, and the sentence of hanging, drawing and quartering passed. The condemned were returned to the Tower to await imminent death.

That day a friend visited Okey to find him 'not in the least disquieted' by his sentence, 'but thankfully owned the Providence of God in bringing them from the place where they were beyond the sea, to their present condition, wherein he professed himself to be much satisfied, and declared he had rather lay down his life here, than to have been buried in another nation'.[24]

There were moments of profound sadness. Okey was refused permission to see the daughter from his first marriage on the day of his sentencing. He wrote to her:

My dear daughter,
   . . . I am something troubled at the cruelty of wicked men that will not let me see you in such a day as this is; but it's not to be wondered at, for you know what the Scripture saith, *The mercies of the ungodly*

are cruelty itself. But blessed be our good God, though they can keep our relations from us, they cannot keep us from coming to our heavenly father; within a few days we shall be out of their hands, where they shall afflict us no more … I thank you for your love to me as much as if I had seen you: and although we are kept one from another in the body, yet we are not so in the spirit, but do rejoice in one another.

Okey asked her to pray for him to be brave at his end, 'that I may not dishonour the Lord, nor bring a reproach to the glorious Gospel of our Lord Jesus Christ, and his cause, which the Lord hath from Heaven so gloriously owned, by scattering of his enemies so often as he hath in the sight of the sun, in bringing many of them to justice, so that the sound of it is gone through the whole world'.[25] After apologising for not being able to leave her an inheritance, and having asked her to be kind to his wife (his daughter's stepmother), and a good example to her children, he signed off: 'Your loving father, in bonds for the Cause of God and his People, till death.'[26]

Barkstead admitted to those visiting him in his final days that he had been deeply troubled by 'the greatness of the sufferings I was yet to go through', but he too found solace in religion. He settled on biblical passages that made him accept his human weakness, and left his heart 'filled with ravishing joys and rejoicings'.[27] Later in his brief imprisonment he was recorded as saying:

Certainly if I had known the comforts of this sweet communion with God in a prison before, I had run to a prison long ago. If I had suffered when my brethren did suffer, I had had little or no blood in my body to have spilt for Jesus Christ in this good Cause; but God carried me into Germany, and there made us to sow a good seed, which will never die; and now God hath brought me back again, with more strength to suffer for his name and cause; indeed, the Lord hath made me in some measure now fit to go through sufferings for him, and it is indeed He alone who hath done this.[28]

Barkstead looked back with regret and shame on his time as
Lieutenant of the Tower, and was particularly conscious of his
cruelty to Fifth Monarchy prisoners. One of the points he was
keenest to pass on to his friends in his final days was the need to
accept all Christian beliefs, and to be free from religious prejudice.
He felt that the intensity of his ordeal – comprising arrest, close
imprisonment and imminent death – was granting him a clear,
divine perspective that he needed to share, as part of his legacy, with
those still caught up in earthly concerns.

The night before his execution, Barkstead and his wife dined with
their family and friends. Mrs Barkstead asked her husband to wash his
hands before eating; Barkstead refused, telling her that the next day
would see his hands impaled on spikes above the City gates, 'and then
the rain would save him that labour'.[29] Then he asked another of his
relatives to air what he referred to as the last shirt he would ever wear.
The humour may have been macabre, but it helped him to make the
grim reality of what would happen the next day somehow acceptable.

Meanwhile, sympathetic pamphleteers had Corbet justifying his
case to the end. 'The day before his death,' Ludlow recorded, 'he
assured his friends, that he was so thoroughly convinced of the
justice and necessity of that action for which he was to die, that if
the things had been yet entire, and to do, he could not refuse to act
as he had done, without affronting his reason, and opposing himself
to the dictates of his conscience.'[30] Aged sixty-seven, Corbet told
friends that he was old enough to be approaching the inevitability
of a natural death, and pointed out that he was lucky to have
outlived many of his contemporaries: 'Alas! I might have died long
since of some noisome disease, or lingering sickness; might have
lain long weltering, and at last been as it were smothered to death in
a feather-bed, and perhaps with the loss of my senses too, and the
use of my reason and memory, as it happens to many that die in
age.' Instead, he was set 'to become a seasonable, holy and lively
sacrifice unto God: and as for the pain of it, I reckon it far less than
what is usually felt in an ordinary sickness.'[31] When friends
suggested that he give the executioner a bribe, so that he would act

with compassion, Corbet would have none of it. 'Let him be as cruel as he will,' he said, 'the more bloody he is, the better for me.'[32] He calculated that an angry hangman would do his work roughly, and so speed him to his death.

As for his capture, which had led to his return to England, he claimed to welcome it. 'Had I continued abroad,' he said, 'I might have died in obscurity, and have been carried out into some hole in a dust basket, where my death would have signified nothing.' He had just one concern: 'All my desire is, that I may not faint, nor any way dishonour the Cause that I am to suffer for, by my weak and unworthy carriage, which I confess I am afraid of, and therefore earnestly desire the prayers of friends on my behalf, that God will be pleased to support me, and carry me well through this so hard and difficult task.'[33]

Corbet slept until two in the morning the night before his day of execution, followed by two further, brief naps before his wife, Mary, appeared in his cell at six o'clock. She had endured much on account of her husband's allegiances, having long been libelled by enemy propagandists, who enjoyed portraying the leading Parliamentarians' wives (particularly Oliver Cromwell's wife, Elizabeth) as voraciously promiscuous. Even before the King's trial, a Royalist writer had taunted Corbet with the pretence that he knew a man who would 'rather go to your house than a bawdy house, because it is a great deal cheaper'.[34]

The evening before her husband's execution Mary Corbet stayed in a room in the Tower, kept awake all night by her dread of what the morning must bring. The couple prayed together for an hour, before breakfast arrived. According to one account, Corbet drank a glass of burnt claret, then picked at the food on offer, concluding with a hardboiled egg; he threw its shell away with the words, 'Farewell, creature comforts, I shall use you no more.'[35]

At eight o'clock in the morning of 19 April – just three days after their trial, and thirty-six hours since they had been informed of the time of their execution – the prisoners heard the rattle on the cobblestones as their sledges arrived in the courtyard, the sound of the horses' hooves resonating round the walls.

Barkstead, who had been chosen to be the first to meet the hangman at Tyburn, asked his wife to help button up his cloak. He was led to the door of the lieutenant's lodgings, where he had once lived in supreme command of the Tower with an annual income of £2,000. Without looking at his former seat of power, Barkstead allowed himself to be secured to the sledge, then headed off for his degrading and agonising end.

The colonel maintained the appearance of brave and proud acceptance throughout his final hours: 'When he was brought to confirm with the testimony of his blood that cause for which he had fought, he performed that part with cheerfulness and courage, no way derogating from the character of a soldier and a true Englishman.'[36] As his sledge turned out of the Tower he looked back and spied his wife in a window above, waving at him with her handkerchief. He removed his hat in a final farewell, shouting up to her, 'To Heaven, to Heaven, to Heaven, my Love, and [I] leave you in the storm!'[37]

Barkstead was the victim of much abuse throughout his final journey, and it continued while he stood on the cart awaiting his two companions at the place of death. A Royalist lord was heard to shout out, 'Goodbye, Barkstead, goodbye!' in a tone of mock distress, to which the colonel replied, 'Sir, you are no gentleman, to triumph over a dying man.' Another onlooker – one of the King's courtiers – ridiculed him for taking fortifying swigs from a flask of alcohol. 'O Barkstead,' he jeered, 'you have got the comforter!'[38] Barkstead countered by saying that it was God who was his true comforter.

One of the guards escorting Barkstead thought he looked so ill that day that he suspected the prisoner had poisoned himself. This soldier shouted out, 'He is almost dead; if he be not quickly hanged, he will be dead before: therefore hang him, hang him, before he be quite dead: see how he looks!'[39] But the hangman said he would hang the trio together. Barkstead waited, clearly unwell, till his comrades joined him.

Okey was the first to arrive. As he dismounted his sledge at Tyburn, a friend asked him how he was feeling. 'I bless the Lord, I am very well,' he replied, holding up his hand, 'and do no more value what I am now going about, than this straw. I have made many a charge in my time,' the veteran colonel continued, 'but now I have but one charge more to make, and then I shall be at rest.'[40] Half an hour after Barkstead's arrival the hurdle bearing Corbet drew up. He was clutching a Bible, and wearing new gloves – a final gift from his wife. She had clung to him as he had been summoned from the Tower crying, 'Oh my dear husband! My precious husband! What an husband shall I now lose! Whom I have not prized, whom I have not improved as I ought and might have done!' Corbet had tears in his eyes as he said his last consoling words to her, before turning to his son. He held the young man's hands, and blessed him. Corbet asked a close friend to stay behind, to comfort his wife and son. He then turned on his heels and strode purposefully towards his sledge, eager to escape the howls of distress of those he loved most, and determined to see through his terrible ordeal.

There were so many come to see the executions that the condemned men had each been forced to get off their sledges and be escorted by foot through the throng, to the executioner's cart. There, their hands were tied with black ribbons, their wigs were removed, and caps were placed on their heads. They were told that they would be permitted to address their final words and prayers to the crowd, but that any attempted justification of what they had done would not be tolerated. The three men stood in the executioner's cart, onto which others had clambered, eager to catch their last words.

The speeches were long enough to irritate the sheriff, who was keen to be done with his duties. Okey asked forgiveness from any he had ever wronged. He clearly remained deeply perplexed by Downing's hand in his capture and death. 'Whoever hath proceeded against my life,' he said, near the conclusion of his speech, 'either in England or Holland (for there was one – who formerly was my chaplain – that did pursue me to the very death, where I remained but two nights, and was going back again, for I had done my business). But both him, and all others upon the Earth, I forgive as freely as I desire the Lord to forgive me. I have no malice either to judge or jury, but desire that the Lord would forgive them; as also those in Holland, that sent us over, contrary to what they did engage to my friends.'[41]

Okey assured the crowd witnessing his end that, if he had as many lives as he had hairs on his head, he would happily risk all of them for the good of his cause. But he also admitted his crime, and encouraged all present to submit to the returned house of Stuart.

When the three men had completed their speeches and their public prayers, the executioner told all others to dismount the cart. He then pulled the prisoners' caps down over their eyes, and waited for them all to lift their hands as a sign that they were ready for the execution to take place. As the cart was drawn away, Barkstead shouted: 'Lord Jesus, receive our souls!'

There were none of the triumphant cries that had accompanied earlier executions of the regicides. Chroniclers commented rather that the overriding emotion at the death of these three captured fugitives was one of great sadness.

They remained hanging for fifteen minutes, before being cut down and quartered in the same order that they had earlier left the Tower: Barkstead first, followed by Okey, and then Corbet. In late afternoon their bodies were taken to Newgate, where they were boiled. Barkstead's head was placed on a spike overlooking the Tower of London, where once he had been supreme, but, more recently, where he had been its lowliest prisoner.

As a reward for Okey's welcome message of obedience to the restored monarchy, the King allowed his family to have his head and quartered body returned for Christian burial, where they thought fit. His widow planned to have the colonel interred in Stepney, next to his first wife, in a family vault that he had bought as his final resting place. But, while Okey's butchered carcass rested near to Newgate prison, awaiting its final journey, news of his funeral buzzed through the City, and a vast crowd (sympathetic pamphleteers claimed improbably that it numbered 20,000 people) assembled. Some were curious, others respectful, while still more were nostalgic for the age of the republic. The throng threatened to turn into an immense and unruly procession that would trail the colonel's remains all the way to his tomb. This support for a slain traitor led to consternation at court, and a swift about turn by the King.

Secretary of State Nicholas wrote to the sheriffs of London, 'The King having observed that the relations of Col. Okey, abusing his clemency, are making preparations for a solemn funeral, and intend a great concourse of people to attend it, desires that his head and quarters when given to his relations, be privately interred in the Tower, and that the names of those who have designed the said solemnity and tumultuous concourse be inquired into.'[42] The five parts of Colonel Okey were buried that night in the grounds of the Tower of London, in a private ceremony conducted by Mr Glendon, the parish priest of Barking.

Charles II's advisers could not help but note the public display of support at Okey's planned funeral. The grisly ritual of hanging, drawing and quartering had been acceptable in October 1660, when the great majority wanted to celebrate the royal return, and were happy to send unpopular republicans to die in the most terrible manner. However, Bishop Burnet, who was a young man during the early 1660s, wrote much later that:

In one thing the temper of the nation appeared to the contrary to severe proceedings. For, though the Regicides were at that time odious beyond all expression, and the trials and executions of the first that suffered were run to by vast crowds, and all people seemed pleased with the sight, yet the odiousness of the crime grew at last to be so much flattened by the frequent executions, and most of those who suffered dying with such firmness and show of piety, justifying all they had done, not without a seeming joy for their suffering on that account, that the King was advised not to proceed farther, at least not to have the scene so near the Court at Charing Cross.[43]

Charles remained determined to make the killers pay for his father's death. As the public scaffold was producing a succession of sympathetic martyrs, he began to look to other means by which he could catch up with the remaining fugitives.

Chapter 11

A Swiss Sanctuary

Having been constrained by the late extraordinary revolution of
affairs in England, the place of our birth, for avoiding the storm
that threatened us and the good people there, to quit that land,
after we had used our utmost endeavours for the advancement of
God's glory and the good of our country, we find cause to admire
the goodness of the Almighty, for inclining your Excellencies to
succour and protect us in this time of our distress . . .

Address by English refugees to the Lords of Berne, 1663

Samuel Pepys wrote with a mixture of wonder and disgust at the conduct of George Downing, the man who tricked, then trapped, John Okey, his former commanding officer and generous benefactor. The diarist called Downing 'a perfidious rogue; though the action is good and of service to the King, yet he cannot with any good conscience do it'.[1] Delighted with his three-man haul, and eager to encourage further hunting down of escaped regicides, Charles II awarded Downing a baronetcy the following year, and added to the diplomat's growing finances: soon he was buying up London property, part of which would become the street bearing his family name, which would in time leave a first-rate traitor for ever linked to the official address of British prime ministers.

Ludlow and the other regicides in Switzerland were shaken when they learnt of the Dutch hand in Barkstead, Corbet and Okey's repatriation for execution. They feared that Louis XIV of France – Charles

II's first cousin, and commander of Europe's mightiest army – might pressure the Swiss into giving them up, too. But Monsieur Voisin, the chief governing officer of Geneva, offered some reassurance: he quietly promised the refugees that he would not only protect them, but also pass on any letters received if they contained threats to their safety. He also undertook that, if the regicides were suddenly in danger in the night, he would use his key to the watergate, and so provide them with that safe passage out of the city. If a threat occurred in the daytime, they would be free to exit by any of the city's gates. Further, he pledged to work with his colleagues to make the Englishmen's lodgings as safe as they could be.

This was reassurance enough for Ludlow and several of his comrades. However, John Lisle and William Cawley (who had taken as their aliases, respectively, 'John Ralpheson' and 'William Johnson') still felt vulnerable, and chose to press for a public commitment from the Council of Geneva that it would defend them, whatever the cost. Despite the overwhelming sympathy of the Swiss representatives, this was not something they could agree to, and so Lisle and Cawley hired a boat to take them away.

Shortly afterwards Ludlow had a very uncomfortable audience with Voisin, who was disappointed that his previously private dealings on the regicides' behalf had been made public. He made it clear to Ludlow that, with Charles II now inevitably aware of these engagements, and likely to act, Geneva could no longer guarantee any of the exiles' safety. Ludlow decided to follow Lisle and Cawley to Lausanne. He was named alongside them in the Act of Protection quickly passed by the Lords of Berne.

Lausanne was now a rare safe haven for the fugitives. The Netherlands, so weak over Barkstead, Corbet and Okey, were now actively dangerous, having signed a treaty with Britain: one of its conditions was the extradition of any of Charles I's judges.

Meanwhile it was clear there would be no let-up in the manhunt for the regicides. Tales arrived from England of state-orchestrated campaigns to break potential enemies to the Crown. The exuberance that surrounded the Restoration had dissolved into disenchantment at the immorality of the returned court. This included unease at the political influence that Charles II's pre-eminent mistress, Barbara Palmer, Lady Castlemaine, and her faction, had over the King, who Pepys recorded, 'hates the very sight or thoughts of business'.[2]

There was also the perceived failure of the monarch to uphold the best interests of the people. The King's popularity plunged on news that he had, in October 1662, sold the French port of Dunkirk to Louis XIV for £320,000, in order, critics claimed, to pay for his glaring personal extravagance. English merchants were furious at the gratuitous loss of this important continental foothold, which had been secured by Cromwell shortly before his death: they correctly foresaw that Dunkirk would revert to its historic role as a base for enemy privateers, from which their shipping would be attacked.

Keen to distract critics of the Crown, and eager to draw their sting should matters deteriorate further, Charles's subordinates pointed to a series of contrived and fictional plots against the King. Major General Browne, who had testified so devastatingly against Scroope and Scott, now busied himself in flushing out potential rebels in the army through crude subterfuge. Middlemen bearing arms and cash led the gullible to believe a rising was imminent, which would be led by Ludlow, with Charles II's death its initial objective. This was appealing to some of Cromwell's former soldiers, particularly those struggling to make a living after the disbanding of their units. There was, in truth, little threat of a serious rebellion at this time. 'However,' Ludlow noted, 'this served the Court for a pretence to seize five or six hundred persons; to disarm all those they suspected; to require those they had taken to give bonds of £200 each, not to take up arms against the King, and to increase their standing guards.'[3]

Ludlow's alleged involvement in imaginary insurrections showed that he retained his status as one of the Crown's main bogeymen, his hand inevitably seen in the darkest of deeds. They said he had landed in Essex with Major General Whalley, another feared and elusive regicide. A further false report had him hiding in the City of London. Most fantastically, he was said to be preparing to rise up with an army of 40,000 disbanded Parliamentarian troops; all this, despite his reality being that of a distant and powerless refugee.

While peddling such fictions at home, the King's men were working to arrange the death or capture of Ludlow where they now knew him to be – in Switzerland. Fortunately for the lieutenant general, he had loyal local support: this was something he first appreciated when a merchant from Lausanne revealed to him that Charles I's youngest daughter, Henrietta, the Duchess of Orléans, had offered a man of his acquaintance 10,000 crowns to have him assassinated.

In the autumn of 1662, Ludlow and his associates were joined in Lausanne by eight other fugitives, several of them legal officers who had acted in the case against the late King at his trial: Edward Dendy, who had found his way safely south after his speedy flight from Rotterdam; William Say, who had, with Harrison and Lisle, been one of the first three to be excepted from the Act of Indemnity, and who had helped frame the warrant of Charles I's execution; Cornelius Holland, who had worked alongside Say, and amassed a fortune during the interregnum; Andrew Broughton, the clerk of the Court in January 1649, who had read out the charge against the King; John Phelps, the acting clerk of the Commons at the trial, who had quit England before the Restoration; Nicholas Love, a diligent member of several of the committees of the High Court of Justice, whose escape route had taken him to Norway, then Hamburg, and who had survived attacks by pirates and terrible storms along the way; Slingsby Bethel, a republican merchant who had not been involved in the King's death, but who, because of his recent support for Lambert's attempted rising, thought it wiser to be abroad than not; and a single military man, Lieutenant Colonel Biscoe, who had been part of the storming party at Basing House and an MP in Richard Cromwell's Protectorate, and who was a known conspirator against the Stuart Restoration.

The settling in one area of so many wanted men made for an irre-sistible target. All were aware of the great rewards given to Downing for apprehending Barkstead, Corbet and Okey. Fortune-hunters and fervent Royalists made plans to strike. On advice, Ludlow and five other regicides – Bethel, Cawley, Holland, Lisle and Say – moved eleven miles south-east from Lausanne to the town of Vevey. The remainder elected to stay in Lausanne: Biscoe and Phelps decided to use Switzerland as the base of their new trading activi-ties, which they planned to operate throughout Germany and the Netherlands; Broughton and Dendy promised to keep in close touch with their friends in Vevey.

The wanted men gravitated towards the most sympathetic Swiss communities for, as one who was engaged in tracking them down wrote, 'the people in the cantons of Fribourg, Lucerne and those others which are not Puritan would hang these assassins, if they had it in their power.'[4] Even the Protestant cantons contained many citizens 'earnestly desiring a good correspondence with that King [Charles II],' as a burger of Zurich wrote, 'who is the crown of our head, and to be as well beloved of his Majesty, as we have been of all his predecessors ever since [the] Reformation'.[5]

In Vevey the regicides were warmly received and given ready reassurances as to their safety. The magistrates explained that, as Ludlow wrote: 'the principal motive that inclined them to offer their services in so hearty a manner was the consideration of our sufferings for the liberties of our country.'[6] They moved into a house at the southeast corner of the town's marketplace, before relocating to a more secure property abutting the town's eastern gate. Ludlow was told to sound the alarm bell next to their lodgings if they ever felt in danger. More importantly for the pious group, their religious needs were also met, with places quickly arranged for them in Vevey's two churches, St Claire's and St Martin's.

The refugees thought it correct to go to Berne to express their gratitude and relief at the sanctuary offered by the canton. Here they were feted by members of the senate, who felt great sympathy for the English refugees and expressed their dismay that the Dutch had sacrificed three of the regicides' comrades in return for mere trading rights. In a public demonstration of their pride at providing sanctuary to such esteemed guests the lords escorted the regicides to church, and insisted they take the principal seats during the service.

Over dinner that evening, Ludlow and one of Berne's senators, Colonel Weiss, discussed the situation in England; Weiss asked how it was that the Parliamentarians had been removed from power without a fight? Ludlow explained that 'most of those persons who had first engaged in the war, having made their own peace, had endeavoured to deliver us and the cause itself into the hands of our enemies; and though they had many opportunities to have ended the dispute by destroying the King's army, they neglected all, and only endeavoured to reduce the crown to their own terms.'[7] He remained convinced that he and his fellow regicides were true believers in the cause, offered up for sacrifice by self-seeking comrades who had betrayed them and forfeited their honour.

The Englishmen returned to troubling news in Vevey. Major Germaine Riordane, an Irishman who had served under the Duke of York when fighting for Spain against the French and English in the 1650s, was reported to be in Turin. There, he had let slip that his mission was to capture or kill the regicides being harboured by the Swiss.

Reports of other such plots came in from several cities in nearby cantons, as well as from Italy and France: assassins were heading towards Switzerland, eager to make their names and their fortunes by harvesting regicides. Ludlow learnt that the French had written to the senators of Berne, asking what might persuade them to hand over the exiles. Charles II had also communicated with Louis XIV, claiming he could never feel that his life was safe while such prominent traitors were still alive and at large. He would be grateful for his cousin's aid in seizing and killing those within France's reach. The sheer number of threats was overwhelming, and for none more so than Ludlow. A friend passed him stark advice from an anonymous source: 'If you wish the preservation of the English general at Vevey, let him know that he must remove from thence with speed, if he have any regard for himself.'[8]

The Englishmen met to discuss their predicament. All agreed they should not move to any country with a crowned head, since any such ruler might well feel he had common cause with Charles II and hand them over. After further discussion they decided that Vevey was the safest haven they knew of, and they resolved to stay there. The town's upcoming fair, when the place would be awash with strangers, was identified as a potential opportunity for assassins to gain access to them. They would find new lodgings for that night and ask the magistrates to double their protection.

On the evening of the fair, 14 November 1663, the assassins made their move. A dozen men arrived in Vevey at six o'clock, an hour after sunset, having crossed Lake Geneva from the Duchy of Savoy – where the nobility was sympathetic to the English Crown. They separated from their boatmen, divided into two groups to lessen suspicion, and took rooms in separate inns. Some claimed to be Catholics, en route for Fribourg, where they would be honouring a saint renowned for miracle-working. To lend credibility to this ruse, they hired horses for the journey that they knew they would never make.

Informants reported that the strangers stayed up all night at an inn, and were 'being instructed by a spy (whom we had observed sometimes in the town)'. The men seemed to have good knowledge of the regicides' routines and daily lives. The plan was to strike the next day, a Sunday, when the assassins 'placed themselves upon the avenues from our house, some before and some behind and some upon the crossways, that they might fall upon us, [and] surprise and assassinate us, going to the church'.

The owner of the lodgings where the regicides had been staying was a Monsieur Dubois. It was his custom to set off for church after the majority of the congregation had assembled there. That Sunday morning he left later than was usual for him, in the company of a friend. Dubois was surprised to see a boat by the lake, with four men standing nearby, oars at the ready. He noticed six other strangers, loitering in pairs, trying to look nonchalant. These were, in the words of one of the regicides, 'ruffian-like fellows, desperados with long cloaks and carbines under them ... and looking behind him he [Dubois] saw more of the like crew, and walking a little further perceived the avenues of his house guarded, and the way to the church beset with the rest'.[9] Dubois pretended to have forgotten something and doubled back to alert the Englishmen.

After discussions the regicides elected to attend church that morning, but to go by a different route to normal. One of them could not resist going to get a glimpse of their would-be murderers, and so he 'walked some few steps towards them, as if we intended [to go] the usual way, and having seen what we were informed of we suddenly returned another way, and so disappointed the surprise'.[10] The regicides were sitting safely in church when they noticed one of the gang creep in to check where his intended victims had gone. He then left to report back to his colleagues that their prey had already reached the shelter of the service. The twelve would-be killers were later seen at an inn, 'where they sat disconsolate for losing their enterprise'.[11]

On leaving church, and hearing that those sent to kill him were busy indoors, eating lunch, Ludlow took the opportunity to steal down to the lake with some men, to examine the waiting boat. He noted that the gang's boatmen remained at the ready, next to their oars, and saw that the bottom of the boat contained a generous amount of straw. Beneath this, he could make out a large cache of weapons. Ludlow also noticed that the boatmen had cut the ropes securing the oars of all the other boats along the lakeside, so they would be unable to give pursuit to the assassins' vessel. When the local people saw this had happened they tackled the boatmen and threatened to have them arrested, 'which made them presently call their masters, who made great haste to their boats, and rowed away with all speed, otherwise they would have been taken'.[12]

The regicides made immediate enquiries into this chilling incursion. Their contacts discovered that the plot had been masterminded by Major Riordane, who had paid for everything that the men had needed in Vevey. Other key figures included Louis Deprez, a ne'er-do-well from Savoy, and two inhabitants of Lyons. The whole endeavour had been funded by Charles II's sister, the Duchess of Orléans, just as she had been behind the earlier, aborted, plan to pay 10,000 crowns for Ludlow's death.

The people of Vevey treated the attempted assassinations of their English guests as an appalling affront to their community. The town's leaders ordered a thorough tightening of security: all inn-keepers were obliged to give a nightly, sworn, account of those lodging in their premises. Vevey's boats were to be kept in readiness for any attempted return by Riordane's men, and all suspicious craft coming from Savoy would, from that point on, be searched. One of the boatmen who had transported the assassins was captured in the harbour of Morges, in the canton of Vaud. On 1 January 1664, Ludlow and his comrades were invited to this man's interrogation by the bailiff of Vevey. His initial silence was broken by the threat of torture, and he was able to confirm the identity of the three main conspirators, while revealing that Deprez had told all aboard on their return to Savoy that the botched attempt had deprived them all of a very significant bounty.

Ludlow now received a fresh warning: it was he who was the assassins' principal target. 'You are hated and feared more than all the rest of your companions,' a friend informed him; 'your head is set at a great price: 'tis against you they take all this pains to find assassins, and 'twas on your account they contrived the late attempt; so that upon the whole matter I cannot but advise, that you would resolve to retire to some place where you may be unknown, there being, in my opinion, no other way to secure you from the rage of your enemies.'[13] Meanwhile Edmund Steiger wrote from Berne, saying he felt responsible for being one of those who had recommended somewhere as exposed as Vevey for Ludlow's asylum. He realised now that it was easy for the enemy to cross the lake from France or Savoy, and so be upon him and his comrades before anyone could spring to their defence. He urged them to move to somewhere more secure, and suggested Yverden, or a return to Lausanne, where he could provide more comprehensive security.

With his customary sangfroid Ludlow refused to run: he calculated that he was safe in Vevey; he knew the place and its people, and they knew him; it would be safer to stay put than to start again in a new place, ignorant of his surroundings, unprotected and distrustful. He formally released Steiger from any responsibility for his and his comrades' safety. From now on they would be sure to look after themselves.

John Lisle listened to the repeated warnings with increasing fear. He felt that the other regicides would be left alone were it not for the feared and hated Ludlow's presence in their midst. He therefore decided to return to Lausanne, pretending that this was because his wife, Alice, was coming to visit him that spring: if she came to Vevey she would most likely be spotted, and this could make life difficult for her on her return to England.

'Before he left us,' Ludlow remembered, 'he made his will, and took leave of the magistrates and of all his friends in the town in a solemn manner.' Ludlow knew that the leading lawyer, who had sat by Bradshaw's side in 1649, was another prized scalp for the Royalists. 'At our parting, I took liberty to desire him to take the best care he could of himself, and not to be too confident of his security, upon supposition that I was the only person marked out for destruction; since he well knew, that at a consult held by our enemies at Chatillon, they had enquired after him as well as myself,' he continued.[14] Ludlow's last words to Lisle, before he left, were that he should never drop his guard.

In late 1663, Major Riordane travelled to France to meet with Henrietta, the Duchess of Orléans, and establish why Deprez had failed in his attempt on the regicides' lives. Riordane next continued on to England, to pass on to Charles II the lessons learnt. The King welcomed him to court, listened to him with interest, and encouraged him to try again.

Riordane's written report of 29 December[15] most likely reflects his conversations with Henrietta and Charles II. It is interesting to note how flawed some of his basic intelligence had been, including incorrect identification of some of those hiding in Vevey. His letter mentions Ludlow first, and also accurately records John Lisle's presence. The Irishman noted how impressed the Swiss were by the titles of these two men – Ludlow being a general, and Lisle still calling himself 'Chancellor of England' – and by the religious devotion of the distinguished pair. However, Riordane also stated, erroneously, that major generals William Goffe and Edward Whalley were part of the group in Vevey. Goffe, whose religious zeal had been so obvious at the Putney debates, and Whalley, from whose custody in Hampton Court Charles I had escaped, were not, and never would be, in Switzerland.

Riordane's spies had carefully recorded the regicides' activities: their reluctance to travel, except to and from church on Sundays – something they only did after careful reconnaissance of the safest routes by one of their number, in the company of Monsieur Dubois; their ingratiation to the citizens of Vevey, who seemed to be in their thrall; their regular receipt of large quantities of letters, by boat, from Geneva; and the enormous amount of time they spent composing their own correspondence. Riordane reckoned that these fugitives constituted a seditious cell, their numerous letters surely fanning the flames of future insurrection against Charles II. To illustrate his point, he reported that Ludlow had seemed close to death with sadness after hearing of the failure of a planned republican rising in Yorkshire earlier that year.

The Irishman urged Charles II to write to the cantons of Berne and Zurich, asking 'with all the force of a sovereign power for the return of parricides to whom all of Europe has refused asylum'.[16] Riordane thought such letters would succeed because he believed the Swiss were easily influenced and, at heart, believers in justice. He also pointed out that Vevey was an easy place in which to catch the fugitives, since it only had two paths leading in and out of it, one of which was effectively closed now that the garrison commander at Fort l'Ecluse was actively looking out for suspicious Englishmen. This left Lake Geneva as the only means of escape. If the Swiss persisted in granting asylum to the fugitives, Riordane suggested the best plan would be to wheedle a spy into their group who could report back on the layout of their house – revealing where any hiding places and false doors might be. If he had this information, Riordane was confident he and his men could storm the building and do their worst, before any help arrived.

Riordane's men returned to Vevey in the summer of 1664 with Ludlow uppermost in their minds. The main ringleaders met in woodland on the eve of their attack to discuss their options. Any approach by boat had a strong chance of interception, and a large band of men arriving in town would be bound to excite suspicion too. They therefore decided to access Vevey by foot, in a small group, with horses on hand to help aid their escape.

Those selected to do the killing arrived to find the regicides extremely well guarded and in the highest state of alert. Ludlow had been receiving excellent intelligence about Riordane's plans from a disgruntled associate of Deprez; he knew the names of the six men most intimately involved in the hunting down of his colony of regicides, and he knew when they were on their way. When two of Riordane's men tried to gain access to Sunday worship, Ludlow sounded the alarm and the town magistrate removed the assailants at gunpoint.

When Riordane arrived in the town, pretending to be a Burgundian, he found that he could move around incognito; but he was unable to penetrate the protective barrier constructed by the people of Vevey around their English guests. The watchfulness of Vevey's citizens proved of repeated benefit to the regicides. One of them, a Monsieur Moulin, was riding towards Lausanne accompanied by servants when he saw four men coming the other way, three on horseback and the other on foot. Moulin got off his mount and pretended to find a problem in one of its hooves, before turning back to warn the Englishmen of the suspicious group approaching. By the time an armed posse had arrived from Vevey to apprehend the group of four, they had fled on a boat heading back towards Savoy. It was later established that their role had been to help the escape of two assassins in the town once they had completed their mission; but this duo also bolted for safety on realising their plans had been compromised. There were other attempts, but none were successful. The assassins now began to look elsewhere.

On Thursday 11 August 1664, John Lisle was walking to the church of St François in Lausanne, wearing the robes of the Chancellor of England: this distinctive attire rather undermined his caution in having recently taken a pseudonym – 'Mr Field'.

A man in a less eye-catching cape emerged from the barber's shop where he had been lurking. Seeing Lisle approach, he walked towards him, and greeted him as he passed. When Lisle entered the churchyard this man followed him, and, according to a contemporary news-sheet, pushed back his cloak and pulled out a musketoon, a short carbine with a flared barrel. He shouted out Lisle's name and ordered him, by the authority of the King of England, to surrender or die. 'Whereupon,' the report continued, 'Lisle with some of the rest presented their pistols, but one of the gentlemen was too quick for him, and shot him into the body with 5 bullets out of a musqueton, so that he fell dead upon the place.'[17] Chaos ensued. As Lisle collapsed, mortally wounded, the assassin, having discharged his blunderbuss, tripped and fell. Shouting, '*Vive le roi d'Angleterre!*' the murderer got back to his feet, then ran towards a mounted accomplice, who threw him the reins of the spare horse by his side. The pair turned towards the nearby city gate, and disappeared at a gallop.

Lisle had been alerted to the suspicious pair in town. They had been spotted waiting outside a church service earlier in the day, scanning the faces of the members of the congregation for someone in particular. One of them had reportedly been heard to say, 'The bastard won't be coming', before sloping off. Lisle had been warned not to go to his regular place of worship: it was too dangerous to stick to a predictable routine with such people about; but he had refused to listen, reminding friends that he had committed his safety into God's hands. He added that he also considered his life safe while Edmund Ludlow lived, since the lieutenant general was the Royalists' prime target. Only when Ludlow was slain would he take extra care, since he would then, he accepted, become the most wanted of the remaining runaways.

According to Ludlow, the assassins had not gone two miles when they came across workers in a vineyard. They bid them thank the governors of Lausanne for helping them in their task that day, and said they would drink their health that night. There was never any proof of complicity between the Swiss officials and the assassins, and this may have been an attempt by the killers to leave discord in their wake. They were pursued by a large force on horseback, but eventually reached safety in Gex, just over the French border.

The Newes of London on 8 September 1664 reported: 'This signal act of just vengeance is applauded by all people that have any sense of generosity, and [is] looked upon as a most remarkable manifestation of God's displeasure against these wretches, to see them pursued into their securest retreats, and cut off by the stroke of divine justice in the very arms of their protectors. (To their shame be it spoken, that harboured them, and made a Protestant canton a sanctuary for such impious parricides.)'[18]

The regicides in Switzerland were left deeply shocked by the loss of one of their leading figures, in broad daylight, while guarded: none of them could now feel safe. A report from Paris summed up their fears: 'However these regicides may for a while trifle with the blood of kings, and outface their wickedness, we see that Divine vengeance finds them out at last.'[19]

Chapter 12

Vengeance at Last

We have considered the Nature of Your Majesty's Declaration
from Breda; and are humbly of opinion, that Your Majesty ought
not to be pressed with it any further; because, it is not a Promise
in itself, but only a gracious declaration of Your Majesty's inten-
tions.

Address of the House of Commons to Charles II,
27 February 1663

In London, there was ambivalence about what to do with the
remaining regicides. There were those who felt the thirteen public
executions comprised enough of a blood sacrifice to atone for the
years of civil war; others pushed for further acts of retribution,
among them the King and his inner circle of advisers who used the
supposed threat of a republican resurgence in their drive to extract
more revenue from Parliament.

In March 1662, Charles II summoned the Commons to Whitehall: 'Gentlemen,' he said,

I need not put you in mind of the miserable effects which have
attended the wants and necessities of the Crown: I need not tell you,
that there is a Republican Party still in the Kingdom, which have the
courage to promise themselves another Revolution: and, methinks, I
should as little need to tell you, that the only way, with God's
Blessing, to disappoint their hopes, and indeed to reduce them from

those extravagant hopes and desires, is, to let them see that you have
so provided for the Crown, that it hath wherewithal to support itself,
and to secure you; which, I am sure, is all I desire, and desire only for
your preservation.[1]

The continued punishment of those who had killed Charles I was
crucial in reminding everyone how terrible things had been, and
could be again, if his son was left inadequately funded. Meanwhile
Nature was steadily reducing the number of those who needed to
be held to account.

At the Restoration the majority of the regicides were in their
fifties and sixties. Grim prison conditions and the stress of their
situations added to a steady cull, of whom the defiant Sir John
Bourchier had been an early example. Simon Mayne, a Bucking-
hamshire MP who was related to six other regicides – including
Oliver Cromwell and Henry Marten – had concealed himself in a
hideaway in his family seat, Dinton Hall, before surrendering in
June 1660. He claimed at his trial that Thomas Chaloner had forced
him into signing the death warrant, threatening that if he failed to
do so his estate would be confiscated. Mayne's health was never
robust; he had been granted a special dispensation in the mid-1630s,
allowing him to eat meat instead of the statutory fish on Fridays,
because of his 'notorious sickness'. Condemned to death, he cheated
the executioner by succumbing to gout, complicated by fever and
convulsions, in the spring of 1661. His body was released to his
family, provided he was buried 'without ostentation'.

The rotund Colonel Vincent Potter had cut a very sorry figure at
the regicides' trial. A founding member of the Massachusetts Bay
Company, he had fought in the Pequot War in the 1630s, when
English settlers in conjunction with Native American allies attacked
the Pequot tribe. The strict Puritan had returned to England in time
for the Civil War. He took an active role as a cavalry officer in
Parliament's army, before finding his true calling: controlling military logistics. Potter's particular contribution to the cause was
insisting that the New Model Army pay its way when on campaign,

so that it did not alienate the local inhabitants, something the King's forces were often guilty of.

Potter had signed not only Charles's death warrant, but also those of the Royalist lords who followed him to the block after the Second Civil War. Arrested at the Restoration, Potter arrived in court in anguish at his plight – 'I pray that the passing [of] the sentence for execution may be suspended' – and racked with severe pain from kidney stones – 'My Lord, my condition requires ease for my body.' His request for permission to be excused from the courtroom so he could urinate was cruelly denied: the Lord Chief Baron allowed only that a chair be brought for him. When it arrived the shackled Potter was instructed to sit. 'I hope I may be freed from irons,' Potter continued, 'I am in pain, and a man of bulk.'[2] Pleading for mercy, his appearance in court was frequently punctuated by tears. It ended in the inevitable guilty verdict and death sentence. He was spared hanging, drawing and quartering by dying of natural causes within a year.

Christmas Day 1661 saw the death in prison of Owen Rowe, a silk merchant who also had trade ties to the American colonies: he dealt in tobacco from Virginia, and was another early investor in the Massachusetts Bay Company. Rowe had long intended to emigrate to New England, but events kept him rooted to London where he simultaneously served as a colonel of militia and arranged rich supplies for the Parliamentary cause. From his trading activities in the Atlantic, Rowe reported that the people of Bermuda remained vehemently opposed to the late King's execution. He had countered this by effectively taking control of the colony. After casting himself on Charles II's mercy – 'I have heard he is a gracious King, full of lenience and mercy, [and] so I hope I shall find it'[3] – he died, aged sixty-nine, in the Tower.

Sixty-two-year-old Gilbert Millington, the MP from Nottinghamshire, who had previously married a sixteen-year-old 'alehouse wench', had said in mitigation at his trial, 'My Lord, I am an ancient man and deaf.'[4] This had not been enough to gain mercy, but his subsequent grovelling apology to the King would spare his life, if not his property. He was sent to Mont Orgueil Castle on the east coast of Jersey, where he died within a few years – certainly before the autumn of 1666, but no record of the exact date survives. He was joined in this, Jersey's main prison, by four fellow regicides: Thomas Waite, Rutland's MP and commander of militia (who had hacked the hands off, and killed, Charles I's chaplain, Hudson); Henry Smith, a Leicestershire MP and infantry colonel; James Temple, an MP and the New Model Army's governor of Arundel Castle; and Sir Hardress Waller, one of Oliver Cromwell's most loyal cronies, who had played a central part in Pride's Purge, and who had been first to plead guilty to high treason at trial.

George Fleetwood, brother of General Charles Fleetwood, had expected to be pardoned: he had refused to take part in Lambert's last rising; Monck had entrusted him with a regiment in the months leading up to the Restoration. When sentenced to death he had pleaded for mercy, pointing to his youth and reluctant endorsement of the death warrant: he had only been twenty-five and, he insisted, had been bullied into signing by Cromwell. Monck's support saw Fleetwood's sentence commuted to life imprisonment, and confiscation of his property. In 1664 an order was drawn up for him to be transported to Tangier, the North African territory that had come to Charles II as part of the dowry of his Portuguese wife, Catharine of Braganza. Prison life there was hot and hellish, the regicides' families fearing it as a 'barbarous and distant'[5] destination for their loved ones. It is not certain if Fleetwood died there, or whether the pleading of his second wife, Hester, managed, as some claim, to secure his secret freedom; according to this version Fleetwood crossed to America and lived in Boston for the rest of his life.

The lawyer Augustine Garland had been chairman of the committee behind the King's trial – something he tried to explain to his own judge by pointing to the chaos of the time: 'My Lord, I did not know which way to be safe in any thing, without doors was misery, within doors was mischief.'[6] Garland had been accused of being the man who spat in Charles I's face during his trial, a charge he categorically rejected. Given his prominence in the proceedings,

and the astonishing disrespect he had allegedly shown the martyred
King, Garland was lucky to have his death sentence quashed. He
was instead given life imprisonment. In 1664 he was transported to
Tangier. He was ordered to be returned to Portsmouth's grimly
utilitarian Southsea Castle in 1677, at which point he drops out of
sight.

Others who had been men of enormous power, but who eked out
their final years in imprisoned anonymity, included Robert
Lilburne. Monck's predecessor as commander-in-chief of Scotland,
Lilburne had surrendered in the statutory two-week period in June
1660. He was sent to Drake's Island in Plymouth Sound the next
year, where he died four years later.

It was a similar tale with John Downes, who had pleaded with
the High Court of Justice to hear Charles I before he was condemned
– an intervention that had drawn Cromwell's intense anger. Downes
claimed at his own trial that he had only signed the King's death
warrant under duress, during a time of military dominance. 'When
those times were,' Downes explained, 'how impetuous the soldiers,
how not a man that durst either disown them or speak against them,
I was threatened with my very life, by the threats of one that hath
received his reward, I was induced to it.'[7] Downes was spared
execution and committed to the Tower. He came close to release in
early 1662, but was disappointed. Downes was still on the roll-call
of prisoners in late 1666, yet when he died after that is not recorded.

For some the sentences that sent them into nameless obscurity
were punctuated by deliberate, public, humiliation. 'We walked
with thousands of people to Tyburn,' wrote the visiting Dutch
artist William Schellinks on 27 January 1662, 'and saw there Lord
Monson, Sir Henry Mildmay and Mr Wallop lying in their tabards
on a little straw on a hurdle being dragged through under the
gallows, where some articles were read to them and then torn up.
After that they were again dragged through the streets back to the
Tower. Their sentence is that they are to be dragged through under
the gallows on this day every year.'[8] The House of Commons had
handed down this punishment to the trio, each of whom was a

former MP, six months earlier. All of them were spared execution because they had neither been in court on the day of the King's sentencing, nor signed the death warrant. But they were told they had done enough wrong by sitting as commissioners of the High Court of Justice to forfeit their freedom for ever, and also that they would have to undergo the annual humiliation witnessed by Schellinks. Their appeal to the Lords against this 'most ignominious' ordeal was dismissed.

Mildmay was one of the most unlikely to have his life spared: he was a significant enemy of the Crown, having assisted Thomas Scott as Parliamentary spymaster, and he had loudly opposed any compromise with the King in the weeks preceding Charles's trial. In 1664 it was ordered that he be imprisoned in Tangier, but he died en route in Antwerp.

Monson had been given his Irish title in the third year of Charles I's reign, but he had opposed the Crown for years, before siding with Parliament during the Civil Wars. He attended the first three days of the King's trial and then declined to take any further part. This change of heart saved his life, after he surrendered himself in June 1660. But his claim that he had only taken part in the High Court of Justice in order to save Charles by preventing 'that horrid murder'[9] was rejected. He was stripped of his titles and possessions, and sent to the Fleet prison, an institution he knew well, having been locked up there during the Commonwealth when convicted as a debtor. This was where he died in the early 1670s.

Robert Wallop, a Hampshire MP, was a cousin of Monson's. Wallop had mounted a similar defence to that of his relative, maintaining that he had sat as a commissioner 'only at the request of his Majesty's friends, in order to try to moderate their furious proceedings'.[10] The Commons disregarded this excuse and he was imprisoned in the Tower, dying there in 1667.

Colonel John Hutchinson had been quickly forgiven by the Commons, thanks to the carefully pitched speech in which he presented himself as having had a reluctant and insignificant role in the drama of the King's trial. He had also benefited from the campaign of vocal support orchestrated by his wife and by his brother-in-law, Sir Allen Apsley, one of Charles II's hard-living set. Attention in mid-1660 had been on finding just seven scapegoats to atone for the days of rebellion against the Crown, and this Nottinghamshire gentleman-soldier was never going to warrant inclusion in such a select number.

His forgiveness was secured in that tiny window between Charles's restoration becoming inevitable, and the insistence that all involved in his father's death should be punished. In retrospect, many believed Hutchinson's pardon to have been over-hasty, ill-considered and incorrect. The chancellor, the Earl of Clarendon, rated him one of the most dangerous men in the kingdom. When bureaucrats retrieved the trial records from the bowels of Parliament it quickly became clear that Hutchinson had been intricately involved in its procedure. He was seen to have sat on key committees, and to have been present during most of the hearings. As the net had widened, and every signatory to the death warrant had been found answerable for his hand in Charles I's demise, so Hutchinson's escape became increasingly galling. When Scroope's initial forgiveness was overturned, thanks to later testimony, many wondered if Hutchinson would be similarly up-ended.

Much would depend on Hutchinson's attitude: the Royalists wanted to see him openly and sincerely repent for his part in the King's trial and death. Also, with the rest of the regicides coming to trial, he was expected to repay the leniency shown to him by assisting in their prosecution.

But Hutchinson felt guilt, not gratitude, at escaping the fate being prepared for his comrades. He had come to resent his wife for having persuaded him to purchase his life with what had, at heart, been a lie. He had obeyed her in a moment of understandable weakness, but he remained proud of his cause, and his profound religious beliefs made his conscience prickle at his dishonest path to mercy. He took to reading his Bible more, finding in it many passages that confirmed his belief that what he had done in the cause of

Parliament – including being one of the King's judges – had been correct, and should be a source of pride, not shame.

Sir Geoffrey Palmer, the attorney general, summoned Hutchinson from his Nottinghamshire estate to help him prepare for his case against the twenty-nine men that were now held in custody. At their meeting Palmer suddenly produced the King's death warrant and urged Hutchinson to share his eyewitness account of what had happened at its signing: he wanted to build a picture of each regicide's attitude and actions at that critical event.

Hutchinson, still smarting at Colonel Ingoldsby's life-saving lie, drily replied to Palmer that he could not even remember the moment when Cromwell allegedly 'forced' Ingoldsby to sign. 'And then, Sir,' said Hutchinson, 'if I have lost so great a thing as that, it cannot be expected less eminent passages remain with me.'[11] Palmer next urged Hutchinson to confirm the identity of each of the signatories. Hutchinson claimed this might not prove possible, since he had not corresponded with most of them, so was unfamiliar with their handwriting. When pressed to look more closely, the colonel said some of the signatures looked like ones he had seen before – but the only ones he verified were those of Cromwell, Ireton and Lord Grey of Groby – all three of whom were safely dead.

This absolute refusal to assist the prosecution was reported to Charles II, who was furious with Hutchinson, saying that the colonel would surely do to him what he had done to his father, 'for he was still unchanged in his principles, and readier to protect than to accuse any of his associates'.[12] Ingoldsby recommended that the stubborn Hutchinson be brought to court as a witness. He walked into the packed courtroom and was forced to pass in front of the defendants. Hutchinson's feelings of fellowship with the accused, and pride in their mutual cause, were matched by his revulsion at those judges who had sided with Parliament but were now assembled to condemn their former comrades. He felt particular disgust for Monck, 'that vile traitor who had sold the men that trusted him',[13] especially because he had supported Monck on his march south, believing that he had come to save Parliament. Hutchinson was so sickened by the level of treachery and hypocrisy on show in the courtroom that, he told his wife, had he been called to give testimony, he would have spoken for the Parliamentary cause.

At the conclusions of that first day's hearing, Hutchinson decided he would not repeat the unedifying experience. He left London, sending a pert message to Palmer that, as he had no evidence to give, he would no longer be attending the trial. The attorney general wrote a withering critique of Hutchinson, and sent it to Charles II and Clarendon. It sealed his fate.

Hutchinson experienced a recurring dream at this time. Its central image was a boat on the River Thames which men were struggling to steer against the wind and tide, in order to bring it safely to the borough of Southwark on the far side. In the dream Hutchinson barked at his companions to stop what they were doing: 'Let it alone, and let me try.' He pushed the boat with his chest, his efforts easing the vessel across, allowing him to reach the far bank, where he stepped onto 'the most pleasant lovely fields, so green and so flourishing and so embellished with the cheerful sun'.[14] Here he encountered his father, who presented Hutchinson with laurel leaves. These had words written on them that he could never decipher.

Hutchinson's wife, Lucy, felt the dream's interpretation was clear: the boat represented the Commonwealth; the other men aboard were those who had hijacked and compromised its cause for their own benefit; while Hutchinson denoted the martyrs who could make the cause come good again – but only through the ultimate sacrifice. Having saved his life by timely pleading and influential allies, Hutchinson now seemed set on forfeiting it for a cause that he believed blended the politically desirable with God's will. His insulting refusal to bow to the King's wishes presented his enemies with the perfect opportunity to act against a hated and feared enemy. Clarendon admonished Sir Allen Apsley for having acted on his brother-in-law's behalf: 'Oh Nall! What have you done? You have saved a man that would be ready, if he had opportunity, to mischief us as much as ever he did.'[15]

All those who had supported the colonel's plea were similarly reproached. The next time she was in London, Lucy Hutchinson found her carriage next to that of a cousin who was an influential courtier. From her window she called out, asking him to help her husband come to no harm. 'I could wish it had been finished last time,' the relative replied, 'for your husband hath lately so behaved himself that it will pass against him.' Startled, Mrs Hutchinson countered, 'I pray, let my friends but do their endeavours for me, and then let it be as God will.' The Royalist cousin replied, ominously: 'It is not now as God will, but as we will.'[16]

Another relative suggested that Lucy could save her husband if she secretly handed over any useful information she could glean from him, in particular if she had any intelligence relating to Sir Henry Vane, William Pierrepoint or Oliver St John, three political enemies of the Crown; this would be of such great value that it would save her family from its otherwise inevitable loss and ruin. Lucy refused to be part of a transaction that traded her husband's wellbeing for the lives of others. Her cousin warned that, if that were the case, the colonel must flee England as soon as possible: if he did not, it had been determined that he would be arrested on the slightest pretext, and once that happened he would have no hope of release. When Lucy passed on this advice, the colonel declined to contemplate escape, claiming that God, who had always protected him in the past, would use him as he saw fit. This was the same way of thinking that had ended in disaster for Lisle.

On a Sunday in October 1663, Colonel Hutchinson led his household's Sunday religious service at his family seat, Owthorpe Hall, and read a New Testament lesson to his family and servants. After the ceremony, one of his retainers returned in an agitated state: soldiers were approaching. Hutchinson calmly remained in his parlour until the troops arrived. They were from the local militia, and their officer brandished a search warrant for arms, as well as an order insisting that the colonel accompany them.

For two hours the soldiers ransacked the house, turning up

nothing more than four shotguns hanging in the kitchen, which were used for killing game for the pot. By the time they had finished it had become, in the words of Lucy Hutchinson, 'as bitter a stormy, pitchy, dark, black, rainy night as any [that] came that year'.[17] But the Royalists refused to allow John Hutchinson to wait till the morning, when his coach might be made ready, and had his son lead him on a horse through the hostile night. They reached the Talbot Inn in Newark at four in the morning, where Hutchinson was shown to a 'vile' room, which he was forced to share with two guards.

He was kept there for several days, while the Royalists returned for further searches of his house – some official, others nothing more than plundering parties. They also stationed spies to keep Owthorpe under surveillance. Meanwhile, in London, a case was being built against Hutchinson, the essence of which was that his traitor's heart was unchanged. It became clear that the colonel had few remaining friends, even among the Parliamentarians: they suspected he had done a deal with the Crown; how else to explain his being spared the vicious death suffered by his fellow regicides?

Hutchinson was taken under cavalry escort to meet the Marquess of Newcastle. Newcastle had commanded the King's forces in the north of England during the Civil War, at one point offering Hutchinson £10,000 and a peerage if he would surrender Nottingham. Hutchinson had refused, so keeping a key Parliamentary stronghold alive in a largely Royalist landscape. The marquess had gone into voluntary exile after the Royalist defeat at Marston Moor in 1644, returning to his previous eminence with the Restoration, although his colossal wealth had been trimmed: his wife Margaret, a playwright, estimated that supporting the King's cause had cost the family nearly £1 million.

Newcastle was at a loss to explain Hutchinson's arrest, confiding to him, 'Colonel, they say you desire to know your accusers, which is more than I know.'[18] Since the Crown had no case, Hutchinson dared hope that he would soon be released. Newcastle showed him a letter he had received from the Duke of Buckingham. In October

1663 the duke had helped suppress the Farnley Wood plot, a small insurrection in Yorkshire by anti-monarchists who planned to take control of the prosperous market town of Leeds, hoping this would lead to a return to the days of the republic. It was part of a minor revolt that occurred simultaneously in two other northern counties, Durham and Westmorland, involving just a hundred men, many of them former Parliamentary soldiers who mistakenly believed they would be led to glory by their old commander-in-chief, Lord Fairfax. But Fairfax was not involved in any way in this feeblest of rebellions – which did not embrace 'one person of talent or consideration' (Sir James Mackintosh wrote, 170 years later, in *The History of England*) – and the suspicion quickly arose that the entire enterprise had been one of the Royalists' ruses to flush out enemy sympathisers. At the same time the backlash to such imagined threats gave the authorities a chance to haul in other undesirables, by pretending they were guilty by association. Charges of setting up the innocent were strongly refuted at the time, Royalist propagandists stating that only 'Pens that were dipt in the blood of the late King'[19] could dare write such outrageous lies. But what happened to John Hutchinson proves otherwise.

Newcastle had released Hutchinson on the basis that there was no charge to answer. A few days later, though, having been advised by Buckingham that, 'though he could not make it out as yet, he hoped he should bring Mr Hutchinson into the plot',[20] the marquess sent his apologies along with a fresh arrest force to Owthorpe, to bring the colonel in once more. This time he was placed under close arrest and forbidden use of pen or paper. He was kept in a harsh prison in Newark, where his fragile health quickly crumbled, before being taken south to the Tower of London.

There, Hutchinson was questioned by one of the senior politicians in the land: the newly ennobled Lord Arlington was a favourite of Charles II, and part of his duties was the securing and managing of the King's mistresses. Arlington presented a bizarre face to the world, choosing to cover a wound he had received on the bridge of his nose, in a Civil War skirmish, with a prominent black plaster. Arlington received Hutchinson in his rooms in Whitehall and presented him with fifteen questions relating to his political and religious beliefs, the identity of his friends, and his recent whereabouts. Dissatisfied with the colonel's replies, Arlington warned that he would be recalled for further interrogation.

Hutchinson was eating supper in his cell one evening when Arlington made good his threat. A strong escort arrived and took him by boat from the Tower to Whitehall. There, he was informed, he would be questioned again, within the hearing of the King. After a long wait Arlington arrived and steered Hutchinson away from the guards in the room towards a window. 'Mr Hutchinson,' he said, 'you have now been some days in prison. Have you recollected yourself any more to say than when I last spoke to you?' The colonel said he had nothing to offer. 'Are you sure of that?' continued Arlington.

'Very sure.'

'Then you must return to prison.'[21]

Now he came under the full oppressiveness of Sir John Robinson's rotten regime in the Tower of London. For several weeks he was denied visits from his wife and when at last they were reunited, it was in the presence of a warder. The Hutchinsons' children were allowed to see their father after the payment of bribes.

It was a freezing winter, and Hutchinson was frail. He was kept in a cell that had reputedly held the 'Princes in the Tower'. The only open windows there were high above his bed. These let in the cold while giving him little light. His poor health was greeted with indifference by his guards. One day, while huddled by his fire, Hutchinson was approached by one of the sentries. 'Sir,' he said, 'God bless you! I have sometimes guarded you in another manner at the Parliament House, and am grieved to see the change of your condition, and only take this employment now to be more able to serve you, still hoping to see you restored to what I have seen you [be].'[22] Hutchinson suspected this was an attempt at entrapment and said he had no need of the man's services. The guard slipped

away, saying he would only reappear once he had established his
dependability. He approached Frances Lambert, wife of the imprisoned Parliamentary general, for whom he had smuggled messages.
She happily vouched for him, before being persuaded by her
daughter that what she had done was naïve in the extreme: clearly,
she said, her mother was the victim of a Royalist deception.

To save herself, Frances Lambert reported the soldier for trying to
trick 'her under colour of a message from Colonel Hutchinson'.
Robinson set about rooting out the man in his ranks who was secretly
helping the prisoners and their families. Hutchinson was presented
with a line-up of those under suspicion, but refused to identify the
guilty man. It did not help: one of the Lamberts' maids was less
protective, quickly pointing him out; he turned out to be a former
Parliamentary soldier, who had taken his current job because he
needed the money. He had secretly maintained his former loyalty,
and helped the prisoners as best he could. For this, he was cashiered
and imprisoned. Meanwhile Hutchinson's custodians again noted his
impenetrable obstinacy, and felt confirmed in their belief that the
colonel could never be reformed, and should never be released.

The few implicated in the Farnley Wood plot had been quickly
dealt with – some hanged from chains, before being beheaded and
quartered. Hearings followed to establish who else might have had
a hand in the uprising. To the disappointment of the Duke of Buckingham there was no evidence of Hutchinson having been involved
in any way as a conspirator.

Lucy Hutchinson secured an audience with Arlington, asking
that her husband be released: apart from the effect on his health, she
said, his estate in Nottinghamshire was suffering greatly because he
was unable to administer it while kept close prisoner. Arlington
told her that her husband should blame his current suffering on his
former crimes. She countered that he was no criminal – a fact proven
by his having been excused under the Act of Oblivion. As she left
their meeting Arlington told Sir Robert Byron, a cousin of Colonel
Hutchinson's, 'that he had heard Mrs Hutchinson relate the sad
condition of her husband and his house', 'and,' said he, 'you may

here take notice how the justice of God pursues those murderers, that, though the King pardoned both his life and estate, by the hand of divine justice they were now like to come to ruin for that crime'.[23]

Two men who had been arrested after the Farnley Wood plot, named Neville and Salloway, were granted their freedom after signing an oath of complete and undying obedience to Charles II. Hutchinson now took the final step away from possible redemption. Presented with the same document, he refused to put his name to it. He told his wife that 'this captivity was the happiest release in the world to him', because through it he had retrieved his honour and conscience. His beliefs were confirmed by the reports he heard about Charles II and his dissipated court: he viewed them with utter disgust.

Sir Allen Apsley asked Lord Clarendon one final time to release his brother-in-law, saying there was no difference between Hutchinson and the pardoned Mr Salloway. 'Surely there is a great difference,' Clarendon replied; 'Salloway conforms to the government, and goes to church, but your brother is the most unchanged person of the Parliamentary party.'[24]

Hutchinson now told his wife and Apsley to stop their representations on his behalf. He had accepted his lot. Hearing that he and the other regicides were to be moved to far-flung prisons – he was earmarked for the Isle of Man – he began writing an account of his five and a half months of poor treatment at the hands of the Royalists. Every week in the custody of Sir John Robinson added to Hutchinson's litany of complaints: on one occasion the lieutenant had extorted £50 from him in order to allow his children to visit.

Robinson lost no opportunity to incriminate Hutchinson further. On 19 April 1664, according to Hutchinson's son, Robinson 'told the King, that when Mr Heveningham and others [of the regicides] were carried out of the Tower to be shipped away, Mr Hutchinson, looking out of his window, bade them take courage, they should yet have a day for it'.[25] This was, quite simply, a lie. Its malicious dishonesty infuriated the colonel more than all the other slights he had suffered up to that point.

Having decided he had little to lose, Hutchinson wrote to

Robinson listing the many corrupt practices he knew him to be guilty of and threatening to expose him. The immediate consequence of this was the soldiers of the Tower being given fifteen of the twenty-two months' wages due to them. The guards knew Hutchinson was responsible for their payment, and were grateful. But Robinson was quick to gain his vengeance. He ordered the colonel to be searched, and found a note with the first verse of the 43rd Psalm on it, concealed in his clothes: 'Judge me, O God, and plead my cause against an ungodly nation: O deliver me from the deceitful and unjust man.' Robinson made public his belief that the 'deceitful and unjust man' was the King, knowing in his heart that the reference was to him.

Out of spite, Robinson took away Hutchinson's retainer, and forbade Lucy from visiting her husband. This ban was only overturned when she threatened to publish the colonel's letter about his ill-treatment. For the first and only time during the imprisonment they were allowed a day together, undisturbed.

One night Robinson's deputy, Cresset, came to Hutchinson's cell to tell him that the next day he would be moved to Sandown Castle in Kent. Hutchinson was too ill to go by horse, but a sympathetic Royalist officer paid for him to be transported by boat to Gravesend. His wife and children followed in another vessel.

'When he came to the castle,' Mrs Hutchinson recalled, 'he found it a lamentable old ruined place, almost a mile distant from the town, the rooms all out of repair, not weather free, no kind of accommodation either for lodging or diet, or any conveniency of life.' This grim prison was garrisoned by half a dozen third-rate troops under the command of an impoverished lieutenant, who lived with his family in the keep. With Hutchinson's arrival, 'a squadron of foot were sent from Dover to help to guard the place, pitiful weak fellows, half-starved and eaten up with vermin, whom the governor of Dover cheated of half their pay, and the other half they spent in drink'. Hutchinson's accommodation was wretched, his cell part of the castle's intricate system of passages. He had to buy bedding from a nearby inn, and organise for his windows to be glazed. The air was 'so unwholesome and damp', Lucy Hutchinson noted, 'that even in the summer time the colonel's hat-case and trunks, and everything of leather, would be every day all covered over with mould'.

There was nowhere in the castle for the Hutchinson family to stay: they lodged in Deal, making daily visits to and from the colonel on foot. Hutchinson's wife and daughter would often scour the beach for seashells, which the colonel enjoyed sorting and tracing. His chief pastime though was studying the Bible: it became his exclusive reading during the remainder of his imprisonment. Buoyed by what he read, the colonel told his wife of his confidence that the cause he believed in so passionately would rise again one day, because 'the interest of God was so much involved in it'. Mrs Hutchinson agreed, but said she feared that, given his poor health, he would die in prison before this could come about. 'I think I shall not,' he replied, 'but, if I do, my blood will be so innocent, I shall advance the cause more by my death, hasting the vengeance of God upon my unjust memories, than I could by all the actions of my life.'[26]

George Hutchinson, the colonel's brother, arrived at Sandown Castle with good news: Lord Arlington had signed an order allowing the prisoner to walk along the beach, provided he was accompanied by guards. The colonel spent his shoreline strolls discussing the likely future of England with his family.

During his time in captivity on the south coast, Hutchinson's heart remained hundreds of miles further north, at Owthorpe Hall. When his wife planned to visit the family home, he gave her plans for new plantings in the garden, and for modifications to the structure of the house. 'You give me these orders, as if you were to see that place again,' she said. 'If I do not,' he replied, 'I thank God I can cheerfully forgo it, but I will not distrust that God will bring me back again, and therefore I will take care to keep it while I have it.'

Lucy Hutchinson set off for home, worried that she had seen her husband for the last time: she suspected the government was keeping him on the south coast before sailing him away to final imprisonment in Tangier.

While she was gone, in early September, Hutchinson fell into a violent fever after a walk on the beach. His grave illness was punctuated by moments of lucidity, during which he turned to his Bible. Dr Jachin, a famous physician, was summoned from Canterbury to tend the distinguished prisoner. He knew the castle, and asked his companion two questions: what sort of man was the colonel? And in what room was he being kept? When told Hutchinson was frail, and that he was being detained in his passageway cell, the doctor said this would prove to be a wasted journey, 'for that chamber had killed'. He gave Hutchinson a potion to help him sleep, and placed poultices on his temples. Seeing no improvement in his patient, Jachin warned the colonel's brother that he would 'soon fall into ravings and die'. When informed of this Colonel Hutchinson replied, 'The will of the Lord be done: I am ready for it.'

He became ever weaker, his pulse flickering. When someone mentioned his wife's name, he summoned his final energy and said, lucidly, 'Alas, how will she be surprised!'

Those were his last words. Eleven months after his arrest on a fabricated charge, he died.

When doctors cut him open to inspect his innards, they noted two or three purple spots on his lungs, as well as that he had an enlarged gall bladder. His body was taken back to the family vault at Owthorpe for burial.

Lucy Hutchinson was overcome by the tragic trajectory of the colonel's life: 'I have often admired, when I have considered the abounding of God's favour in the want of all things, that he who had had a comfortable house of his own, attendants, and all things that any gentleman of his quality could require from his infancy till his imprisonment, should come to die in a vile chamber, untrimmed and unhung, in a poor wretched bed without his wife, children, servants and relations about him, and all his former employments taken from him.'[27] The Royalists had let Hutchinson go prematurely during the first, heady, days of the Restoration – but they got their man, in the end.

Chapter 13

An Ocean Away

It is as hard a thing to maintain a sound understanding, a tender
conscience, a lively, gracious, heavenly spirit, and an upright life
in the midst of contention, as to keep your candle lighted in the
greatest storms.
Richard Baxter, theologian, and chaplain to Colonel Whalley's
Regiment of Horse

William Goffe opened his journal for 1662[1] with a list of sixty-nine names associated with the killing of the King, written in his own hand. There was no mention of the ten regicides executed by this point. The rest were divided into groups: seventeen men, including Bourchier and Deane, who he marked as 'all deceased'; next were the four whose bodies had been marked for posthumous revenge: Cromwell, Ireton, Bradshaw and Pride; the seven names following were of men who Goffe noted had been 'degraded' through harsh punishment, but not condemned to death; there were three men together, whose fate he was perhaps unsure about – Lisle, Say and Walton; and then there were two lists, each of nineteen names, the first of which detailed those in prison in the Tower of London, while the other was a roll call of those he had marked simply as 'Fled'. In this column were the three men recently captured by Downing in Delft, as well as Ludlow, but also two referred to only by their initials: 'E. W.' and 'W. G.' – Edward Whalley, and himself. The journal was written

in hiding, in America, its author employing shorthand, pseudo-
nyms and codes.

Goffe and Whalley were among that inner core of Cromwell's
confidants drawn tight together by family connections: Whalley's
mother, Frances, was Oliver's aunt; while Whalley's daughter,
another Frances, had married Goffe. The father-in-law and
son-in-law were both first-rate soldiers. Whalley had served as a
major in his cousin Cromwell's cavalry regiment and was one of the
men of humble birth and strict piety to be promoted through merit.
This process had attracted criticism from the snobbish on his own
side: 'Colonel Cromwell [in the] raising of his regiment makes
choice of his officers, not such as were soldiers or men of estate, but
such as were common men, poor and of mean parentage, only he
would give them the title of godly precious men . . . If you look
upon his own regiment of horse, see what a swarm there is of those
that call themselves the godly; some of them profess they have seen
visions and had revelations.'² Whalley had no pretentions to
nobility, but he was a natural leader of men, Cromwell reporting to
Parliament in the aftermath of the battle of Gainsborough, in 1643,
'The honour of this retreat is due to God, as also the rest: Major
Whalley did in this carry himself with all gallantry becoming a
gentleman and a Christian.'³

At Naseby, Whalley's ferocious charge dispersed two divisions
of the Royalist cavalry. As a reward, in January 1646, when
Cromwell's regiment divided into two, Parliament made Whalley
colonel of one of the resulting units. He led it with distinction at the
storming of Bristol and Banbury, where his bravery was recognised
by a gift of £100 from Parliament, which he used to buy two
warhorses. He was lionised by his cause as a symbol of unbounded
courage, John Milton writing, 'You, Whalley, whenever I heard or
read of the fiercest battles of this war, I always expected, and found,
among the thickest of the enemy.'⁴ Only the most fanatical Puritans
treated him with distrust, claiming he was a Presbyterian. When
Whalley heard Hugh Peters was behind this attack on his sincerity,
he threatened to hunt down the preacher and give him a thrashing.

Whalley had been entrusted with overseeing the defeated Charles I's detention in 1647, which he did with charm and efficiency until his flight to the Isle of Wight. Before that escape, he had been open in wishing to preserve the King's life. It is possible that Whalley was, as the historian Mark Noble wrote in the 1780s, 'the abject tool of Cromwell's ambition, perhaps without his own knowledge', because Cromwell 'employed him in carrying all the petitions of the army to the Parliament, to prepare for the tragic death of the King'.[5] Certainly Whalley attended all but one of the King's trial sessions, and signed his death warrant.

William Goffe was the radical son of a Puritan divine from a village near Brighton, Sussex. Religion remained the backbone of his life, leading contemporaries to call him 'Praying William'. As a young man he had served as an apprentice to a London dry-salter, curing hides and meat, before joining Parliament's army. He served in the Civil Wars with distinction, being promoted first to quarter-master, before becoming an infantry colonel.

Goffe's had been an earnest voice at the Putney debates, persistently warning that to stray from God's way was to invite his wrath against the Parliamentary cause: 'There are two ways that God doth take upon those that walk obstinately against him: if they be obstinate and continue obstinate, he breaks them in pieces with a rod of iron; if they be his people and wander from him, he takes that glory from them and takes it to himself.'[6] He worried that negotiations with the King were breathing new life into the Royalist cause. Like Whalley, he was open to drastic measures to bring about peace in the kingdom. Convinced long before the trial that the path to a settled nation involved the trial and death of the King, he was a fully persuaded signatory of the death warrant.

Goffe's military support of Cromwell in his Scottish campaign of 1650 was heroic, the lord general recording that, during the battle of Dunbar, Goffe 'at the push of pike, did repel the stoutest regiment the enemy had there'.[7] (At the same action Whalley was one of the infantry commanders, acting with his customary bravery, and receiving a wound in the wrist.) Goffe was present a year later, at Worcester, when he accepted the surrender of the Royalist Sir Henry Washington, a cousin of George Washington's grandfather. After Lambert's fall from grace Goffe was promoted Major General of Foot.

Goffe approved of Cromwell's political ruthlessness, supporting his and Harrison's expulsion of the Rump Parliament as well as his loss of patience with the well-intentioned but unproductive Barebone's Parliament. During the Commonwealth, Cromwell's dependence on Whalley and Goffe was demonstrated when, in the 1650s, he appointed them as two of his administering major generals. Goffe believed his duties to mean that he was 'called of God to serve him and his people in the country'.[8]

Even after the failure of the major-generalships the pair remained uncompromising champions of the regime's religious and political beliefs. John Evelyn remembered being hauled before Goffe and Whalley in 1657 for breaking Cromwell's ban on celebrating Christmas: 'When I came before them they took my name and abode, examined me, why contrary to an Ordinance made that none should any longer observe the superstitious time of the Nativity (so esteemed by them) I durst offend, and particularly be at common prayers, which they told me was but the Mass in English, and particularly pray for Charles Steward [Stùart], for which we had no Scripture.'[9]

They had both been created peers in the House of Lords formed by Oliver Cromwell earlier that year. This chamber was greeted with contempt by the republican element that had rushed to abolish the original House of Lords, Lucy Hutchinson seeing its appearance as evidence of Cromwell's lamentable self-glorification. 'At last he took upon himself to make lords and knights,' she wrote, 'and wanted not many fools, both of the army and gentry, to accept of, and strut in, his mock titles.'[10] Whalley was among those who, it was noted, took to his new status with a particular swagger.

Goffe was one of the seven authors responsible for the Instrument of Government, which was written as a template for the Protectorship in 1657. He grew rich, buying up confiscated Crown lands, as well as 7,000 square miles of Newfoundland.

Goffe and Whalley were among those at Oliver Cromwell's deathbed, when he proclaimed his son Richard as his heir. They (along with the pardoned regicide, Richard Ingoldsby) were known as the most loyal supporters of the new Lord Protector. This allegiance proved isolating when Richard's regime quickly folded: in November 1659, Goffe and Whalley were sent by the army to talk with the enigmatic Monck, but Monck – knowing their hatred for the royal family – was not interested in what they had to say.

Goffe had two brothers in the enemy camp: John, an Anglican clergyman, and Stephen, who worked in Europe as an agent for Charles II, before becoming a Catholic priest and a chaplain to Charles I's widow, Henrietta Maria. However, he had little confidence that they could help him survive the changes being ushered in by the Restoration: nervous at what was implied by the mistier subclauses of the Declaration of Breda, he decided, with Whalley, to cross to New England. They were confident that they could find a home in this outpost of orthodox Puritanism. They would also have the option, from there, of slipping south to New Amsterdam (soon to be taken by the British, and renamed 'New York'), where the King, as yet, had no authority.

The two exiles also had a fair knowledge of, and some close ties to, the American colonies: Whalley's sister Jane had married William Hooke, who had lived in Taunton, Massachusetts, and moved to New Haven, before returning to England in the 1650s. The Hookes were close friends of Connecticut's governor, John Winthrop. The two major generals had also met Richard Saltonstall while they were accompanying Cromwell in Scotland, nine years earlier. Saltonstall was an inhabitant of Ipswich, Massachusetts, and would prove useful to the two men in the future.

They secretly set sail from Gravesend on 13 May – the day before the House of Commons ordered their arrest – aboard the *Prudent Mary*, a seventy-six-foot ship that had seen action in the First Anglo-Dutch War. She was under the command of a Captain Pierce. They used aliases, Goffe calling himself 'Stephenson', Whalley, 'Richardson': their fathers had been baptised, respectively, Stephen and

Richard. On the same vessel was William Jones, son of the regicide Colonel John Jones. The colonel was at that time released on bail and enjoying the weeks before his sudden and disastrous re-arrest. William Jones was accompanied by his new wife, Hannah, a daughter of Theophilus Eaton, the first governor of the New Haven Colony: Governor Eaton had died two years previously, and Hannah and her husband were coming to claim his estate, and live in his house. Also aboard was Captain Daniel Gookin, a member of the General Court that governed the Massachusetts Bay Company. Gookin invited the two men to stay with him in his house in Cambridge, four miles from Boston, when they reached New England.

'July 27,' Goffe wrote in his journal, after the ten-week voyage, 'we landed between Boston and Charlestown, between eight and nine in the morning. All in good health through the hand of God [being] upon us.'[11] They dropped their aliases and reported as their true selves to the seventy-two-year-old governor of the Massachusetts Bay Company, John Endecott, a strict Puritan famed for defacing the English flag (the cross of St George) because he thought he detected symbols of the papacy in it. He embraced both men, and declared his hope that more like them would cross the Atlantic to New England. Endecott's enthusiastic welcome led other leading figures in the colony to greet the two new arrivals with great respect. John Crowne noted how Goffe and Whalley were met with 'universal applause and admiration', and 'were looked upon as men dropped down from Heaven'.[12]

There was a ready appreciation of the danger the two men faced, on the other side of the Atlantic. Two weeks after their arrival in Boston the Reverend John Davenport, the leading Puritan minister in New Haven Colony, wrote a letter to Governor Winthrop in which he secreted a secondary message: 'Sir, I mistook in my letter, when I said Col. Whalley was one of the gentlemen, etc. It is Commissary-General Whalley, sister Hooke's brother, and his son-in-law who is with him is Col. Goffe; both godly men, and escaped pursuit in England narrowly.'[13] The two fugitives were far from discreet about their past, Crowne reporting that he heard

Whalley say on several occasions that, if presented with the question again, he would still approve of Charles I's execution.

The pair lived in Cambridge for seven months, honoured with the 'liberty of the House' of the General Court, mixing with the lawgivers and preachers of Massachusetts, their piety and integrity acclaimed by the colony's leaders. When, during a visit to Boston, a Royalist shouted insults at them, he was arrested and bound over to his good behaviour.

Stories relating to the venerable guests soon circulated. One told how a brash showman arrived in Boston, his special skill fencing. He set himself up upon a stage, sword in hand, loudly challenging all comers to try their luck against him. Goffe was unable to resist the lure of showing off the skills honed by the Civil Wars. Holding a shield that was nothing more than a large cheese in a sack, Goffe got onto the stage with a dripping broom in his sword hand. The fencing master told his challenger – whose identity he did not know – to be gone, so proper fighters could take him on. When Goffe refused to stand down he went at him with his small sword, assuming this would be enough to send his disrespectful opponent scurrying back onto the street.

Instead, Goffe caught the blade in his cheese, then counter-thrusted with his dirty broom, smearing a muddy moustache along the assailant's top lip. Enraged, the showman now attacked Goffe with purpose, the major general lithely side-stepping, then rubbing the broom above his eyes. A third bout ended similarly, Goffe covering his opponent's face in sludge. Humiliated by the laughter of the crowd, the man now reached for his broadsword. 'Stop, sir!' warned Goffe. 'Hitherto you see I have only played with you, and not attempted to hurt you; but if you come at me now with the broadsword, know, that I will certainly take your life!'

The fencer, clearly frightened, shouted, 'Who can you be? You are either Goffe, Whalley, or the Devil, for there was no other man in England that could beat me.'[14] Goffe got down from the stage and melted away into the crowd.

* * *

When news arrived from the English colony of Barbados that only seven of the late King's judges would be executed, it seemed unlikely that the two major generals would be among the condemned.

For now, Goffe and Whalley could feel safe in this, the most independent of the established American colonies, one that had taken the opening of the English Civil War as an excuse to dispense with the swearing of allegiance to the King. Once Charles I had been militarily defeated, Massachusetts Bay's governors had dared to go further, claiming that their people lay outside of the reach of Parliament's laws, or the King's writ. Since 1652 the colony had minted its own coins with no mention of England on them, just 'Massachusetts' and a tree on one side and 'New England' with the date on the reverse. British royal power had not been felt for more than a decade, but such brazen assertions of colonial independence would now be tested, with the regicides at the centre of a power struggle with the newly restored Crown.

Whalley and Goffe had been among the forty-four men cited in Charles II's proclamation of 6 June 1660 which demanded that all those listed hand themselves in within two weeks, or else forfeit their lives and estates. The two men were excluded from the Act of Indemnity in August, and were then specifically addressed by another of the King's decrees of 22 September, 'For their execrable creations in sentencing to death, signing the instrument for the horrid murder, or being instrumental in taking away the precious life of our late dear father.'[15] A reward of £100 was offered for either man's arrest in any of the British dominions. If they resisted, the proclamation continued, they should be killed.

These developments transformed their status in New England from one of honoured guests to that of contagious fugitives. In November, news of Goffe and Whalley's exception from pardon reached Boston, and it was common knowledge that those who helped traitors would share their fate of hanging, drawing and quartering. There was considerable unease in Massachusetts as to what to do now. Many of the governors were anxious not to bow to the wishes of Charles II and the nation they termed 'the State of England', since this would set a precedent: they did not want to acknowledge that duty of obedience to the Crown which many had purposefully rejected when crossing the Atlantic. The colonists had not felt the royal yoke for nearly two decades, and they were unwilling to have it reapplied now. Others felt it best to hand over the duo in order to placate the new King: their security and trading rights, both of which were threatened by Dutch and French rivals, were underpinned by English arms. Captain Thomas Breedon was of such a belief, insisting to Governor Endecott that the two regicides be arrested and transported back to England, in the interests of justice and for the good of the colony.

Endecott at first avoided making the difficult decision by claiming he could not act until a properly executed commission arrived from London. This prompted the marshal general of the colony, Edward Michelson, to turn on Breedon with the sing-song taunt, 'Speak against Whalley and Goffe if you dare, if you dare, if you dare!'[16]

Breedon set sail for England, keen to report in person to the King the regicides' whereabouts and the names of those in New England who were blocking their arrest. His account was greeted in London with surprise and anger. The governor and his juniors soon heard rumours that Charles planned to bring the colony to heel. On 11 February, Endecott sent a 'Humble Petition and Address to the King', which implored Charles not to rush to judgment until he had heard Endecott's detailed defence of his administration's conduct. Soon afterwards Endecott and the Court of Assistants met to discuss what to do about Goffe and Whalley, while the two men awaited their fate in Cambridge.

The members of the Court were unable to come to a conclusion. The fugitives thought it best to remove themselves from Massachusetts. They entrusted their possessions, which included a herd of cattle, to Daniel Gookin, their host in Cambridge. They asked Gookin and Captain Pierce (who had brought them to New England) to look after their affairs for them. Charles II's commissioners later established that the two regicides then 'were furnished with horses and a guide and sent away to New Haven'.[17]

The colony of New Haven had been founded in the late 1630s, as a nursery bed for the religious aspirations of the Reverend John Davenport.* Davenport was an Oxford graduate who came from a wealthy family from Coventry in the English Midlands. His Puritan beliefs put him increasingly at odds with Charles I's religious leaders and, taking the same path that had attracted Hugh Peters, he moved to what he assumed would be the more tolerant Netherlands (where he served as co-pastor of the English Church in Amsterdam), before further religious difficulties persuaded him to relocate to New England. Arriving in Boston he was disappointed with what he judged to be Massachusetts's sloppy theology, and looked to establish a fresh community elsewhere, with religious orthodoxy at its core.

The location of this 'new haven', arranged round a bay in the Long Island Sound that had once been a Dutch beaver-trading outpost, came about largely through Native American rivalries. The local Quiripi tribe had been reduced to just forty males by attacks from their Mohawk and Pequot enemies. These few survivors were persuaded by the wealthy London merchant, Theophilus Eaton – a former ambassador of Charles I and a childhood friend of Davenport's – to give up enough land to 500 European settlers for the building of seven settlements, in return for armed protection. They also received exotic European gifts: a dozen coats, alchemy spoons, hatchets, hoes, porringers, as well as two dozen knives, and a further four cases of French knives and scissors. At the end of 1638 an additional purchase – this time involving thirteen coats, handed to the Monotowese tribe – secured a further 130 square miles for the new colony. Both the tribes of Native Americans who sold to the settlers were allowed to grow crops on part of the land, and to hunt over all of it: effectively, this was the first occasion

---

* After whom Davenport College, at Yale University, is named.

when indigenous North Americans were placed on a reservation by white settlers.

The administration of New Haven was placed under the control of the newly elected Governor Eaton, who organised a union with surrounding towns, and formulated a legal code for the new colony. Eaton was returned to the post of governor each year until his death in 1658. He was succeeded by Francis Newman, before Newman died in November 1660. Goffe and Whalley would arrive in this religious utopia while the governorship of New Haven was vacant. The man overseeing things in the meantime was Deputy Governor William Leete, a forty-seven-year-old lawyer who had emigrated from England as a young man, disgusted by Charles I's treatment of the Puritans. Leete was a committed republican.

Goffe and Whalley left Boston, riding through snowfall towards New Haven. On the way they spent several nights in Hartford, where Governor Winthrop received them with kindness. They reached their destination on 7 March, and went immediately to meet the Reverend John Davenport. Davenport had prepared the people for the outsiders' arrival as best he could, addressing the meeting house before their arrival with an exhortation inspired by a passage from the Book of Hebrews: 'Withhold not countenance, entertainment, and protection, from such, if they come to us from other countries, as from France or England or any other place. Be not forgetful to entertain strangers, for thereby some have entertained angels unawares. Remember them that are in bonds, as bound with them, and them who suffer adversity as being yourselves also in the body ... While we are attending to our duty in owning and harbouring Christ's witnesses, God will be providing for their and our safety, by destroying those that would destroy his people.'[18]

Probably as part of a prearranged plan, it was not until several days after the pair had left Boston that Endecott finally made a show of doing the King's bidding. He prepared an arrest warrant, which he committed to Edward Michelson to execute as he saw fit: Endecott was well aware that Michelson's sympathies lay with the regicides.

On 27 March news that the search for Goffe and Whalley was under way reached them in New Haven. The following day, in an attempt to mislead their pursuers, they bade a noisy farewell to friends, letting everyone know that they were heading for New Amsterdam. Proceeding to the new settlement of Milford, they very publicly announced their arrival there, again spreading the falsehood that they were en route for 'the Manhados' (Manhattan). That night, they retraced their footsteps and hid in Davenport's home. They stayed there for five weeks. This was when they learnt of the horrific executions carried out on their ten fellow regicides. Shock at what they heard must have been tempered by the realisation that fleeing their homeland had saved their lives.

After learning from Captain Breedon how some in New England were aiding or sheltering his father's killers, Charles II had sent a sharp communication to Governor Endecott:

Trusty and well-beloved, We greet you well. We being given to understand that Colonel Whalley and Colonel Goffe, who stand here convicted for the execrable murder of our Royal Father, of glorious memory, are lately arrived at New England, where they hope to shroud themselves from the justice of our laws; Our will and pleasure is, and we do hereby expressly require and command you . . . to cause both the said persons to be apprehended, and with the first opportunity sent over hither under a strict care, to receive according to their demerits. We are confident of your readiness and diligence to perform your duty; and so bid you farewell.[19]

The key word in this message was 'command', with its reminder of 'duty'. There was absolute expectation that this matter would be dealt with quickly and conclusively.

When Endecott received the letter he realised he must act in order to protect his colony from royal wrath and retribution. He therefore appointed 'two zealous Royalists' – Thomas Kellond, a merchant, and Thomas Kirke, a ship's master – to oversee the capture of the major generals. The two commissioners were told to disseminate copies of the King's letter to the governors of the surrounding English colonies, as well as to Pieter Stuyvesant, the Dutch director general of the colony of New Netherland, who was based in New Amsterdam.

Kellond and Kirke left Boston with a guide on the evening of 7 May, in their words, 'in search after Colonels Goffe and Whalley (persons declared traitors to his Majesty)'.[20] They arrived in Hartford three days later and met with Governor Winthrop, who proved supportive. 'The honourable governor carried himself very nobly to us,' they reported, 'and was very diligent to supply us with all manner of conveniences for the prosecution of them, and promised all diligent search should be made after them in that jurisdiction, which was afterwards performed.'[21] Winthrop informed them that the two regicides had left the town some time previously, but he would be happy to organise a sweep of the area in case they had somehow returned, without his knowledge.

Keen to catch their men, Kellond and Kirke pushed on to Guilford, the capital of New Haven, where, on 11 May, they showed Deputy Governor Leete papers explaining their mission. Leete read these out aloud in front of men visiting his home, prompting the Royalists to advise, 'It is convenient to be more private in such concernments.'[22] They feared he was intentionally broadcasting the confidential information, so those listening could get word to the fugitives. Leete took the pursuers aside and told them that Goffe and Whalley had not been seen in his jurisdiction for nine weeks. Kellond and Kirke countered that this differed from what they had heard. They demanded that Leete assist them by making out the arrest warrant and providing fresh mounts for their sixteen-mile journey on to New Haven.

Kellond and Kirke retired to an inn, awaiting the horses and the authorisation to bring the regicides in. There they were approached by Dennis Scranton, a Guilford resident who bore a grudge against Leete for having had him publicly whipped. Scranton shared with them that – as he was sure Leete knew – Goffe and Whalley were staying with the Reverend John Davenport, in New Haven. This,

Scranton said, would explain Davenport's recent purchase of £10 worth of fresh provisions, which he was storing in his home. Others now confirmed to Endecott's men that they, too, had seen the two fugitives outside Davenport's house, and also travelling to and from the nearby dwelling of William Jones. It was believed, Scranton revealed, that one regicide was living with Jones, the other with Davenport.

The Royalist agents rushed back to Leete, demanding immediate delivery of the warrant and the horses, as well as reinforcements. Leete said he would happily help them with their transport, but he needed to consult colleagues about the legal paperwork. He pointed out that, unfortunately, it being a Saturday evening, there was nothing that could be done in this regard until the Monday morning, as the Sabbath must be observed. A furious Kellond and Kirke threatened to push on without the warrants before the major generals could flee. Leete pointed out that if they tried to do that, he would have to have them arrested for breaking the Sabbath.

As they kicked their heels that weekend, the Royalists were kept up to date with developments by the vengeful Scranton. He warned them that there was an old Native American and a man called John Meigs who seemed, separately, to be preparing to ride to New Haven, no doubt to warn Goffe and Whalley of the imminent danger. Kellond and Kirke demanded that Leete bring both men in for questioning, but the governor said he had no reason to do so, and refused.

As the commissioners had feared, these delays gained a head start for the regicides. 'To our certain knowledge,' Kellond and Kirke reported, 'one John Meigs was sent a-horseback before us, and by his speedy and unexpected going so early before day was to give them an information; and the rather because by the delays which were used it was break of day before we got to horse; so he got there before us.'[23] The arrival of this news prompted the preacher to transfer care of both regicides to William Jones, who moved them by night to a remote mill he owned, two miles northwest of New Haven.

Knowing that Leete could only delay their pursuers for a while, Goffe and Whalley showed themselves in the street the next morning before laying another false trail in the direction of Guilford. They had not gone far when they were cornered by the marshal, Thomas Kimberly, who had set off after them in solitary pursuit. When he tried to take them prisoner the two old warriors stood with their backs to a tree, cudgels in hand, poised to fight. Kimberly realised he needed reinforcements, and returned to New Haven.

At a crossing point known as Mill River, Goffe and Whalley heard horses galloping towards them: Kimberly and a posse of men. With no cover in sight, they ran back to the bridge. The base of the crossing was only a foot above the waterline, but there was nowhere else to conceal themselves, so the pair jumped into the water and remained there while their pursuers charged on overhead. When it was safe, they clambered onto the riverbank and headed quietly back to Jones's mill.

Earlier that same day, Kirke and Kellond had ridden from Guilford to New Haven where Leete was due to summon the local magistrates to hear their requests. Kellond and Kirke demanded once more that Leete come to authorise their arrest warrants, but were met with more excuses and stalling. The pair noted that the deputy arrived only 'within two hours or thereabout after us, and came to us to the court-chamber, where we again acquainted him with the information we had received, and that we had cause to believe they were concealed in New Haven, and thereupon we required his assistance and aid for their apprehension; to which he answered, that he did not believe they were. Whereupon we desired him to empower us, or order others for it; to which he gave us this answer, that he could not, nor would not, make us magistrates.'[24]

Leete again advised them that they were wasting their time: the men they sought were not in New Haven. The Royalists insisted they at least be allowed to search the homes of Davenport and Jones. When Leete wavered, they reminded him of his duty and loyalty to the King. Leete retired to discuss the matter with his colleagues, saying that he was troubled at the precedent he would be setting if he complied with a proclamation addressed to the 'Governor of New England', since there was no such person, or office. After five or six hours, Leete returned, still not prepared to cooperate. Noting that the deputy was declining to help them in ways that the governors of Connecticut and Massachusetts had readily done, Kellond and Kirke warned Leete, 'how ill his sacred Majesty would resent such horrid and detestable concealments and abettings of such traitors and regicides as they were'. They asked him 'whether he would honour and obey the King or no in this affair, and set before him the danger which by law is incurred by anyone that conceals, or abets traitors, to which the Deputy Leete answered: "We honour His Majesty, but we have tender consciences." To which we replied, that we believed that he knew where they were, and only pretended tenderness of conscience for a refusal.'[25]

Leete now retired for a further two hours of deliberations. Still blocking the Royalists' demands, he confided to one of them that he wished he had been a simple ploughman rather than an elected official, because he found his duties such a burden. Kellond and Kirke would have none of it. 'We told him,' they reported, 'that for their respect to two traitors they would do themselves injury and possibly ruin themselves and the whole colony of New Haven.'[26] Leete said he would summon the General Court for the Jurisdiction which, given the distance that some of its members lived from the town, would not be able to meet for four days.

During this protracted delay Kellond and Kirke received a tip-off that the regicides had been seen entering the home of a widow, Mrs Johanna Allerton, whose husband had been a leading figure in the Plymouth colony, having crossed from England on the *Mayflower* four decades earlier. As the pursuers approached her house, Goffe and Whalley exited Mrs Allerton's home and then doubled back. Mrs Allerton beckoned them into a large kitchen cupboard that had a false front, which she hung with a screen of kitchen utensils. When the Royalists arrived, demanding to know where the regicides were, she said they had just left through her back door. Her matter-of-fact manner was so convincing that the agents and their redcoats continued on. Goffe and Whalley then returned to the proven safety of Jones's isolated mill.

Kellond and Kirke had, by now, had their fill of this wild goose chase: they guessed that the fugitives would make their way to Manhattan, where the King of England's edicts held no sway and where it would be easier to hide. This was a community that was, as Russell Shorto wrote in *The Island at the Centre of the World*, 'not a city with its own structure of governance but literally a company town: its inhabitants were considered less citizens than employees, and there was no real legal system'.[27] Pieter Stuyvesant promised to watch for the judges' arrival in his ramshackle jurisdiction, and forbade all shipping from transporting the runaway Englishmen out of New Amsterdam. At the same time he arranged discreet inspections of ships at anchor, hoping to discover Goffe and Whalley stowed on board.

Returning to the more amenable Governor Endecott, Kellond and Kirke reported their failure to track down the wanted men. As a reward for their efforts, each of the commissioners received a farm of 250 acres – a hint of the bonanza they would have secured had their mission been successful. Meanwhile, the General Court had assumed that the regicides were no longer in the colony of New Haven, and felt it safe at last to authorise wide-ranging search warrants. Kellond and Kirke listed the obstructions that Leete had thrown up in a sworn affidavit that they handed to Governor Endecott on 30 May. By that time Leete had been confirmed as governor of the colony. He and Davenport were both under the strongest suspicion of having aided the regicides, and were put under careful watch.

Thanks to Kellond and Kirke, and the commotion they had stirred up during their determined manhunt, everyone in the surrounding communities knew two things for sure: the regicides were not far away, and rich prizes awaited those who helped in their capture. The pursuers' parting shot had been to leave open offers of 'great rewards to English and Indians who should give information that they might be taken'.[28]

Chapter 14

Into the Wilderness

*Nowadays Monarchs pretend always in their Titles, to be Kings
by the grace of God: but how many of them to this end only
pretend it, that they may reign without control; for to what
purpose is the grace of God mentioned in the Title of Kings, but
that they may acknowledge no Superior?*

John Calvin, 1561

The regicides saw their sufferings in biblical terms, convinced
that they were the 'witnesses' described in the eleventh chapter
of the Book of Revelation – prophets who would be sent as the
forerunners of the Second Coming. According to this text, the
witnesses would be granted a period of divine authority and protection, but,

When they have finished their testimony, the beast that comes up out
of the abyss will make war with them, and overcome them and kill
them. And their dead bodies will lie in the street of the great city
which mystically is called Sodom and Egypt, where also their Lord
was crucified. Those from the peoples and tribes and tongues and
nations will look at their dead bodies for three and a half days, and
will not permit their dead bodies to be laid in a tomb. And those who
dwell on the earth will rejoice over them and celebrate; and they will
send gifts to one another, because these two prophets tormented
those who dwell on the earth. But after three and a half days, the

breath of life from God came into them, and they stood on their feet; and great fear fell upon those who were watching them. And they heard a loud voice from heaven saying to them, 'Come up here.' Then they went up into heaven in the cloud, and their enemies watched them. And in that hour there was a great earthquake, and a tenth of the city fell; seven thousand people were killed in the earthquake, and the rest were terrified and gave glory to the God of heaven.

'The beast that comes out of the abyss' could readily be interpreted as the restored monarchy. The phrase, 'And their dead bodies will lie in the street of the great city', equated with the anguish of those who had been publicly butchered then displayed in London. This had been the period of the regicides' greatest torment, but soon they would be revitalised by 'the breath of life from God'. That was when they would be summoned from heaven to his glory, and would then be able to witness their enemies either suffer cruel destruction, or reach out for spiritual salvation.

Much of this faith dovetailed with the Fifth Monarchist expectation that the year 1666 would include the Day of Judgment. Whalley and Goffe were two who subscribed to this belief and both yearned for the beginning of that fateful year. In the meantime, as they moved from hiding place to hiding place, successfully evading the King's men, it seemed that their faith in God was being repaid.

On 13 May 1661, according to tradition, while waiting for a more permanent sanctuary, the two men were in a remote area, desperate to find some shelter; looking up longingly at the boughs of the trees above them, one of them said, 'Would to God we had a hatchet.'[1] Just then they found an axe lying on the ground, probably dropped by a Native American. The major generals used it to lop off branches and made a basic roof over their heads. They referred to this place, which they believed had only come into being through God's care, as 'Hatchet Harbour'.

The fugitives knew that spending time in anyone's home was likely to lead to discovery or betrayal so decided to live in the wilderness until immediate danger had passed. Goffe's diary records the preparation of another of their refuges, 'a cave or hole in the side of a hill'.[2] It was surrounded by trees, with a freshwater spring just thirty yards away. Goffe called this hideaway 'Providence'. They stayed in what is now known as 'Judges' Cave', West Rock, from May to early June. Once during those four weeks, startled in the night by a prowling mountain lion, the pair bolted for the shelter of a nearby house. A sympathetic farmer sent his son out towards West Rock every morning with instructions to leave a bucket of food near the same tree stump each day. He said this was for some men working in the wilderness. Each evening the boy retrieved the bucket, which was empty. He was kept in the dark about the true identity of those he was feeding – in case he were tempted to gossip, and to spare him from punishment if the fugitives were discovered.

The Englishmen began to despair of escaping their pursuers for much longer. They became increasingly concerned that they would drag others down with them, when their inevitable capture came about. On 11 June they went to Guilford, sending a message to Deputy Leete that they had come to surrender: he should hand them over to Charles II. Leete was loath to do this, and hid them in his stone cellar for three days and nights while he tried to come up with an alternative plan. After sounding out trusted friends, Leete decided that the fugitives must continue in their efforts to evade capture; but they should also keep him informed of their whereabouts in case he ever had to call them in for arrest, to spare others from punishment on their behalf.

On 22 June, the judges showed themselves in public in New Haven before attending church there the following day. Appearing at this distance from Guilford was designed to absolve Davenport and Jones of the prevailing suspicion that the wanted men were hiding in their homes. They then returned to their cave on 24 June, staying there and at other hideouts for a further eight weeks until the Royalist searches began to lose momentum. As agreed with Leete, the governor always knew where they were.

In August, they moved to the house of Micah and Mary
Tompkins, the parents of nine children, who were pioneer settlers
in Milford. This would be their safe house for the next two years.
At the Tompkins', Goffe heard much about what had happened to
his fellow regicides since his and Whalley's flight from England; it
was while in hiding here that he wrote down the names of all those
he could remember as having been involved in the trial and execution of Charles I, along with the tidings he had received regarding
their fates. As Ezra Stiles, an eighteenth-century Master of Yale,
wrote, 'Goffe's list . . . shows that he had pretty just information, as
to the number in 1662 dead; the number whose ashes were to be
dishonoured; those adjudged to perpetual imprisonment, who were
fled, and in the Tower. Enough to show Whalley and Goffe what
would be their fate if taken.'[3]

The two major generals endured a bleak existence. Goffe recorded
in his journal that he and Whalley never once dared to go outside
during their two-year stay; they did not even venture out into the
Tompkins' orchard. They remained hidden in the house's basement,
while upstairs the daughters of the house busied themselves spin-
ning yarn. Goffe and Whalley heard them at their work, often
singing popular ballads brought over from England, some of which,
to their amusement, ridiculed the regicides.

There were a few trusted visitors, including Davenport who led
them in prayer during their grim confinement. Occasional letters
passed between the fugitives and their families in England, through
the hands of another minister, the Reverend Increase Mather, who
was based in Boston. The voice of Frances, the wife of Goffe and
the daughter of Whalley, was bravely upbeat in one of the first
letters she sent to her husband; hope, longing and the agony of
separation all call clearly from the page:

My dearest Heart,
    I have been exceedingly refreshed with your choice and precious
letter of the 29 May, 1662 . . . The preservation of yourself and my
dear father, next to the light of his own countenance is the choicest

mercy that I enjoy. For, to hear of your welfare gives, as it were, a new life to me ... I shall now give you an account of your family, as far as I dare. Through mercy, I and your little ones are in reasonable health, only Betty and Nan are weakly, and I fear will be lame a little, the others are very lusty ... I do heartily wish myself with thee, but that I fear will make be a means to discover thee ... and therefore I shall forbear attempting any such thing for the present, hoping that the Lord will, in his own time, return thee to us again ...

My dear, I know you are confident of my affection, yet give me leave to tell thee, thou art as dear to me as a husband can be to a wife, and, if I knew anything that I could do to make you happy, I should do it, if the Lord would permit, though to the loss of my life ... I know not whether I may ever have another opportunity to send to you this season or not, which makes me [write] the longer now ... and though it is an unspeakable comfort to me to hear of thy welfare, yet I earnestly beg of thee not to send too often, for fear of the worst; for they are very vigilant here to find out persons ... And now, my dear, with 1,000 tears, I take my leave of thee, and recommend thee to the great keeper of Israel, who neither slumbers nor sleeps, who, I hope, will keep thee, and my dear friend with thee, from all your enemies ... and in his own time return you with safety to your family. Which is the daily prayer of thy affectionate and obedient wife, till death, F.[4]

In another letter, Frances asked her husband to 'be careful what you write, for all the letters we receive come from the post house', to which he replied, 'glad you informed me of it, for I would not make my letters too chary to you'.

It was at the Tompkins' home that the regicides learnt of the capture and execution of Barkstead, Corbet and Okey. This dismal news reinforced their view that the only safe course was to remain in hiding, hopeful that the reign of the Stuarts would somehow be overthrown once more by God. Only such an event would enable them to return to their homeland and their families, and so live openly once more. In the meantime their boredom, isolation and fear were punctuated by gratifyingly inaccurate reports arriving from London: one had them assassinated in Switzerland, where the Royalist agent Riordane had mistakenly placed them in his dispatches, while others swore they had seen the major generals skulking in the Spanish Netherlands. However, the King's 'Searchers' in New England remained certain that the fugitives were near at hand, and continued to look for them, reminding people of the rewards for betraying them and the punishments for assisting them. Three such commissioners, Colonel Thomas Temple, Captain Richard Lord and John Pynchon, swore never to give up the hunt for the fugitive pair.

On 4 July 1661, a month before Goffe and Whalley's arrival at the Tompkins' home, Edward Rawson, the Secretary of the Council of the Bay who had taken the sworn deposition of Kellond and Kirke, wrote to Leete from Boston. He wanted to notify Leete of Charles II's great unhappiness with New Haven, given its reluctance to show him the loyalty he expected as King: had Leete, he wanted to know, even taken the trouble to proclaim the King's accession to the throne?

Rawson also warned that there were rumours crossing from London that, such was the royal displeasure, Charles was planning to sell New Haven to Spain. 'Further,' Rawson continued, 'I am required to signify to you, as from them, that the non-attendance with diligence to execute the King's warrant for the apprehending of Colonels Whalley and Goffe will much hazard the present state of these colonies and your own particularly, if not some of your persons, which is not a little afflictive to them.' Rawson stressed that the only way to counteract such dangers would be to ensure that the two regicides were found and handed over. He knew they had been spotted in New Haven in the previous two weeks, and the continued failure to seize them was threatening not just New Haven, but also its neighbouring colonies.

Rawson could not have made his exasperation any clearer, asking Leete for his 'guidance and direction in [a] matter of such moment, as his Majesty may receive full and just satisfaction, the mouths of all opposers stopped, and the profession of the truth that is in you and us may not in the least suffer by you acting [in this way]'. There was a postscript to this letter: 'Sir, since what I wrote, news and certain intelligence is come hither of the two Colonels being at New Haven, from Saturday to Monday and publicly known, and however it is given out that they came to surrender themselves.' Rawson said it was further reported that, 'nobody setting a guard about the house nor endeavouring to secure them', they had been allowed to slip away once more. 'Sir, how this will be taken is not difficult to imagine, to be sure not well, nay, will not all men condemn you . . .?'[5] Rawson's message was simple: hand over the two men immediately, or face the consequences for yourself, New Haven and its surrounding colonies.

On 1 August, a General Court was held in New Haven, attended by the governor and thirteen of his senior officers, to compose a reply to Rawson. It contained the reassurance that New Haven would readily

> engage to [the King] full subjection and allegiance . . . with your-
> selves and the other neighbouring colonies . . . upon which grounds
> we both supplicate and hope to find a like protection, privileges,
> immunities and favours from his Royal Majesty. And as for that
> [which] you note of our not so diligent attention to his Majesty's
> warrant, we have given you an account of before, that it was not done
> out of any mind to slight or disown his Majesty's authority, &c. in
> the least, nor out of favour to the colonels, nor did it hinder the effect
> of their apprehending, they being gone before the warrant come into
> our colony, as is since fully proved.[6]

They blamed the King's officers for arriving 'without commission', since their paperwork was incorrectly addressed to the nonexistent 'Governor of New England', while at the same time emphasising their embarrassment at failing to capture the two regicides: 'We must wholly rely on the mercy of God and the King, with promise to do our endeavour to regain them if opportunity serve.' In conclusion the colony of New Haven urged its neighbours to share the expense of sending an advocate to England, to counter all the misinformation that was being peddled there against New England.

Davenport sent a further separate petition claiming that, in his capacity as a religious minister, he could see God's hand in Goffe and Whalley's many escapes. 'Not for myself alone do I make this humble request,' he wrote to a Royalist officer, 'but also on behalf of this poor colony & our Governor & magistrates, who wanted neither will nor industry to have served his Majesty in apprehending the 2 Colonels, but were prevented & hindered by God's overruling providence, which withheld them that they could not execute true purpose therein; And the same providence could have done the same,' he added blithely, 'in the same circumstances, if they had been in London, or in the Tower.'[7]

A month later, Leete was one of the seven signatories of the 'Declaration of the Commissioners of the United Colonies concerning Whalley and Goffe'. Preferring an act of dishonesty to bringing down further wrath upon himself and his increasingly vulnerable colony, he put his hand to a document that claimed:

> diligent search hath been made for the said persons in the several colonies (as we are informed) and whereas, notwithstanding it is conceived probable that the said persons may remain hid in some parts of New England, these are therefore seriously to advise and forewarn all persons whatsoever within the said colonies, not to receive, harbour, conceal or succour the said persons so attainted, or either of them, but that, as they may have any knowledge or information where the said Whalley and Goffe are, that they forthwith make known the same to some of the Governors or Magistrates next residing, and in the meantime do their utmost endeavour for their apprehending and securing, as they will answer the contrary at their utmost peril.[8]

Despite the written reassurances, Charles II was making little progress in his hunt. In 1664 he sent more commissioners to Boston from England – in four frigates, at the head of 400 soldiers. Their brief consisted of three parts: first, to capture New Amsterdam from the Dutch; secondly, to resolve various land disputes in New England; and thirdly, to round up any regicides that remained at large. 'You shall make due enquiry,' their commission ordered, 'who stand attainted here in Parliament of high treason, have transported themselves thither, & do now inhabit or reside or are sheltered there, and if any such persons are there, you shall cause them to be apprehended and to be put on shipboard and sent hither; to the end that they may be proceeded with according to law ... (for we will not suffer the Act of Indemnity to be in any degree violated).'[9] This instruction was clear in its general intent, but its hesitant wording – '*if* any such persons are there' – shows that the King's advisers in London were no longer sure as to which (if any) of the regicides still made New England their refuge.

Learning of the arrival of the commissioners, the major generals moved again, this time back to Providence, their West Rock cave. They had only been in this trusted hideout for ten days when it was compromised. A Native American hunting party stumbled across their bedding there, and reported the find to the authorities. Goffe and Whalley knew they could never return to what had been their safest sanctuary.

During their investigations, the King's commissioners heard that many of the cattle grazing Daniel Gookin's pastures in Cambridge were the property of the two fugitives. They ordered the seizure of the herd, but Gookin insisted on his rights and blocked what he claimed to be an arbitrary and illegal confiscation of his property. He was told to report in person to London, but refused to go. Something of the difficulty of dealing with challenging settlers from very far away is shown in the fact that he went unpunished for this disobedience.

However, when it came to truly significant matters, the Atlantic proved no impediment to Charles II and his government: partly for its role in hiding the regicides, partly because he wanted to formalise New England's subservient relationship to the British Crown, in

1665 Charles II deprived the colony of New Haven of its independence. It had been formed without any charter or commission from England. It had consistently flouted the King's demands to have two of his father's most prominent killers tracked down and handed over. For these reasons the colony was forcibly and permanently absorbed into Connecticut.

Eighty miles north of New Haven lay Hadley, a tiny community of a hundred or so houses covering a square half-mile on the River Connecticut. It had been settled five years earlier by a preacher, John Russell, and his followers – disaffected Puritans from the Connecticut towns of Hartford and Wethersfield. Russell had met Goffe and Whalley previously, and offered his new, isolated, settlement as a sanctuary. Now, in October 1663, Goffe and Whalley left for a new life in Hadley.

Russell sheltered them in his home, and kept them hidden from the other inhabitants. His simple, two-storey, dwelling was adapted to provide the Englishmen with hiding places on both floors, in the narrows behind the central chimney stack. Goffe and Whalley spent their days on the upper floor, where small windows allowed in daylight. The floor there had retractable floorboards which allowed speedy access into an enclosed space. This was where the secret house guests went whenever they needed to hide, and where they slept.

The two men's lives were, however, no better than they had been in Milford. They lived in discomfort and isolation, in constant fear of discovery, again an invisible part of the household, secluded from the world. They relied on the generosity of friends and were particularly grateful to their old acquaintance Richard Saltonstall: when he returned to England with his family in 1672, he gave the two fugitives £50. The climate brought its own challenges: the winters in Hadley were extremely harsh. Frances Goffe suggested to her husband that he buy a wig for warmth; he replied patiently that her proposal, though thoughtful, would be of little use against the intense cold he faced, which was very much crueller than anything she would ever have encountered in England.

They also had to live with profound disappointments. Goffe and Whalley had remained confident in the prediction that 1666 would witness the Second Coming: then, all would be put right in the world, and they would be reunited with their loved ones. When 1666 came and went, it proved to be a year just like all others; the Great Fire of London was its one brush with cataclysm.

Life was equally difficult for the regicides' relatives back home. Frances Goffe lived off the charity of an aunt, in poverty, thinking constantly of her husband and her father. To the former she wrote of one of their sons, Frederick, who 'with the rest of thy dear babes that can speak, present their humble duty to thee, talk much of thee, and long to see thee'.[10]

In 1674, Goffe wrote to Frances, taking on the voice of a son writing to his mother, in case the correspondence was intercepted by the authorities. He began by thanking her for her letter of 29 March that year, which had reached him four months later. He mentioned further correspondence that he had sent in the meantime, which he hoped she would have received – while being grateful that all but one of his recent letters seemed to have made it safely to her. With the Third Anglo-Dutch War taking place predominantly at sea, Goffe acknowledged that they had been lucky that their correspondence got through to one another as often as it did.

Goffe's wife had written with momentous family news: one of their daughters had died; while another daughter, Frances, had married. Goffe was happy to give his blessing to a union that he felt sure was blessed by God, since he understood his son-in-law to be a devout Christian: 'I pray remember my most tender and affectionate love to them both, and tell them that I greatly long to see them, but since that cannot be at present, you may assure them that whilst they shall make it their great work to love the Lord Jesus in sincerity, and love one another for Christ's sake.' He offered passages in the Bible to encourage his wife and family in their faith, begging her not to worry about the lack of material things in their life, but to concentrate on spiritual matters instead. 'Dear mother,' he wrote, 'I have been hitherto congratulating my new married sister, but I must now turn aside to drop a few tears upon the hearse of her that is deceased, whose loss I cannot choose but lament with tears, and so share with you in all the providences of God towards us, but my dear mother let me not be the occasion of renewing your grief, for I doubt not but you have grieved enough, if not too much already.' He then moved on to family news from Hadley, bringing his wife up to date with details of her father's ill health (he had probably suffered a stroke): 'Your old friend Mr R. is yet living, but continues in that weak condition of which I formerly have given you account, and have not now much to add,' he wrote:

He is scarce capable of any rational discourse, his understanding, memory and speech doth so much fail him, and seems not to take much notice of any thing that is either done or said, but patiently hears all things and never complains of any thing, though I fear it is some trouble to him that he hath had no letter of a long time from his cousin Rich [the codename for Mrs Whalley – the older major general's wife] but speaks not one word concerning it, nor any thing you wrote of in your last. Only after I had read your letters to him, being asked whether it was not a great refreshment to him to hear such a gracious spirit breathing in your letters, he said it was none of his least comforts, and indeed he scarce ever speaks any thing but in answer to questions when they are put to him, which are not of any kinds, because he is not capable to answer them, the common and very frequent question is to know how he doth, and his answer, for the most part is, 'very well, I praise God', which he utters with a very low and weak voice; but sometimes he saith, 'not very well', or 'very ill', and then if it be further said, 'do you feel any pain any where?', to that he always answereth 'no', when he wants any thing he cannot well speak for, because he forgets the name of it, and sometimes asks for one thing when he means another, so that his eye or his finger is oftentimes a better inter-preter of his mind than his tongue, but his ordinary wants are so well known to us, that most of them are supplied without asking or making signs for them, and some help he stands in need of in every thing to which any motion is required, having not been able of a long time, to dress or undress himself, nor to feed, or ease nature either way orderly, without help, and it is a great mercy to him that he hath a friend that takes pleasure in being helpful to him, and I bless the Lord that gives me such a good measure of health and strength, and an opportunity and a heart to use it in so good and necessary a work; for tho' my help be but poor and weak, yet that ancient servant of Christ could not well subsist without it, and I do believe, as you are pleased to say very well, that I do enjoy the more health for his sake.

Goffe indicated that the end could not be too far off for his old friend and father-in-law, and said that in his most coherent moments it was Whalley's fervent wish that his wife, family and friends keep him in their prayers. As for himself, Goffe stated openly, 'The greatest thing I need is a heart to abide patiently in this condition until it is expended. I cannot but account it a great mercy that in these hard times you should be able to be so helpful to your poor children, but I beseech you let not your love to them make you to forget yourself, in parting with what is necessary for your own comfort in your old age.'

He signed off this letter affectionately, knowing that it would be passed around his immediate family and closest friends. He then added a postscript, for his wife's eyes only. It was full of playful teasing that his dear, long-suffering, spouse could have misinterpreted an earlier letter he had sent as bearing anger towards her:

But oh, my dear mother, how could you fear such a thing from me? Yourself knoweth I never yet spake an angry word to you, nay I hope I may never say (without taking the name of God in vain) the Lord knoweth I never conceived an angry thought towards you, nor do I now, nor I hope never shall, and in so saying I do not commend my self, for you never gave me the least cause, neither have you now, and I believe never will, therefore, dear mother, the whole praise belongs to yourself, or rather to the Lord, who, blessed be his name, hath so united our hearts together in love, that it is a thing scarce possible to be angry with one another.[11]

Whalley died in 1675. The major generals had learnt of the dishonouring of Bradshaw, Cromwell and Ireton's tombs and, in a bid to stop similar outrages happening to their remains, had elected to have secret graves. Two traditions exist relating to Whalley's burial place: that it is either in the cellar of the regicides' hosts, the Russell family (where unidentified human bones were found during an excavation decades later), or else under the boundary wall between two settlers' farmsteads, so that neither landholder could be said to be the concealer of such a prominent outlaw, should his body ever be discovered.

In the summer of 1675, the frontier town of Hadley was placed in grave danger by a major rising of Native Americans. 'King Philip's War' (named after the chief of the Wampanoag, Metacom, whose adopted name was Philip), would continue for almost three years. It saw the people of some of the northern tribes, including the Nipmug and Quanbang, rise up in an effort to wipe out the communities of European settlers that had taken root across their ancestral lands.

According to popular tradition, on 1 September the people of Hadley were observing a day of fasting, during which they were gathered together in prayer in the meeting house. Suddenly the town was attacked by Native Americans and, although the people had weapons to hand, they were panic-stricken at the thought of impending death. It was then that an unknown, elderly, man was said to have appeared in the meeting house. Taking command of the situation, and showing soldierly expertise, he organised everyone into a successful repulse of the attack.

Once the settlers were safe, the anonymous man slipped away: he sought no thanks, and was never seen again. This mystery figure became known as 'the Angel of Hadley'. It was only when John Russell died in 1692 that it became common knowledge that the two regicides had lived in Hadley. After this 'the Angel' was quickly assumed to be the old New Model Army hero, Major General William Goffe. He was said to have brought to bear his military know-how for the salvation of a community that had been largely ignorant of his presence in their midst. After years of living in secret he had come into the open, to offer his fighting skills to the beleaguered settlement.

This story subsequently attracted the attention of romantics. Sir Walter Scott used the tale of Goffe's intervention in his longest novel, *Peveril of the Peak*, in 1823. Some historians have painstakingly reconstructed the events of King Philip's War to claim that Hadley was not in fact attacked on the day linked with this miraculous deliverance. However, others still prefer to believe that Goffe was involved in such an event; the exact timings, they argue, would be hard to synchronise, given that the events would have been covered up at the time by Goffe's protectors.

What is certain is that after this time Goffe felt unable to remain in Hadley. In 1676 he informed Dr Increase Mather in Boston that he was leaving, after fifteen years hiding out in this remote backwater. He reappeared in 1678 in Hartford, where he was recognised and only narrowly avoided arrest. Even after nearly two decades on the run, he was still one of the English-speaking world's most wanted men. In April 1680, a Royalist called John London would claim that Goffe still remained in Hartford, hidden in the house of a Captain Bull. Search warrants turned up nothing however. There were further unsubstantiated reports of his being in Narragansett (modern-day Rhode Island), Pennsylvania and Virginia. The Virginian theory is the most plausible and corresponds with a word-of-mouth tradition passed down among the eighteenth-century inhabitants of Hadley.

It seems certain that the hunt for the major generals continued after both were dead. Edward Randolph was sent to New England five times between 1676 and 1683 as inquisitor general. His remit was to break down the colonial settlements' civil rights and religious freedoms, and bring them more firmly under the control of the British Crown. On his last mission, in 1683, he was specifically charged with making yet another search for Goffe and Whalley. The following year the governor expressed surprise that the pair were still being pursued: he told Randolph he had heard on good authority that they had travelled to Manhattan some time previously, en route for the Netherlands. That was the end of all searches for the pair, elusive even beyond death. The final testimony to Goffe's success in avoiding capture lies in the fact that there is no record of when and where he died.

Sir Edmund Andros had been made governor of a new 'super colony', 'the Dominion of New England' in 1686, having served the Crown as governor of New York and New Jersey. During a tour of Connecticut he was attending morning service in New Haven one Sunday when his attention was drawn to a distinguished-looking man in his late seventies, standing in his eye-line. There was something about him. Andros was convinced of two things: 'He has been a soldier, and has figured somewhere in a more public station than this.'[12] When Andros appeared at that afternoon's ceremony, keen to have a second look at the intriguing figure, he was nowhere to be seen. The local preacher recalled that Andros's interest in him had so troubled the old man that he had 'brought sundry papers (as he said of importance) sealed up, which he requested [me] to take into safe custody and not to suffer the seals to be broken till after [his] decease, declaring it was not so safe under present changes [that] those writings should be found in his hand'.[13]

The man had first surfaced in New Haven in 1670, then in his sixties, calling himself 'James Davids'. He claimed that he had spent his working life as a merchant. Davids had money but no relatives, and chose to lodge with a childless couple, Mr and Mrs Ling, passing his day in solitary study (his favourite reading was said to be *The History of the World* by Sir Walter Raleigh) and quiet walks. His easy temper and obvious piety (he fasted every Friday) made him a popular addition to New Haven society. The same preacher remembered the newcomer as 'an aged person of manifest great education, who called himself James Davids, but was generally supposed to be of another name; his observable wisdom and great knowledge in the English Law, state policy and European affairs made his conversation very valuable ... and rendered said gentleman honourable with all that knew him'.[14]

When Mr Ling died in 1673, he left a request that the kind Mr Davids look after his widow, Joanna. Later that year Davids married Mrs Ling, but she only lived for a very short time after the wedding, leaving her husband of two weeks in possession of the £900 estate bequeathed to her by her first husband. Four years later, when aged seventy, he married again. This late second marriage produced a son and two daughters.

Andros had been correct in his deductions: Davids indeed had a military past, and he had held a prominent role in society. His true identity was Colonel John Dixwell, regicide.

A gentleman from Folkestone, Kent, Dixwell had enjoyed wealth and prominence in England, studying as a lawyer, serving as Sheriff of Kent, and then as an MP at different times for his county and for Dover. He was a stalwart Parliamentarian, being both a commissioner of the New Model Army and an active officer in the militia. He had attended all the days of Charles I's trial, and had signed the death warrant.

In the summer of 1660 he had ignored the King's proclamation to turn himself in, and secretly organised his affairs so he could fund his escape and time in hiding. In exile he had initially joined fellow refugees; first, in the free city of Hanau, before migrating to Switzerland. (He had long been closely aligned to Ludlow's committed republican beliefs.) There, he was believed by Charles II's advisers to have died. Taking advantage of this misinformation, and nervous at the vulnerability of the regicides to assassination in Switzerland, he moved unnoticed to New England.

Dixwell visited Goffe and Whalley in Hadley in February 1665, staying with them for some time – perhaps for the entire five years when his movements are otherwise unaccounted for. A letter from Davenport suggests Dixwell was one of 'three worthies' in Hadley that he hoped to see in December of that year.

Fragments of Dixwell's correspondence survive. His principal point of contact in London was his niece, Elizabeth Westrow, who used the pseudonym 'Elizabeth Boyce' in her letters. He also wrote to her husband and son. A man called Humphrey Davie, a resident of Boston, received money from family and friends in England to pass on to Dixwell: the colonel had avoided all employment since his arrival in New England, and steadily worked his way through his financial reserves. A receipt from the fugitive details the way in which money reached him: 'Received now and formerly of Mr Hum. Davie, by the direction of Mr Increase Mather, thirty pounds New England money, by the order of Madam Elizabeth Westrow, in England.'[15]

Throughout his long exile Dixwell had remained steadfast in his beliefs, writing that, 'the Lord will appear for his people, and the good old cause for which I suffer, and that there will be those in power again who will relieve the injured and oppressed'.[16] His dreams seemed to have come true with the Glorious Revolution of November 1688: Charles II had died suddenly of a kidney infection in 1685 and been succeeded by his brother, the Duke of York, who reigned as James II.

James's fervent Roman Catholicism was his downfall. It could perhaps be tolerated while his heirs were Protestant, as were the daughters of his first marriage; but the arrival of a son in 1688, whose mother was a Catholic, brought matters to a head. Deserted by his daughters, and by key courtiers and generals, James was forced into exile in a bloodless coup. He was replaced by William of Orange, whose mother had been one of Charles I's daughters, and by William's wife, Mary, who was James II's eldest child.

Dixwell died of the dropsy – a disease of the vital organs, which resulted in swelling caused by excess fluid – in New Haven on 18 March 1689, after twenty-nine years in exile, before news of the change in ruler in England reached him. He left instructions that his gravestone be vague, so his enemies could not disturb his remains. It read:

'J.D., Esq.,
Deceased March the 18th,
In the 82nd Year of His Age,
1689'

During his final illness he was tended by the preacher John Pierpoint, a long-standing friend and neighbour. Aware that he was dying, Dixwell told Pierpoint to open the chest containing his private papers. There he would find confirmation of his true identity.

Dixwell was perhaps the most successful of the regicides, reaching a great age after living in clear sight, leading a normal existence, and leaving behind a family. This was in glaring contrast to Goffe and Whalley, whose terror of being hauled back to England for hanging, drawing and quartering obliged them to endure a succession of miserable confinements, 'banished from all human society'.[17] Dixwell avoided that fate.

The New England regicides are remembered in New Haven, Connecticut, today: there you will find Dixwell Avenue, Goffe Street and Whalley Avenue – with rather more ease than the English redcoats ever had in locating the three gentlemen in question.

Chapter 15

To the Last Man

And they acted their parts like men; they set themselves against
the unruly wilfulness, the rage, the secret designs of an embittered
King; they held the common liberty and safety before their own.
John Milton, 'Defence of the People of England', 1651

Of the regicides whose fates we can follow to the end, Edmund Ludlow was the last survivor. From time to time there had been other attempts on his freedom and on his life; but the wily old soldier's instinct to remain in familiar territory, surrounded by faces he knew, rather than flee into the unknown and be at the mercy of anonymous assassins, proved a sound strategy to the end.

In late 1680 he learnt of the death of Henry Marten. Despite his central role in the preparation of Charles I's trial, and his stern republicanism, Marten managed to escape execution: there was an element of reluctance in Royalist circles to make such a well-known figure into a martyr. There was also an acknowledgement that Marten's advocacy had spared the lives of some of their own number after the King's execution.

Marten's fear of being exiled overseas came to nothing. He was sent first to Holy Island, off the Northumberland coast, before a move to Windsor Castle in 1665. But Charles II baulked at having a regicide kept so near to him and – in an echo of Marten's famous dismissal from the late King's presence, at the racecourse in London – he ordered his removal. From 1668, Marten was imprisoned in

Chepstow Castle, accompanied by his mistress, Mary, while his wife remained behind at the marital home in Berkshire. In his late seventies this man of boundless sensual appetites died, choking on his dinner.

Ludlow's companions in Switzerland all predeceased him. William Cawley, who had been frail at the time of his flight from Restoration England, died in Vevey in 1667, aged sixty-five. He had been one of the commissioners for 'demolishing superstitious pictures and monuments in London',[1] whose brief had culminated in the destruction of the stained-glass windows of Henry VII's Chapel in Westminster, and of Queen Henrietta Maria's chapel in Somerset House; her altarpiece, designed by Rubens, was cast into the Thames. Cawley was laid to rest in the handsome, unfussy Protestant church of St Martin, set back from Lake Geneva on a gentle hill.

Nicholas Love had felt sure before the great trial of January 1649 that Charles I would be acquitted and, when proved wrong, had become rich through the acquisition of confiscated royal and Church property. While friends decided to trust the clemency seemingly promised by the Declaration of Breda, Love wisely fled, 'being resolved not to trust the mercy of enraged beasts of prey'.[2] He died aged seventy-four, at the end of 1682, and was buried near to William Cawley.

Andrew Broughton, one of the clerks at Charles's trial, had arrived in Switzerland in 1662 after initially hiding in Hamburg with Nicholas Love. He, Love and Ludlow had travelled to an audience with the Lords of Berne to present the regicides' thanks to the senators for their protection from Royalist revenge. Broughton died in 1687, aged eighty-five, after quarter of a century in Vevey. He was also committed for burial in St Martin's.

These deaths left Ludlow as the solitary Swiss exile to hear of the death of Charles II, and the even more thrilling news of James II's overthrow. He had remained fascinated by events in Britain, and still maintained an alluring charisma to those who regarded him as the ultimate invincible opponent of the British Crown. In the mid-1660s, the Dutch had sounded out Ludlow to see if he would aid them in their conflict against Charles II. But Ludlow never forgave the Dutch for their betrayal of Barkstead, Corbet and Okey, which he believed left them tarnished with bloodguilt. He refused to help them, despite their common cause.

In 1684, the year before Charles II's death, Ludlow was the man that plotters turned to, asking him to raise the standard against the Stuarts in the west of England. He declined, claiming that he was in 'no ways disposed to the thing, saying he had done his work, he thought, in this world, and was resolved to leave it to others'.[3]

Such a rebellion took place in the southwest of England the following year. It was led by the Duke of Monmouth, Charles II's favourite illegitimate son. Monmouth had been a popular figure in England, as well as commander of its army, before overreaching himself and being banished abroad. On the death of his father he returned to England, hoping that people would flock to his Protestant cause in a stand against his Catholic uncle, James II. But the invasion was premature and poorly planned: the new King had yet to provoke huge unpopularity, and only a ragtag force of 4,000 – many armed with pitchforks – followed the duke. Monmouth resorted to a desperate nocturnal attack on the superior Royalist forces on Sedgemoor, but the element of surprise was lost when a pistol was discharged into the night. James II's favourite, John Churchill, led the King's forces in a complete rout of the rebels, while his commanding officer, Lord Feversham, was delayed from appearing on the battlefield because – it was said – he insisted on eating his breakfast first. (Feversham was further waylaid through problems straightening his wig and cravat.)

Monmouth, despite tearful pleadings, was sentenced to death. He was beheaded in a flurry of inept axe blows on Tower Hill, the first strike a glancing wound that made the duke look up in disbelieving pain. At this Jack Ketch, the executioner, lost his nerve, his repeated hacks failing to do the job. He eventually threw down his blade in defeat, before being forced by the irate crowd to complete his task with the retrieved axe, and then with a knife.

James II was determined to make an example of all the rebels and sent Judge George Jeffreys, Lord Chief Justice of the King's Bench, into the southwest to dispense vengeance in his name. One of those arrested was Dame Alice Lisle, the elderly widow of the regicide John Lisle, who had been felled by a blunderbuss in that Swiss churchyard twenty-one years earlier. She was accused of harbouring fugitive rebels on her property: Richard Nelthorp was discovered hiding behind the chimney in her family home, Moyles Court. John Hicks, a Nonconformist preacher, was also found on her land.

Dame Alice was a lady of some standing in the community. A mother of eleven children, she was in her late sixties when Monmouth invaded. As judge, Jeffreys was of course supposed to remain detached. However, on 27 August 1685, as the case against Dame Alice was heard in Winchester Castle, he revealed himself to be an eloquent addition to the prosecution. He reminded the jury of what the dame's late husband had been guilty of – 'I will not say what hand her husband had in the death of that blessed martyr, she has enough to answer for . . . and I must confess it ought not one way or other to make any ingredient into this case what she was in former times'[4] – but it was clear that Jeffreys was eager to underline her connection by marriage to the shocking execution of King James's father.

The jurors, troubled by the sight of the old lady repeatedly falling asleep while on trial for her life, tried to persuade the judge that they had enough doubt about her guilt to make conviction impossible. But Jeffreys would have none of it, insisting, 'There is as full proof as proof can be; but you are judges of the proof, for my part I thought there was no difficulty in it.'[5] The jury remained in an agitated huddle for fifteen minutes before finally and unhappily declaring Dame Alice's guilt.

She was sentenced to be burnt at the stake, a punishment that, on appeal, was commuted to beheading. Some say she gave a dignified speech from the scaffold, hastily erected in Winchester market square, while others reported her as being 'old and dozy', and reported that she 'died without much concern'.[6] The killing of this venerable pillar of the community appalled many, and while Judge Jeffreys went on to dispatch a further 300 people connected with Monmouth's rebellion, the stain of Dame Alice's blood has clung to his reputation with particular stubbornness. The regicide's widow has the unwanted distinction of being the last woman ever to have been beheaded by order of a court in English history.

Three years later the invasion by William of Orange resulted in the bloodless Glorious Revolution. In 1689 the new regime was looking to suppress support in Ireland for the exiled James II. Ludlow's name was again discussed as a possible leader of the English force: his effectiveness there, thirty years earlier, was recalled with admiration.

Ludlow said goodbye to friends in Switzerland, feeling it was at last time for him to return to England and help the latest manifestation of God's cause. He was greeted with joyful nostalgia by other survivors from the glory days of the New Model Army and the Republic of the Commonwealth. His lodgings in London bustled with family and old colleagues. But there were still powerful enemies for the lieutenant general to contend with.

Ludlow's confiscated estate had been granted to Sir Edward Seymour, an arrogant and unpopular Speaker of the House of Commons. Concerned that Ludlow would look to reclaim his property, Seymour's brother-in-law, Sir Joseph Tredenham, launched a pre-emptive attack in Parliament. Tredenham was quick to remind MPs that Ludlow's arrest warrant was still live: he must, therefore, be punished for high treason. 'To what can these persons pretend,' Tredenham said, in reference to returning exiles like Ludlow, 'but to bring us into the same anarchy as formerly?'[7] While sympathisers tried to delay a vote on his fate, Ludlow slipped away to the Netherlands. Soon afterwards King William announced that Ludlow must indeed be held to account for his part in Charles I's death, and offered a reward of £200 for his arrest.

Ludlow returned to Vevey. He died there in late 1692 at the age of seventy-two. His widow had a Latin inscription borrowed from the works of Ovid placed over the door of their home: '*Omne solum forti patria quia patris*'. It applies equally to the many other pious regicides – those courageous men who dared to kill a king in the hope of bringing peace to their traumatised land; who were forced to live overseas, or face agonising and degrading death at home. Translated, it reads: 'To the brave man every land is a fatherland, because God his father made it'.

NOTES

Chapter 1: Man of Blood

1 Anon., *An Exact and Most Impartial Accompt of the Indictment, Arraignment, Trial, and Judgment (According to Law) of Twenty-Nine Regicides ...*, London, 1660, p. 169.

2 Rev. Francis Peck (ed.), *Desiderata Curiosa*, 'Hudson's Examination by the Committee of Parliament', Thomas Evans in the Strand, London, 1779, p. 359.

3 Ibid., 'Letter of Miles Corbet and Valentine Walton to Speaker Lenthall', 11 May 1646, p. 349.

4 John Rushworth (ed.), *Historical Collections of Private Passages of State, Weighty Matters of Law ...*, Vol. VI – *The Scottish Leaders to Parliament, 6 May 1646*, London, 1701, p. 268.

5 A. L. Rowse, *The Regicides and the Puritan Revolution*, Duckworth, London, 1994, pp. 13–14.

6 Edmund Ludlow, *The Imprisonment & Death of King Charles I, Related by One of his Judges – Extracts from the Memoirs of Edmund Ludlow*, privately printed, Edinburgh, 1882, p. 10.

7 Ibid., p. 11.

8 Ibid., p. 16.

9 Ibid., p. 19.

10 Ibid., p. 20.

11 Lucy Hutchinson, *Memoirs of the Life of Colonel Hutchinson*, Orion, London, 1995, p. 214.

12 Peck (ed.), *Desiderata Curiosa*, 'Letter of Colonel Whalley to Speaker Lenthall', p. 377.

13 Ibid., p. 374.

14 Ibid., p. 375.

15 Ibid., p. 376.

16 Ibid.

17 Ann Geneva, *Astrology and the Seventeenth-century Mind: William Lilly and the language of the stars*, Manchester University Press, 1995, p. 212.

18 Tristram Hunt, *The English Civil War at First Hand*, London, 2002, p. 164.

19 John Fox, *Oxford Dictionary of National Biography (DNB)*, Jane Whorwood, quoting the diarist Anthony Wood.

20 John Fox, 'Jane Whorwood: The King's Smuggler', *History Today*, January 2010.

21 C. H. Firth (ed.), *The Clarke Papers*, Vol. I, Camden Society, 1891, p. 325.

22 Ibid., p. 254.

23 Ibid., p. 256.

24 Earl of Clarendon, *The History of the Rebellion: A New Selection*, edited by Paul Seaward, Oxford, 2009, p. 323.

25 Hutchinson, *Colonel Hutchinson*, p. 225.

26 Rowse, *Regicides*, p. 15.

27 Ludlow, *Imprisonment & Death*, pp. 53–4.

28 Firth (ed.), *Clarke Papers*, pp. 227–78.

29 Ludlow, *Imprisonment & Death*, p. 33.

30 Hutchinson, *Colonel Hutchinson*, p. 231.

31 M. Sylvester (ed.), *Reliquiae Baxteraniae*, London, 1696, p. 54.

32 Anon., *Twenty-Nine Regicides*, p. 54 (a).

33 Clarendon, *Rebellion*, p. 330.

34 Ibid., p. 328.

35 Anon., *Twenty-Nine Regicides*, p. 2.

36 John Jesse, *Memoirs of the Court of England: During the Reigns of the Stuarts*, Vol. II, 1899, p. 256.

Chapter 2: A King on Trial

1 Roger Lockyer (ed.), *The Trial of Charles I: A Contemporary Account taken from the Memoirs of Sir Thomas Herbert and John Rushworth*, Folio Press, 1974, p. 76.

2 Samuel Rawson Gardiner (ed.), *The Constitutional Documents of the Puritan Revolution, 1625–1660*, Clarendon Press, Oxford, 1906, p. 357.

3 Clarendon, *Rebellion*, p. 326.

4 John Alvis (ed.), *Areopagitica and other Political Writings of John Milton*, Liberty Fund Press, Indianapolis, 1999.

5 Clarendon, *Rebellion*, p. 326.

6 Anon., *Twenty-Nine Regicides*, p. 106.

7 Margo Todd, *DNB*, Isaac Dorislaus, quoting 'Letters of Wren' from the National Archives.

8 Sean Kelsey, *DNB*, Nicholas Love, quoting Bodl. Oxf. MS Clarendon 34, fol. 17v.

9 Rowse, *Regicides*, p. 118.
10 Ibid., p. 119.
11 *Mercurius Pragmaticus*, pp. 36–7, 5–12, December 1648.
12 Mark Noble, *Memoirs of the Protectoral-House of Cromwell*, Vol. I, London, 1798, p. 373.
13 Rowse, *Regicides*, p. 90.
14 Clarendon, *Rebellion*, p. 334.
15 John Aubrey, *Brief Lives*, St Edmondsbury Press, Bury St Edmunds, 1998, p. 195.
16 Ibid.
17 Sarah Barber, *DNB*, Henry Marten.
18 Anon., *Twenty-Nine Regicides*, p. 248.
19 Jonathan Scott, *DNB*, Algernon Sidney, quoting from *Sidney Papers*, ed. R. Blencowe (1825), pp. 236–9.
20 For the full wording of the Dutch Act of Abjuration see: http://www.fordham.edu/halsall/mod/1581dutch.asp
21 Gardiner (ed.), *Constitutional Documents*, p. 371.
22 Anon., *Twenty-Nine Regicides*, p. 248.
23 Rowse, *Regicides*, p. 70.
24 Anon., *A Perfect Narrative of the Whole Proceedings of the High Court of Justice, licensed by Gibbert Mabbot*, London, 1649, p. 995.
25 Ibid.
26 Ludlow, *Imprisonment & Death*, p. 62.
27 C. V. Wedgwood, *A King Condemned: The Trial and Execution of Charles I*, Palgrave Macmillan, New York, p. 131.
28 Anon., *Twenty-Nine Regicides*, p. 190.
29 Ibid.
30 Interchange between Charles I and Lord President Bradshaw in Anon., *Perfect Narrative*, pp. 995–7.
31 Ludlow, *Imprisonment & Death*, p. 56.
32 Book of Numbers, chapter 35, verse 33.
33 Ludlow, *Imprisonment & Death*, p. 56.
34 Hutchinson, *Colonel Hutchinson*, p. 234.
35 T. B. Howell, *A Complete Collection of State Trials and Proceedings for High Treason and other Crimes and Misdemeanors*, Vol. IV, T. C. Hansard, London, 1816, p. 1128.
36 Edmund Ludlow, *Memoirs of Edmund Ludlow*, Vol. I, London, 1771, Appendix, p. 17.
37 Howell, *Complete Collection of State Trials*, Vol. IV, p. 1017.
38 Clarendon, *Rebellion*, p. 336.
39 Ludlow, *Imprisonment & Death*, p. 17.
40 Agnes Strickland, *Lives of the Queens of England, from the Norman Conquest*, Vol. 4, James Miller, New York, 1843, p. 126.
41 Anon., *Account of Charles I's Conduct on the Scaffold from: King Charles His Execution*, printed by Peter Cole, London, 1649.

42 Mark Noble (ed.), *The Lives of the English Regicides*, Vol. I, John Stockdale, London, 1798, p. xxxiv.

Chapter 3: The Republic

1 Noble (ed.), *Lives of the English Regicides*, p. xxxiii.
2 E. S. de Beer (ed.), *The Diary of John Evelyn*, Oxford University Press, 1959, pp. 275–6.
3 Clarendon, *Rebellion*, p. 333.
4 Bulstrode Whitlocke, *Memorials of the English Affairs from the Beginning of the Reign of Charles the First*, Vol. 3 of 4, General Books, Memphis, 2010, p. 43.
5 Ibid., p. 51.
6 Ibid., p. 34.
7 Anthony Wood, *Athenae Oxonienses*, Vol. III, London, 1817, p. 667.
8 Clement Walker (writing as 'Theodorus Verax'), *Anarchia Anglicana*, 1649, p. 173.
9 Whitlocke, *Memorials*, pp. 21–2.
10 Thomas Carte, *A Collection of Original Letters and Papers concerning the Affairs of England, from the Year 1641 to 1660*, Vol. I, Society for the Encouragement of Learning, London, p. 291.
11 Ludlow, *Memoirs*, Vol. I, p. 251.
12 *Declaration on their Just Resentment of the Horrid Murther of Isaac Dorislaus*, Acts of Parliament (1648–50), 1.92.
13 De Beer, *Diary of John Evelyn*, p. 556.
14 Anon., *A Salt Teare: or, the Weeping Onion at the Lamentable Funerall of Dr Dorislaus*, London, 1649.
15 Anthony Ascham, *A Discourse, wherein is examined what is particularly lawfull during the Confusions and Revolutions of Government*, 1648.
16 *Calendar of State Papers*, 16 January 1650.
17 *Clarendon State Papers*, 4 June 1650.
18 Alvis (ed.), 'Second Defence of the People of England', *Areopagitica*, p. 381.
19 Ibid., p. 382.
20 Whitlocke, *Memorials*, p. 14.
21 Peck (ed.), *Desiderata Curiosa*, Lib. XIII, p. 485 fn.
22 Ibid., p. 486.
23 Ibid.
24 Ibid., p. 488.
25 Whitlocke, *Memorials*, p. 41.
26 Ibid., p. 14.
27 Andrew J. Hopper, *DNB*, Isaac Ewer.
28 Christopher Durston, *DNB*, John Hewson.
29 Ludlow, *Memoirs*, Vol. I, p. 215.

30 De Beer, *Diary of John Evelyn*, p. 279.
31 Oliver Cromwell to the Honorable John Bradshaw, 16 September, 1649: www.olivercromwell.org/letters_and_speeches/letters/Letter_105.pdf
32 Hutchinson, *Colonel Hutchinson*, p. 182.

Chapter 4: A New Monarchy

1 C. H. Firth (ed.), *The Memoirs of Edmund Ludlow*, Vol. II, Clarendon Press, Oxford, 1894, p. 9.
2 Hutchinson, *Colonel Hutchinson*, p. 239.
3 Ibid., p. 249.
4 Book of Revelation, chapter 13, verse 1.
5 Rowse, *Regicides*, p. 57, quoting from Richard Baxter's *Reliquiae Baxterianae*.
6 Hutchinson, *Colonel Hutchinson*, p. 243.
7 Ibid.
8 Firth (ed.), *Memoirs of Edmund Ludlow*, p. 352.
9 Ibid., p. 7.
10 Ibid.
11 Paul M. Kennedy, *The Rise and Fall of British Sea Mastery*, A. Lane, London, 1976, p. 48.
12 De Beer, *Diary of John Evelyn*, p. 323.
13 Hutchinson, *Colonel Hutchinson*, p. 257.
14 Ibid., p. 246.
15 Ibid., p. 257.
16 Townsend's Annals, MS, p. 285; Prattenton's Coll., Society of Antiquaries.
17 Bodl. Oxf., MS Rawl. A 34, fol. 395.
18 Book of Leviticus, chapter 24, verse 14.
19 Thomas Burton, *Diary of Thomas Burton*, Vol. I, London, 1828, p. 52.
20 Hutchinson, *Colonel Hutchinson*, p. 256.
21 Ibid., pp. 256–7.
22 *Clarendon State Papers, III*, p. 327.
23 Firth (ed.), *Memoirs of Edmund Ludlow*, p. 21.
24 Ibid., p. 24.
25 Ibid., p. 25.
26 Ibid., p. 27.
27 Clarendon, *Rebellion*, p. 385.
28 Burton, *Diary*, Vol. II, p. 388.
29 Ibid., pp. 387–8.
30 Noble, *Memoirs of the Protectoral-House*, Vol. I, p. 279.
31 De Beer, *Diary of John Evelyn*, pp. 394–5.
22 *Weekly Intelligencer*, 1–8 November 1659, London, p. 212.
33 David Farr, *John Lambert, Parliamentary Soldier and Cromwellian Major-general, 1619–1684*, Boydell Press, Woodbridge, 2003, p. 200.
34 Whitlocke, *Memorials*, p. 49.

35 Firth (ed.), *Clarke Papers*, p. 110.
36 Clarendon, *Rebellion*, p. 407.

Chapter 5: The Word of a King

1   Clarendon, *Rebellion*, p. 382.
2   *Calendar of State Papers Domestic, 1654–55*, p. 341.
3   Clarendon, *Rebellion*, p. 414.
4   Farr, *John Lambert*, p. 211.
5   Firth (ed.), *Memoirs of Edmund Ludlow*, p. 257.
6   Noble, *Memoirs of the Protectorate-House*, Vol. I, p. 368.
7   *Journals of the House of Commons*, Vols 8–11, Henry Hughes, London, 1780, p. 829.
8   Hutchinson, *Colonel Hutchinson*, pp. 273–4.
9   Anon., *Twenty-Nine Regicides*, pp. 86 and 87.
10 Ibid., p. 265.
11 Gardiner (ed.), *Constitutional Documents*, p. 465.
12 Clarendon, *Rebellion*, p. 393.
13 Ibid., p. 418.
14 Rowse, *Regicides*, p. 49.
15 *Journals of the House of Commons*, Vol. 8, 14 May 1660.
16 C. H. Simkinson, *Thomas Harrison, Regicide and Major-General*, J. M. Dent, London, 1905, p. 222.
17 Firth (ed.), *Memoirs of Edmund Ludlow*, p. 269.
18 *Journals of the House of Commons*, Vol. 8, 11 May 1660.
19 Ibid., 21 May 1660.
20 Firth (ed.), *Memoirs of Edmund Ludlow*, p. 316.
21 Rowse, *Regicides*, p. 144.
22 J. T. Peacey, *DNB*, Gregory Clements.
23 Firth (ed.), *Memoirs of Edmund Ludlow*, p. 272.
24 *Journals of the House of Commons*, Vol. 8, 31 May 1660.
25 *Proclamation of King Charles*, Whitehall, 6 June 1660.
26 *Journals of the House of Commons*, Vol. 8, 9 June 1660.
27 Hutchinson, *Colonel Hutchinson*, p. 280.
28 Ibid.
29 Anon., *Coll. Henry Marten's Letters to His Lady of Delight*, Oxford, 1663, p. 26.
30 Anon., *Twenty-Nine Regicides*, p. 89.
31 *Journals of the House of Commons*, Vol. 8, 9 June 1660.
32 Hutchinson, *Colonel Hutchinson*, p. 282.
33 Ibid., p. 284.
34 Ibid., p. 282.
35 *Journals of the House of Commons*, Vol. 8, p. 97.
36 Anon., *Twenty-Nine Regicides*, p. 65.
37 The National Archives, PRO, SP 29/71, fol. 20.
38 Hutchinson, *Colonel Hutchinson*, p. 287.

Chapter 6: A Bloody Sacrifice

1 A. B. Worden (ed.), *A Voyce From The Watch Tower, Part Five: 1660–1662*, Royal Historical Society, London, 1978, p. 258.
2 Ibid., p. 266.
3 Anon., *Twenty-Nine Regicides*, p. 232.
4 Geoffrey Robertson, *The Tyrannicide Brief*, Chatto & Windus, London, 2005, p. 286.
5 Anon., *Coll. Henry Marten's Letters*, p. 2.
6 Ibid., p. 3.
7 Ibid., pp. 3–4.
8 Ibid., p. 4.
9 A. L. Rowse, *Four Caroline Portraits*, Duckworth, London, 1993, p. 65, quoting from John Aubrey.
10 Anon., *Coll. Henry Marten's Letters*, p. 6 [Letter 2].
11 Ibid., p. 7 [Letter 6].
12 Ibid., p. 19 [Letter 18].
13 Ibid., p. 14 [Letter 10] and p. 58 [Letter 70].
14 Ibid., p. 66 [Letter 80].
15 Ibid.
16 Ludlow, *Memoirs*, Vol. II, p. 302.
17 Hutchinson, *Colonel Hutchinson*, p. 286.
18 Louis A. Knafla, *DNB*, Sir Geoffrey Palmer.
19 Sir William Blackstone, *Commentaries on the Laws of England*, Book III, 1765, p. 55.
20 Anon., *Twenty-Nine Regicides*, p. 9.
21 Ibid.
22 Ibid., p. 15.
23 Ibid., p. 10.
24 Ibid., p. 15.
25 Ibid., p. 10.
26 Ibid., p. 15.
27 Ibid., pp. 14–15.
28 Ibid., p. 15.
29 Ibid., p. 17.
30 Ibid.
31 Samuel Pepys, *Diary of Samuel Pepys*, 10 October 1660, www.pepysdiary.com.
32 Anon., *Twenty-Nine Regicides*, p. 37.
33 Ibid., p. 39.
34 Ibid., p. 42.
35 Firth (ed.), *Memoirs of Edmund Ludlow*, p. 304.
36 Anon., *Twenty-Nine Regicides*, p. 44.
37 Ibid., p. 46.
38 Ibid., p. 48.

39 Ibid., p. 49.
40 Ibid., p. 50.
41 Ibid., p. 54.
42 Ibid.
43 Ibid., p. 55.
44 Ibid., p. 56.
45 Ibid.

Chapter 7: Men of God

1   Robertson, *Tyrannicide Brief*, p. 286.
2   Howell, *Complete Collection of State Trials*, Vol. V, p. 687.
3   The Earl of Clarendon, *History of the Rebellion and Civil Wars in England*, Vol. II (of II), Oxford University Press, London, 1893, p. 852.
4   Noble (ed.), *Lives of the English Regicides*, Vol. I, pp. 335–6.
5   Firth (ed.), *Memoirs of Ludlow*, p. 304.
6   Worden (ed.), *A Voyce From The Watch Tower*, p. 215.
7   Simkinson, *Harrison*, p. 269.
8   Robertson, *Tyrannicide Brief*, p. 326.
9   Pepys, *Diary*, 13 October 1660.
10 Anon., *Twenty-Nine Regicides*, p. 100.
11 Ibid., p. 100.
12 Ibid.
13 Rowse, *Regicides*, p. 65.
14 Ibid.
15 Book of Revelation, Chapter 20, Verse 4.
16 Rowse, *Regicides*, p. 66.
17 Anon., *Twenty-Nine Regicides*, p. 76.
18 Ibid., p. 79.
19 Ibid., p. 81.
20 Firth (ed.), *Memoirs of Edmund Ludlow*, p. 305.
21 Anon., *Twenty-Nine Regicides*, p. 81.
22 Rowse, *Regicides*, p. 67.
23 *Calendar of State Papers, Domestic, 1625–49*, p. 175.
24 Nathaniel B. Shurtlett (ed.), *Records of the Governor and Company of the Mass. Bay in New England*, Vol. I, Boston, 1853–4, pp. 10 and 12.
25 Eleanor Bradley Peters, *Hugh Peter: Preacher, Patriot, Philanthropist*, New York, 1909, p. 68.
26 John Winthrop, *Journal of John Winthrop, 1630–1649*, Massachusetts Historical Society, 1996, p. 346.
27 Peters, *Hugh Peter*, p. 72.
28 Ibid., p. 68.
29 Anon., *Twenty-Nine Regicides*, p. 166.
30 Guy de la Bedoyere (ed.), *The Diary of John Evelyn*, The Boydell Press, Woodbridge, 1995, p. 68.

31 Anon., *Twenty-Nine Regicides*, pp. 167–8.
32 Pepys, *Diary*, 7 March 1662.
33 Peters, *Hugh Peter*, p. 86.
34 Anon., *Twenty-Nine Regicides*, p. 162.
35 Ibid.
36 Ibid.
37 Peters, *Hugh Peter*, p. 69.
38 Ibid., p. 70.
39 Ibid., p. 71.
40 Anon., *Twenty-Nine Regicides*, p. 30.
41 Ibid., p. 153.
42 Ibid., p. 158.
43 Ibid., p. 163.
44 Ibid., p. 159.
45 Ibid., p. 181.
46 Ibid., p. 160.
47 Worden (ed.), *A Voyce From The Watch Tower*, p. 230.

Chapter 8: A Time to Die

1   Anon., *A Compleat Collection of the Lives, Speeches, and Prayers of those persons lately executed*, London, 1660, p. 30.
2   Robertson, *Tyrannicide Brief*, p. 336.
3   Ibid., p. 337.
4   Worden (ed.), *A Voyce From The Watch Tower*, p. 240.
5   Ibid., p. 249.
6   Ibid., p. 242.
7   Ibid., pp. 243–4.
8   Ibid., p. 247.
9   Ibid., p. 246.
10 Ibid., p. 247.
11 Ibid.
12 Anon., *Twenty-Nine Regicides*, p. 68.
13 Ibid., p. 63.
14 Ibid., p. 71.
15 Hutchinson, *Colonel Hutchinson*, p. 284.
16 Worden (ed.), *A Voyce From The Watch Tower*, p. 249.
17 Ibid.
18 Ibid., p. 265.
19 Anon., *Twenty-Nine Regicides*, p. 276.
20 Firth (ed.), *Memoirs of Edmund Ludlow*, p. 320.
21 Anon., *Twenty-Nine Regicides*, p. 218.
22 Hutchinson, *Colonel Hutchinson*, p. 282.
23 Anon., *Twenty-Nine Regicides*, p. 226.
24 Worden (ed.), *A Voyce From The Watch Tower*, p. 257.

25 Ibid.
26 Ibid., p. 264.
27 Ibid., p. 260.
28 Ibid., p. 262.
29 Anon., *Twenty-Nine Regicides*, p. 287.
30 De Beer, *Diary of John Evelyn*, p. 412.

Chapter 9: Surrender or Else

 1 Firth (ed.), *Memoirs of Edmund Ludlow*, p. 275.
 2 Wilbur Cortez Abbott (ed.), *Writings and Speeches of Oliver Cromwell*, Oxford University Press, USA, 1989, Vol. 4, p. 266.
 3 Firth (ed.), *Memoirs of Edmund Ludlow*, p. 278.
 4 Ibid., p. 279.
 5 Ibid., p. 280.
 5 Ibid., p. 283.
 7 Ibid., p. 286.
 8 *Parliamentary or Constitutional History of England from the earliest times to the Restoration of Charles II, Vol. XXII (of XXIV)*, London, 1751–62, p. 397.
 9 Firth (ed.), *Memoirs of Edmund Ludlow*, p. 286.
10 Ibid., p. 293.
11 Ibid., p. 294.
12 Ibid., pp. 295–6.
13 Ibid., p. 296.
14 Ibid., p. 297.
15 Ibid., p. 298.
16 Ibid.
17 Rowse, *Regicides*, pp. 73–4.
18 Firth (ed.), *Memoirs of Edmund Ludlow*, p. 300 fn.
19 Ibid.
20 Ibid.
21 De Beer, *Diary of John Evelyn*, p. 416.

Chapter 10: Strangers in a Strange Land

 1 Anon., *Twenty-Nine Regicides*, p. 45.
 2 Worden (ed.), *A Voyce From The Watch Tower*, p. 249.
 3 Ibid., p. 154.
 4 Anon., *The Speeches, Discourses, and Prayers, of Col. John Barkstead, Col. John Okey, and Mr Miles Corbet*, London, 1662, p. 24.
 5 Ibid., p. 1.
 6 Jonathan Scott, *DNB*, Sir George Downing.
 7 Worden (ed.), *A Voyce From The Watch Tower*, p. 297.

8   Scott, *DNB*, Sir George Downing.

9   Ibid.

10 Scott, *DNB*, Thomas Chaloner.

11 Firth (ed.), *Memoirs of Edmund Ludlow*, p. 331 fn.

12 Ibid., pp. 330–1 fn.

13 Anon., *Saint George and the Dragon*, published in *Anglice Mercurius Poeticus*, London, 28 February 1659.

14 The Book of Revelation, chapter 21, verse 8.

15 T. H. Lister, *The Life and Administration of Clarendon*, Vol. III, Longmans, London, 1838, p. 169.

16 Anon., *Speeches, Discourses*, p. 2.

17 Ibid., p. 34.

18 Ibid., p. 39.

19 Ibid., unnumbered [p. 26]

20 Rowse, *Regicides*, p. 80.

21 Firth (ed.), *Memoirs of Edmund Ludlow*, p. 332.

22 Anon., *Speeches, Discourses*, 8th unnumbered page after p. 24.

23 Ibid., 9th unnumbered page after p. 24.

24 Ibid., 11th unnumbered page after p. 24.

25 Ibid., 21st unnumbered page after p. 24.

26 Ibid., 23rd unnumbered page after p. 24.

27 Ibid., p. 14.

28 Ibid., p. 17.

29 Ibid., p. 22.

30 Firth (ed.), *Memoirs of Edmund Ludlow*, p. 332.

31 Anon., *Speeches, Discourses*, p. 25.

32 Ibid., p. 25, and unnumbered page before p. 37.

33 Ibid., unnumbered page before p. 25.

34 Anon., *The Parliament Kite*, No. 10, 20–27 July 1648, London, p. 54.

35 Anon., *Speeches, Discourses*, p. 41.

36 Firth (ed.), *Memoirs of Edmund Ludlow*, p. 333.

37 Anon., *Speeches, Discourses*, p. 23.

38 Ibid., p. 24.

39 Ibid., p. 49.

40 Ibid., p. 24.

41 Ibid., p. 57.

42 *Calendar of State Papers, Domestic, 1661–62*, p. 346.

43 Howell, *Complete Collection of State Trials*, Vol. V, p. 317, fn.

Chapter 11: A Swiss Sanctuary

1   Pepys, *Diary*, 12 March 1662.

2   Ibid., 31 October 1662.

3   Firth (ed.), *Memoirs of Edmund Ludlow*, p. 342.

4   Ibid., p. 483.

5 Ibid., p. 484.
6 Ibid., p. 345.
7 Ibid., p. 356.
8 Ibid., p. 360.
9 Ibid., pp. 484–5.
10 Ibid.
11 Ibid.
12 Ibid.
33 Ibid., p. 364.
14 Ibid., p. 367.
15 Ibid., pp. 482–3.
16 Ibid., p. 482.
17 Ibid., p. 488.
18 Ibid.
19 Ibid., p. 489.

Chapter 12: Vengeance at Last

1 *Journals of the House of Commons*, Vol. 8, 3 March 1662.
2 Anon., *Twenty-Nine Regicides*, p. 263.
3 Ibid., p. 253.
4 Ibid., p. 24.
5 Hutchinson, *Colonel Hutchinson*, p. 312.
6 Anon., *Twenty-Nine Regicides*, p. 265.
7 Ibid., p. 262.
8 M. Exwood and H. H. Lehmann (trans. and eds), *The Journal of William Schellincks' Travels in England, 1661–1663*, Camden Society, 1993, pp. 72, 82–3, 86.
9 *Seventh Report of the Royal Commission on Historical Manuscripts*, Eyre and Spottiswoode, London, 1879, appendix 1, p. 150.
10 Rowse, *Regicides*, p. 84.
11 Hutchinson, *Colonel Hutchinson*, p. 312.
12 Ibid., p. 288.
13 Ibid., p. 289.
14 Ibid., p. 295.
15 Ibid., p. 288.
16 Ibid., p. 289.
17 Ibid., p. 297.
18 Ibid., p. 300.
19 Andrew J. Hopper, 'The Farnley Wood Plot and the Memory of the Civil Wars in Yorkshire', *The Historical Journal*, 45 (2), p. 300.
20 Hutchinson, *Colonel Hutchinson*, p. 300.
21 Ibid., p. 305.
22 Ibid., p. 307.
23 Ibid., p. 310.

24 Ibid., p. 312.
25 Ibid., p. 314.
26 Ibid., pp. 319–22.
27 Ibid., pp. 327–33.

Chapter 13: An Ocean Away

1   This journal was destroyed by fire in 1776. These names, and other excerpts, were transcribed beforehand. The list can be found in Ezra Stiles, *A History of Three of the Judges of King Charles I*, Elisha Babcock, Hartford, 1794, pp. 99–100.

2   C. H. Firth, *The Raising of the Ironsides*, Spottiswoode & Co., London, 1899, p. 21.

3   Thomas Carlyle, *Oliver Cromwell's Letters and Speeches, Vol. I, Part II, Letter XII*, Scribner, Welford and Co., New York, 1871, p. 136.

4   Alvis (ed.), *Areopagitica*, p. 405.

5   Noble, *Memoirs of the Protectoral-House*, Vol. II, p. 145.

6   Firth (ed.), *Clarke Papers*, p. 254.

7   Carlyle, *Cromwell's Letters*, p. 170.

8   Bodl. Oxf., MS Rawl. A 38, fol. 125.

9   De la Bédoyère (ed.), *Diary of John Evelyn*, p. 105.

10 Hutchinson, *Colonel Hutchinson*, p. 257.

11 Excerpt from Goffe's diary from css.podsdemo.com/webpages/ftphtmltransfer/judges3.html

12 *Calendar of State Papers, Colonial, America and West Indies, 1661–1668*, no. 161, p. 54.

13 Edward Elias Atwater et al., *History of the Colony of New Haven to Its Absorption Into Connecticut*, The Journal Publishing Company, Meriden Connecticut, 1902, p. 422.

14 Christopher Pagliuco, *The Great Escape of Edward Whalley and William Goffe*, Charleston, SC, 2012, p. 61.

15 *A Proclamation By the King For Apprehension of Edward Whalley and William Goffe*, 22 September 1660, printed by Christopher Baker and John Bill, London, 1660.

16 *The New England Quarterly*, Vol. 60, No. 4, p. 529.

17 Stiles, *Three of the Judges*, p. 60.

18 Lemuel Aiken Welles, *The History of the Regicides in New England*, New York, 1927, pp. 28–9.

19 *Decree of Charles II, March 1661*, Whitehall.

20 Stiles, *Three of the Judges*, p. 52.

21 Atwater et al., *Colony of New Haven*, p. 424.

22 Frederick Hull Cogswell, 'The Regicides in New England', *New England Magazine*, Vol. IX, No. 2, 1893, p. 191.

23 Atwater et al., *Colony of New Haven*, p. 426.
24 Ibid.
25 Stiles, *Three of the Judges*, p. 55.
26 Ibid.
27 Russell Shorto, *The Island at the Centre of the World*, Doubleday, London, 2004, p. 71.
28 Atwater et al., *Colony of New Haven*, p. 428.

Chapter 14: Into the Wilderness

 1 Stiles, *Three of the Judges*, p. 82.
 2 Ibid., p. 74.
 3 Ibid., p. 108.
 4 Welles, *History of the Regicides in New England*, pp. 69–70.
 5 Stiles, *Three of the Judges*, pp. 56–8.
 6 Ibid., pp. 49–50.
 7 Pagliuco, *Great Escape*, p. 77.
 8 Stiles, *Three of the Judges*, pp. 59–60.
 9 Pagliuco, *Great Escape*, p. 84.
10 Noble, *Memoirs of the Protectoral-House*, Vol. I, pp. 425–6.
11 Stiles, *Three of the Judges*, pp. 118–24.
12 Cogswell, 'The Regicides in New England', p. 200.
13 Stiles, *Three of the Judges*, p. 158.
14 Ibid., p. 157.
15 Ibid., p. 164.
16 J. T. Peacey, *DNB*, John Dixwell.
17 Noble, *Memoirs of the Protectoral-House*, Vol. II, p. 152.

Chapter 15: To the Last Man

 1 Rowse, *Regicides*, p. 74.
 2 Firth (ed.), *Memoirs of Edmund Ludlow*, p. 281.
 3 Firth/Worden, *DNB*: Edmund Ludlow.
 4 Antony Whitaker, *The Regicide's Widow*, Sutton Publishing, Stroud, 2006, p. 174.
 5 Ibid., p. 177.
 6 Ibid., p. 190.
 7 M. W. Helms and John P. Ferris, *The History of Parliament, volumes 1660–1690*, www.historyofparliament.org, entry for Edmund Ludlow.

BIBLIOGRAPHY

Manuscript and Archive Sources

Anglice, Mercurius Poeticus, 28 February 1659, eebo.chadwyck.com

Calendar of State Papers, Colonial, America and West Indies, 1661–68, British History Online, www.british-history.ac.uk

Calendar of State Papers, Domestic, 1650; 1654–65; 1660; 1661, British History Online, www.british-history.ac.uk

Clarendon State Papers, Bodleian Library, Oxford, www.bodley.ox.ac.uk

Declaration on their Just Resentment of the Horrid Murther of Isaac Dorislaus, E. Husband, Printer to the House of Commons, 1649

Journals of the House of Commons, Vol. 8: 1660–1667, British History Online, www.british-history.ac.uk

Mercurius Pragmaticus, 5–12 December 1648, The Bodleian Library Record, Volume 17

PRO, SP 29/71, fol. 20, The National Archives, Kew

Proclamation by the King for Apprehension of Edward Whalley and William Goffe, London, 22 September 1660, printed by Christopher Barker and John Bill, London, 1660

Proclamation of King Charles, Whitehall, 6 June 1660, printed by Christopher Barker and John Bill, London, 1660

Published Sources

Alvis, John (ed.), *Areopagitica and Other Political Writings of John Milton*, Liberty Fund Press, Indianapolis, 1999

Anon., *A Perfect Narrative of the Whole Proceedings of the High Court of Justice*, London, 1649

— *A Salt Teare: or, the Weeping Onion at the Lamentable Funerall of Dr Dorislaus*, London, 1649

— *Account of Charles I's Conduct on the Scaffold from: King Charles His Execution*, London, 1649

— *An Exact and Most Impartial Accompt of the Indictment, Arraignment, Trial, and Judgment (According to Law) of Twenty-Nine Regicides*, London, 1660

— *A Compleat Collection of the Lives, Speeches, and Prayers of those Persons Lately Executed*, London, 1660

— *The Speeches, Discourses, and Prayers, of Col. John Barkstead, Col. John Okey, and Mr Miles Corbet*, London, 1662

— *Coll. Henry Marten's Letters to his Lady of Delight*, Oxford, 1663

Ascham, Anthony, *A Discourse, wherein is examined what is particularly lawfull during the Confusions and Revolutions of Government* (three parts), London, 1648

Atwater, Edward Elias et al., *History of the Colony of New Haven to its Absorption into Connecticut*, The Journal Publishing Company, Meriden Connecticut, 1902

Aubrey, John, *Brief Lives*, St Edmondsbury Press, Bury St Edmunds, 1998

Blencowe, R. W. (ed.), *Sidney Papers*, John Murray, London, 1825

Bremer, Francis J., *Building a New Jerusalem: John Davenport, a Puritan in Three Worlds*, New Haven: Yale University Press, 2012

Burton, Thomas, *Diary of Thomas Burton*, Vols I and II, London, 1828

Carlyle, Thomas, *Oliver Cromwell's Letters and Speeches* (two volumes), Wiley & Putnam, New York, 1845

— *Oliver Cromwell's Letters and Speeches* (two volumes), Scribner, Welford and Co., New York, 1871

Carte, T., *A Collection of Original Papers*, 2 Vols, 1739

Clarendon, The Earl of, *The History of the Rebellion and Civil Wars in England*, Vol. II (of II), Oxford University Press, London, 1893

— *The History of the Rebellion: A New Selection*, edited by Paul Seaward, Oxford, 2009

De la Bédoyère, Guy (ed.), *The Diary of John Evelyn*, The Boydell Press, Woodbridge, 1995

De Beer, E. S. (ed.), *The Diary of John Evelyn*, Oxford, 1959

Eliot, Samuel, *New England Magazine*, Vol. IX, No. 2, NP, 1893

Exwood, M. and Lehman, H. H., (trans. and eds), *The Journal of William Schellincks' Travels in England, 1661–1663*, Camden Society, London, 1993

Farr, David, *John Lambert, Parliamentary Soldier and Cromwellian Major-General: 1619–1684*, Rochester, New York, 2003

Firth, C. H. (ed.), *The Clarke Papers, Vol. I*, Camden Society, London, 1891

— *The Memoirs of Edmund Ludlow, Vol. I and Vol. II*, Clarendon Press, Oxford, 1894

— *The Raising of the Ironsides*, Spottiswoode & Company, London, 1899

Fox, John, *The King's Smuggler, Jane Whorwood, Secret Agent to Charles I*, The History Press, Stroud, 2010

— 'Jane Whorwood: The King's Smuggler', *History Today*, January 2010

Gardiner, Samuel Rawson (ed.), *The Constitutional Documents of the Puritan Revolution, 1625–1660*, Clarendon Press, Oxford, 1906

Goffe, William, *Diary*, www.css.podsdemo.com/webpages/ftphtmltransfer /judges3

Helms, M. W. and Ferris, John P., *The History of Parliament, Volumes 1660–1690*, www.historyofparliamentonline.org

Howell, T. B., *A Compleat Collection of State Trials, and Proceedings for High Treason and Other Crimes and Misdemeanors*, Vols IV and V, London, 1816

Hunt, Tristram, *The English Civil War at First Hand*, Weidenfeld & Nicolson, London, 2002

Hutchinson, Lucy, *Memoirs of the Life of Colonel Hutchinson*, John C. Nimmo, London, 1885

— *Memoirs of the Life of Colonel Hutchinson*, Orion, London, 1995

Jesse, John, *Memoirs of the Court of England: During the Reigns of the Stuarts*, Vol. II, Lea and Blanchard, Philadelphia, 1840

Kennedy, Paul M., *The Rise and Fall of British Sea Mastery*, A. Lane, London, 1976

Lister, T. H., *The Life And Administration of Edward, First Earl of Clarendon*, Longmans, London, 1838

Lockyer, Roger (ed.), *Trial of Charles I: A Contemporary Account taken from the Memoirs of Sir Thomas Herbert and John Rushworth*, Folio Press, 1974

Ludlow, Edmund, *The Imprisonment & Death of King Charles I, related by One of his Judges – Extracts from the Memoirs of Edmund Ludlow*, Edinburgh, 1882

— *Memoirs of Edmund Ludlow*, London, 1771

— *Memoirs of Edmund Ludlow, Vol. I*, Sands, Murray and Cochran, Edinburgh, 1751

Maccioni, P. Alessandra and Mostert, Marco, *Isaac Dorislaus (1595–1649): the Career of a Dutch Scholar in England, Transactions of the Cambridge Bibliographical Society*, Vol. 8, No. 4, Cambridge, 1984

Marshall, Henrietta Elizabeth, *This Country of Ours: the Story of the United States*, George H. Doran Company, New York, 1917

Noble, Mark (ed.), *The Lives of the Regicides*, Vols I and II, John Stockdale, London, 1798

— *Memoirs of the Protectoral-House of Cromwell*, Vols I and II, G. G. J. and J. Robinson, London, 1787

Oxford Dictionary of National Biography (DNB), www.oxforddnb.com

Pagliuco, Christopher, *The Great Escape of Edward Whalley and William Goffe*, Charleston, SC, 2012

Parliamentary or Constitutional History of England from the earliest times to the Restoration of Charles II, Vol. XXII (of XXIV), London, 1751–62

Peck, Rev. Francis (ed.), *Desiderata Curiosa*, Thomas Evans, London, 1779

Pepys, Samuel, *Diary of Samuel Pepys*, www.pepysdiary.com

Peters, Eleanor Bradley, *Hugh Peter: Preacher, Patriot, Philanthropist*, New York, 1909

Peters, Hugh, *The Case of Mr Hugh Peters Impartially Communicated to the View and Censure of the World: Written by his own Hand*, London, 1660

Raithby, John (ed.), *Statutes of the Realm*, Vol. 5, The Record Commission, London, 1819

Robertson, Geoffrey, *The Tyrannicide Brief*, Chatto & Windus, London, 2005

Rowse, A. L., *Four Caroline Portraits*, Duckworth, London, 1993

— *The Regicides and the Puritan Revolution*, Duckworth, London, 1994

Rushworth, John (ed.), *Historical Collections of Private Passages of State, Weighty Matters of Law*, Volumes VI, VII and VIII, London, 1701

Seventh Report of the Royal Commission on Historical Manuscripts, Eyre and Spottiswoode, London, 1879

Shorto, Russell, *The Island at the Centre of the World*, Doubleday, London, 2004

Shurtlett, Nathaniel B. (ed.), *Records of the Governor and Company of the Mass. Bay in New England*, Boston, 1853–4

Simkinson, C. H., *Thomas Harrison, Regicide and Major-General*, J. M. Dent, London, 1905

Stiles, Ezra, *A History of Three of the Judges of King Charles I*, Elisha Babcock, Hartford, 1794

Sylvester, M., (ed.), *Reliquiae Baxteraniae*, London, 1696

Walker, Clement, *Anarchia Anglicana*, London, 1649

Wedgwood, C. V., *A King Condemned: The Trial and Execution of Charles I*, Palgrave Macmillan, New York, 2011

Welles, Lemuel Aiken, *The History of the Regicides in New England*, New York, 1927

Whitaker, Antony, *The Regicide's Widow*, Sutton Publishing, Stroud, 2006

Whitlocke, Bulstrode, *Memorials of the English Affairs from the Beginning of the Reign of Charles the First*, Vol. III, Memphis, 2010

Winthrop, John, *Journal of John Winthrop, 1630–1649*, Massachusetts Historical Society, 1996

Wood, Anthony, *Athenae Oxoniensis*, London, 1817

Worden, A. B. (ed), *A Voyce From the Watch Tower, Part Five: 1660–1662*, Royal Historical Society, London, 1978

Acknowledgements

The subject of this book came to me when reading an 'On this day' website recording the 350th anniversary of John Barkstead, Miles Corbet and John Okey's execution for their part in the death of Charles I. Okey's name jumped out at me, as I wrote a little about his Civil War exploits in an earlier work. Wondering what happened to the rest of the killers of the King, and who they all were, led to this book.

I am grateful for the wholehearted encouragement of Andrew Kidd and Gillon Aitken, my literary agents, to pursue the topic. Also to Michael Fishwick, Anna Simpson and their colleagues at Bloomsbury, for their enthusiasm for it all.

My wife, Karen, has been the most intelligent and receptive of sounding boards, enduring my passion for this subject with grace and humour, and always giving superb advice.

Final thanks to the extremely brave men who put a defeated and distrusted king on trial, and saw through what they sincerely believed had to be done. Charles I had many personal qualities – many of which he displayed at his noble and dignified end – but I believe he was, in his final years, an execrable ruler. It is striking how many fascinating and notable figures colluded to end his life. They deserve, in my view, to be remembered with respect for their sacrifices: this book is my tribute to them.

Index